elvis *Culture*

CULTURE AMERICA

Karal Ann Marling & Erika Doss, *series editors*

elvis
Culture
Fans, Faith & Image
Erika Doss

UNIVERSITY PRESS OF KANSAS

© 1999 by the
University Press of Kansas
All rights reserved
Published by the
University Press of Kansas
(Lawrence, Kansas 66049),
which was organized by the
Kansas Board of Regents and
is operated and funded by
Emporia State University,
Fort Hays State University,
Kansas State University,
Pittsburg State University,
the University of Kansas,
and Wichita State University

Library of Congress
Cataloging-in-Publication Data
Doss, Erika Lee.
Elvis culture : fans, faith, and image / Erika Doss.
    p.   cm.—(CultureAmerica)
Includes bibliographical references and index.
ISBN 0-7006-0948-2 (cloth : alk. paper)
1. Presley, Elvis, 1935–1977—Influence.   2. Rock
music fans—United States.   3. Popular culture—
United States.   I. Title.   II. Series.
ML420.P96D68   1999
782.42166′092—dc21
[B]   98-31730

British Library
Cataloguing in Publication Data is available.

Printed in the United States of America

10   9   8   7   6   5   4   3   2   1

The paper used in this publication
meets the minimum requirements of
the American National Standard for
Permanence of Paper for Printed Library
Materials z39.48-1984.

CONTENTS

ILLUSTRATIONS

ACKNOWLEDGMENTS

So many have contributed so much to this project that I scarcely know where to begin my sizable debt of thanks. These acknowledgments have been a huge part of this book all along.

I'd especially like to thank David Morgan, whose illuminating insights about visual piety kick-started this project on a Saturday afternoon in September 1992. David was the first to say "go with it" when I told him of the Elvis epiphany I'd had during his talk; I'm grateful for his steady encouragement and good advice.

One of the most invigorating aspects of this project has been the many opportunities it has given me to make new acquaintances in different fields and different places, and to really experience the crossover dynamics that are possible in contemporary cultural studies. Longtime friends and colleagues in the art world have also been enormously influential in shaping the critical discourse this book hopefully provides. Thanks to Michelle Bogart, Norm Girardot, William Henderson, Mark Hirsch, Stewart Hoover, Joy and John Kasson, Ayako Maeda, Greil Marcus, Karal Ann Marling, Marty Mertens, Gil Rodman, David Sanjek, Barry Shank, Tom Tweed, Alice Wondrak, and Adrienne Young for generously sharing information and pointing me in different directions; thanks to Claire Farago, Linda Herritt, Stewart Hoover, Jim Johnson, Susan Krane, Antonette Rosato, Paul Shankman, and other colleagues at the University of Colorado, Boulder, as well as John Gennari, Mark Pittenger, Rickie Solinger, and the members of the American Studies Reading Group, for good advice and astute criticism; thanks to Donna Gartenmann, Vanessa Jones, Evelyn and Gene Kane, Lesley Sharp, and many other friends who kept my mailbox full of Elvis stuff; thanks to Billie Gutsgell, my indispensable chauffeur, and Leland Rucker for great conversation; thanks to Elaine Tyler May for sharing her memories of meeting Elvis backstage at the Hilton Hotel in Las Vegas in 1972.

I owe a special debt to the energetic research assistants and photographers who've helped me with this project, including Bill Anthes (who will never, never go back to Graceland), Jaime Siff, Greg Adams, Jan Kabili, Nick Havholm, Joseph Krettek, and Dinah Zeiger. I'd also like to thank all the people who sent me bits and pieces of Elvis ephemera that I couldn't seem to work into this book: the Waynesboro, Tennessee, high-school marching band, whose repertoire is all-Elvis, no-Sousa (thanks to Carlton Bing); the Elvis shrine backstage at the Washington Shakespeare Company, which helps to "preempt" various theatrical curses (thanks to Catherine Lavender); and the Elvis Revival Festival, held each January in Parkes, New South Wales (thanks to Ian Mylchreest).

I spent the spring of 1996 in the Department of Fine Arts at the University of Sydney, and I'd like to thank faculty, students, staff, and others who made my stay in Australia such a pleasure. Peter Barnes (Elvis artiste extraordinaire), Mick Carter, John Clark, Alan Cholodenko, Kajri Jain, Laleen Jayamanne (who graciously lent me her office), Mary MacKay, Louise Marshall, Catriona Moore, Frances Page-de Mars, Julian Pefanis, Jenny Reeks, Terry Smith, and Virginia Spate gave me the invaluable opportunity to air my ideas and build some enduring friendships.

Some of the material in this book was presented first as conference papers at the American Studies Association (1994), the University of Chicago (1994), the University of Colorado, Boulder (1996), and the Third Annual Elvis Conference in Memphis (1997), and as lectures at the University of Sydney (1996), the University of North Carolina (1997), and the Appleton Art Center (1997); thanks to all for inviting me, listening to my ideas, and providing helpful feedback. I'd also like to thank Lisa Siegrist of *American Art* and David Nye of *Odense American Studies International Series* for publishing abbreviated portions of this book. Research for this project was supported by grants from the University of Colorado's Council on Research and Creative Work, and its Graduate Committee on Arts and Humanities.

I have been especially fortunate to work with a great editor, Nancy Scott Jackson, at the University Press of Kansas, and with a great co-editor, Karal Ann Marling, in the CultureAmerica Series. I hope this book does our series proud.

Most of all, I want to thank the hundreds of fans who generously spent time with me, wrote to me, and shared their own insights about Elvis.

Finally, thanks to Geoffrey for translating Prince's "Face Off/Dead Like Elvis," for uncovering fabulous El Vez CDs, and for just generally putting up with this entire project, including accompanying me to Memphis during Elvis Week 1995 when he could have gone to Cropredy.

Images of *elvis*

"Elvis is everywhere," chanted rock wits Mojo Nixon and Skip Roper in a 1987 semihit single that plumbed the depths of Elvis Presley's abiding cultural presence a decade after his death. Today, judging from all the pictures, plates, stamps, and refrigerator magnets bearing various images of the King of Rock and Roll, and the tribute concerts, greatest-hits re-releases, biographies, art exhibitions, movies, and conferences cashing in on his music, his appearance, and his life, Elvis is still "everywhere" and shows no signs of disappearing any time soon. The future of his image is ensured, too: in 1995, his ex-wife and widow, Priscilla Presley, remarked that she and the folks who run Elvis Presley Enterprises, Inc. (Elvis Inc. or EPE, the corporate outfit that owns Graceland and claims legal copyright on Elvis's name and face), are working "to bring Elvis into the twenty-first century."[1] Already, folklore has it that the three most recognized words around the world are "Jesus," "Coca-Cola," and "Elvis."

Elvis fans are everywhere, too. Some belong to one or more of the 500 or so official Elvis Presley fan clubs that can be found around the world, more than half of them in the United States. Others habitually visit Graceland, Elvis's Memphis home for twenty years, making it the second most popular house tour in America (after the White House). During Elvis International Tribute Week, a Memphis phenomenon that occurs annually on the anniversary of Elvis's death (August 16, 1977), the city swells as thousands of fans gather in grief and celebration around Elvis's grave site at Graceland's Meditation Gardens, displaying a kind of emotional intensity and reverence that clearly intimates his popular culture canonization.

Why Elvis? Why has Elvis Presley become sanctified as the central figure in what some are calling a quasi-religion? Why not some other popular culture martyr who died young, like John Lennon, Buddy Holly, Janis Joplin, Jimi Hendrix, or, more recently, Kurt Cobain or Selena? Why is Elvis—more so than Malcolm X, Martin Luther King, Jr., and J.F.K.—consistently held up as an "icon of the twentieth century"? Why is it Elvis's image that we see on the surface of every

(overleaf) *Joni Mabe, collection of Elvis stuff, as displayed in* Traveling Panoramic Encyclopedia of Everything Elvis, 1988. *Mixed media installation, 1,600 square feet. (Collection of the artist, Athens, Georgia)*

Elvis fan during Elvis Week 1997 at Graceland Crossing shopping mall, Memphis.

conceivable mass-produced consumer item, from black velvet paintings and ceramic statuettes to laminated clocks, liquor decanters,
ashtrays, oven mitts, address books, earrings, checks, flags, key rings?
Why does Elvis's image prevail in contemporary visual culture?

More to the point, why should any of this be taken seriously—why
should any of us even bother with looking at and trying to make sense
of Elvis Culture? The answer, quite simply, is that Elvis Presley oc-

cupies a big space in the daily lives of many Americans. For some, the space that he—or, more specifically, his image—occupies is not especially broad or deep. But for others, especially for fans, Elvis has sweeping significance in terms of personal, social, and even national identity: Elvis is who they want to be, who they most admire, who they mourn for; Elvis is their image of an ideal American. In a contemporary culture where images dominate (some estimate we receive three-quarters of our knowledge from visual sources), it is worth wondering why Elvis's image seems to dominate most of all.

It is worth wondering about because while Elvis's image has been fixed in national popular culture for more than forty years—ever since millions watched him gyrate on *The Ed Sullivan Show* in 1956—there is no particular agreement about what his image really means. Elvis's multifaceted image—rockabilly rebel, teen angel, army private, B-movie idol, family man, Las Vegas superstar, Nixon admirer, drug addict, dead icon—is ambiguous and contradictory, solid but unstable. American popular culture has always been unstable—"a site of conflicting interests, appropriations, impersonations," says Eric Lott—and ever since the mid-1950s, Elvis's image has been continually renegotiated and remade in order to mesh with individual and institutional preferences.[2]

This book asks why Elvis Presley remains the most popular icon in contemporary America more than twenty years after his death. It finds answers in Elvis's image and his fans. Clues to Elvis's abiding cultural symbolism are not to be found, in other words, only in his music or his biography, but among his many diverse and conflicted images and what they mean to the people who look at them, make them, and collect them: his fans.

What Elvis's image means to his fans is predisposed by his history and presence in popular culture, and articulated by the diversity of their responses to his image and his music. Many fans were turned on to Elvis when they first saw him on television. Elvis turned up thirteen times on TV in 1956, each time drawing more viewers, more critical attention, more teenage fans. His first appearance on *The Ed Sullivan Show* in September drew the highest ratings in then-TV history, with over 82 percent of the American viewing public (54 million people) tuning in to watch Elvis sing "Don't Be Cruel" and "Love Me Tender." By the time of the second Sullivan show in October (the third aired in January 1957), Elvis's records were selling at the rate of $75,000 a day (accounting for more than half of RCA's profits).[3] Fans mobbed his concerts (he performed live 161 times in 1956), followed him everywhere, ripped bits of upholstery from his pink and black Cadillacs, and organized "I Love Elvis" clubs.

Reporters could not get enough of Elvis either; magazines and journals from *Modern Screen* to the *New Republic* paid an unprecedented amount of anxious attention to this "whirling dervish of sex" who was making more money than the president of the United States. It wasn't just Elvis's music, in other words, that made fans gush and critics moan: it was the way he moved, it was his body, it was his image. The new medium of television helped facilitate Elvis's mass attention, drawing squeals of desire from fans and prompting howls of protest from critics and clergy: *New York Times* writer Jack Gould said that Elvis had "no discernible singing ability," *Daily News* critic Ben Gross complained that popular music had "reached its lowest depths in the 'grunt and groin' antics of one Elvis Presley," and Francis Cardinal Spellman, the most vocal public spokesman for postwar Catholics, warned that Elvis embodied "dishonesty, violence, lust, and degeneration."[4] But it was what took place between Elvis and his audiences that really accelerated his popular culture hold.

Elvis's music was, of course, absolutely pivotal to his popularity. If he had been only a teen heartthrob and B-movie star, Elvis would never have attracted the adulation that continues unabated. From the start, he courted a singing style that bound his fans and himself in an intensely emotional relationship. From the rocket-fueled and raw-voiced rockabilly energy of the 1950s performances to the gospel repertoire of his 1967 album *How Great Thou Art* and the slick pop of his 1970s arena acts, Elvis's music was always sensual (if not downright erotic) and utterly captivating.[5] Rough and unpolished in the early days and rich and often uncomfortably desperate in the later years, it hinged on Elvis's own personal need to provoke, please, and communicate, and on the reciprocal desires of his fans to respond and become a part of something explosive and experiential, something liberating and connective all at once. Yet if music gave Elvis his start and remains a part of the relationship that fans have with him today, listening to Elvis is never far from looking at him.

Sight is the dominant sense in modern Western culture—how else can we explain the phenomenal popularity of television compared with radio?—and Elvis, perhaps more so than any other performer in the 1950s, recognized this. Just as he skillfully mixed black and white musical forms to create his own influential brand of rock and roll, Elvis consciously blended sound (the rhythm and pulse of his music, the vibrato of his voice) and sight (the look of his body, the style of his movements) into sensual and seductive spectacles. His performances were gestural and affective, the "real physical absolute" that Antonin Artaud imagined for a new kind of modern theater keyed to visual immediacy and felt experience.[6] Shattering musical and theatrical conventions, Elvis set the pace for the predominantly visual aura of contemporary popular culture: within a decade or so of his mid-1950s debut, flamboyant stage acts with Spectra-Color light shows and glitzy special effects became the norm for rock bands ranging from the Rolling Stones to the Grateful Dead. Today we talk about going to "see" Sting or Prince or Madonna, which tells us a lot about how profoundly visualized contemporary popular music has become.

Elvis's manager, Colonel Tom Parker, most sagely recognized his single client's visual appeal. Promoting him as the "Atomic Powered Singer," Parker appropriated Cold War rhetoric to call attention to Elvis's explosive on-stage energy. Others labeled him the "male Monroe" and came a little closer to the sexual aesthetic that had such an electric effect on his fans. *Look* magazine tried to classically contain that sexuality, explaining that the twenty-one-year-old Elvis (who in 1956 weighed 185 pounds and stood just over 6 feet tall) looked a lot like Myron's *Discobolos* or Michelangelo's *David*. *Life* more astutely reported that Elvis was "a different kind of idol," who used "a bump and grind routine usually seen only in burlesque" to "set off" his young audiences into "shock waves of hysteria, going into frenzies of screeching and wailing, winding up in tears." "He isn't afraid to express himself," said one fifteen-year-old fan watching Elvis perform. "When he does that on TV, I get down on the floor and scream."[7]

The 1950s saw an explosion of body-centered performance art. In

Elvis in concert, 1956. (Reprinted with permission of Life Magazine. Copyright Time Warner, Inc.)

Japan, Europe, and the United States, in small-scale venues at art schools and alternative galleries, avant-garde artists—including the Gutai group, Georges Mathieu, Yves Klein, John Cage, Merce Cunningham, Robert Rauschenberg, Allan Kaprow, and, later, Carolee Schneemann—challenged traditional boundaries between theater and audience. Many declared their bodies a new zone of aesthetic experimentation: replicating the action painting of Jackson Pollock, Japanese artist Kazuo Shiraga used his body as a brush and made art by rolling around in piles of mud; organizing the Orgies Mysteries Theater, Austrian artist Hermann Nitsch staged elaborate, participatory acts that urged audiences to liberate themselves from repressive sexual and religious mores via "intoxication, ecstasy and delight."[8]

Elvis did the same with his body in his performances but he did it in front of millions, on national television, in the realm of popular culture. Pouting and sneering, winking his eyes, licking his lips, wiggling his hips, shaking his legs, Elvis was excessive and emotional and defiantly erotic, openly violating mainstream standards of social re-

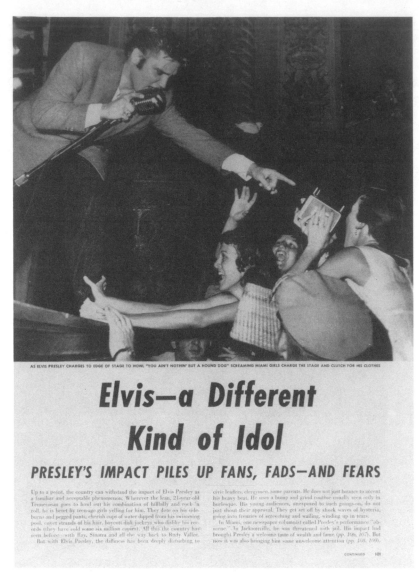

AS ELVIS PRESLEY CHARGES TO EDGE OF STAGE TO HOWL "YOU AIN'T NOTHIN' BUT A HOUND DOG" SCREAMING MIAMI GIRLS CHARGE THE STAGE AND CLUTCH FOR HIS CLOTHES

Elvis—a Different Kind of Idol

PRESLEY'S IMPACT PILES UP FANS, FADS—AND FEARS

Up to a point, the country can withstand the impact of Elvis Presley as a familiar and acceptable phenomenon. Wherever the lean, 21-year-old Tennessean goes to howl out his combination of hillbilly and rock 'n roll, he is beset by teen-age girls yelling for him. They dote on his sideburns and pegged pants, cherish cups of water dipped from his swimming pool, covet strands of his hair, boycott disk jockeys who dislike his records (they have sold some six million copies). All this the country has seen before—with Ray, Sinatra and all the way back to Rudy Vallee. But with Elvis Presley, the daffiness has been deeply disturbing to

civic leaders, clergymen, some parents. He does not just bounce to accent his heavy beat. He uses a bump and grind routine usually seen only in burlesque. His young audiences, unexposed to such goings-on, do not just shout their approval. They get set off by shock waves of hysteria, going into trances of screeching and wailing, winding up in tears. In Miami, one newspaper columnist called Presley's performance "obscene." In Jacksonville, he was threatened with jail. His impact had brought Presley a welcome taste of wealth and fame (pp. 100, 107). But now it was also bringing him some unwelcome attention (pp. 108, 109).

CONTINUED 101

"Elvis—A Different Kind of Idol," article on Elvis fandom in Life, *April 27, 1956. (Reprinted with permission of* Life *Magazine. Copyright Time Warner, Inc.)*

straint and cultural refinement. "His legs weren't solidly planted then, as they would be years later," writes critic Michael Ventura:

> They were always in motion. Often he'd rise on his toes, seem on the verge of some impossible groin-propelled leap, then twist, shimmy, dip, and shake in some direction you wouldn't have ex-

pected. You *never* expected it. Every inflection of his voice was matched, accented, *harmonized* by an inflection of muscle. As though the voice couldn't sing unless the body moved.

Elvis's was a spectacular, rhythmic body, and it was offered for consumption and imitation to millions of visually fixated and physically responsive postwar teens. "It's impossible to sit still while Elvis is on the stage," Janie Butterfield of Beaumont, Texas, told the editors at *Life*. "His belting style drives us wild. We have to do something. Kick the seat in front or let out a 'rebel yell' or something."[9]

"Seeing" Elvis, in other words, was never simply a matter of looking at him. Elvis was never just a picture or a statue, a beautiful object that his fans gazed upon and contemplated. Elvis demanded reaction and response, the physical and emotional participation of an audience that was urged to become more than a body of listeners or viewers, but "an audience of performers." Whether seen and experienced in concert or on TV, Elvis gave his fans "shared access to feeling" in a postwar culture that aimed to keep "people separate and feeling at a distance."[10] Drawing audiences together and encouraging their emotional response, Elvis challenged Cold War containment and invited his fans to do the same. Critics of the 1950s viewed Elvis's body, image, and performances, and the bodies and performances of his fans, with dread: it all blatantly symbolized the sensual subversion of reason and control. But for 1950s fans, that was what it was all about: Elvis's body moved their bodies; Elvis's image mediated their needs and desires.

Fans who saw Elvis in concert or on television in the 1950s especially remember what he looked like, how he moved, how he made them feel. "He was innocent looking but also sexy. His eyes and his voice just thrilled to the bone. When he sang it would almost seem it was directly to me," recalls Georgene Knecht of Los Alamos, New Mexico. "He was the first man to totally excite me; I loved his music but I fell in love with his eyes, his beautiful hair and his creamy, blemish-free skin," says Joyce Noyes of Saginaw, Michigan. "Elvis was drop-dead gorgeous," writes Joann Tumelavich of Bridgeton, New Jersey, who adds that his "singing and gyrating hips were great too." "He was young, charismatic, charming, a rebel and soooooooooo handsome, all the things that would sweep a Southern girl off her feet," recalls Judith Adams of Johnson City, Tennessee. Looking at mid-1950s magazine pictures of Elvis, says Rae Gagnon of Duluth, "awakened in me the sort of fuzzy desire to kiss those lips and somehow touch him romantically." "It was love at first sight, and sound," remembers South Carolina fan Kathy Ruff. "I somehow knew instantly that his smile, his expressive eyes, his voice, his attitude, his whole persona would receive my unconditional love til the end of time."[11]

Newspaper accounts imply that the largest number of fans at the 1950s concerts were young teenage girls, but Elvis's body moved men and boys, too. As Ventura comments, "Presley's moves were body-shouts, and the way our ears heard his voice our bodies heard his body. Girls understood it and went nuts screaming for more. Boys instantly understood it and started dancing by themselves in front of their mirrors in imitation of him."[12] Many boys were lured by how television framed Elvis's body, and immediately set out to copy that look. As Ken Kolarz of Lake View, New York, recalls, Elvis "was *the* coolest guy I had ever seen." Austin fan Edwin Richison had the same reaction: "It wasn't until Elvis appeared on *The Ed Sullivan Show* that I got to place a face with the music. What a night to remember. His clothes, the way he moved and talked. . . . He became an instant icon of rock and roll. After seeing him, his music became secondary."

Contemporary fan feelings for Elvis continue to hinge on his image but now, after forty years of history and mythmaking, Elvis's image is far more nuanced: Elvis the rockabilly vies with Elvis the patriot and Elvis the philanthropist for fan favoritism. Images of Elvis are seemingly direct, providing information and disclosing the "real" Elvis. But if they embody the historical memory, the likeness, of the Elvis that once was, they are hardly uncomplicated. Rather, they are ambiguous and contradictory, straightforward yet confused, substitutes and hallucinations, a tangled hybrid of fact and desire. All of this might suggest that Elvis ultimately "means" nothing but, in fact, the versatility of his image is directly linked to his widespread cultural significance. Elvis's multiformity illuminates the emotional relationships that continue to exist between Elvis and his fans, who insist that his image has significance far beyond simple form and fact.

Today's fans "see" Elvis on many different levels, each of which corresponds to their own constructions of personal and social identity.

Images of Elvis as a great entertainer, interior of GracelandToo, 1996, Holly Springs, Mississippi.

Most view Elvis as a great entertainer, a musical legend. "He was and still is the KING OF ROCK AND ROLL," says Judy Adams of Johnson City, Tennessee. "Imagining rock n' roll without Elvis is like imagining the Revolutionary War without George Washington," writes Geri Elsasser of Broomfield, Colorado. "Elvis is one of the greatest singers of ALL time," says Rick Massa of Bayonne, New Jersey. "He was a dynamic performer who put his heart and soul into his concerts," says Sue

Haver of Superior, Wisconsin. "Elvis has been said to be the Greatest Entertainer on Earth," writes Ron Graham of Piqua, Ohio. "If you have ever been to an Elvis concert you would understand and be a believer or fan also."

Yet if fans celebrate Elvis's legendary rock-and-roll status, his singing, performance style, and musical talents are often less important to them than the strong personal bonds they feel they have with him. Many fans talk about Elvis's charisma and "animal magnetism," about how he "connected" with them individually, or seemed to. "Even in those big sports halls and even on TV," writes a fan from San Jose, "I just knew he was looking and singing just to me." ("Every word of every song that he sang was for you," Alannah Myles croons in her hit single "Black Velvet" [1991], a song that's all about Elvis.)

Some of this sense of intimacy and closeness corresponds to the ways in which many fans claim Elvis on familial terms—as kin, as blood. Minnie Hamlett of Paris, Arkansas, echoes other fans when she remarks that Elvis has always been an essential element in her life: "I remember when he was drafted in the Army, when his Mom died, when he married. It just seems like he was part of my family." Other fans reveal that when Elvis died, it was as though someone in their own family had died: "I cried for days," recalls Gloria Winters of Elizabethton, Tennessee. They talk about how Elvis made them feel like they were always part of *his* family by bonding with them during concerts, by politely signing autographs and inviting them into his home, or by talking with them as though he really liked them and really wanted to get to know them. Now that he is gone, fans complete the family circle by embracing Elvis as an important member of *their* families, by remembering and honoring him, by recalling his extraordinary presence in their lives. Even those who became fans only after Elvis's death tend to shape their fandom around his broader familial image, seeing Elvis, themselves, and other fans as one big "Elvis Family" and claiming the private Elvis—his tastes, his things, even his ex-wife, Priscilla, and his daughter, Lisa Marie—as the stuff of their own personal devotion.

Elvis, in other words, has long-term constancy in the lives of his fans, who often speak of their relationship with him as an intensely personal commitment—the kind of commitment one has to a family member or best friend. Austin fan Jim Rosenfeld best captures the sense in which fans image Elvis as a close acquaintance when he writes, "Every Elvis fan sees what they want to see in the man and his various incarnations. To me he was simply the greatest talent of the century and a person that I would have loved to have known and really feel that I did know even if he never knew me." Elvis's image as an intimate, as someone who shares their secrets and listens to their problems, not only drives the devotion of his fans but shapes their sense of self. As Florida fan Mary Cartaya says, "Elvis not only was the single most driving force in the history of Rock 'n' Roll music, but the single most driving force in my life."

Closely attached to Elvis's image as a rock god cum family member and personal friend are fan readings of Elvis's rags-to-riches life story. Again and again, many fans recite how Elvis started out as a poor white nobody and wound up with money, fame, and a mansion in Memphis. But their accounts of his achievement of this ultimate American dream always include this twist: Elvis stayed the same "real decent, fine boy" that Ed Sullivan introduced on TV in the 1950s; Elvis stayed "true" to his roots. Elvis was a "gentleman who truly loved his mother, believed in family values, never forgot his true friends or his humble upbringing," writes Charles Stevens of Flint, Michigan. "He started out poor, loved his mom and dad, served in the U.S. Army. He seemed honest to me," says Andy Kohler of Westminster, Colorado. "He was always polite, he never cussed," another Colorado fan remarks. "Growing up in a very close knit Italian-American family, we could relate to Elvis's kindness towards his mother, father, family, and friends," writes Hoboken fan Alexander Corrado about himself and his brother. "He loved his fans," writes Cara Striff of Gainesville, Florida. "You never heard Elvis call them fans though. He was too modest to assume that anybody was a fan."

Ascribing to Elvis the honesty, decency, humility, generosity, respect, politeness, and familial devotion that they also ascribe to an idealized American working class, many fans see Elvis as one of them, as a "blue-collar guy in blue suede shoes." They admire, and many certainly envy Elvis's social mobility, but they also believe that he stayed "true" to them, that he rejected the status and privilege of wealth (if not all of its attendant materialism) in deference to his family, his friends, and his fans. "He did not forget where he came from," notes Virginia Blizzard of Bridgeton, New Jersey, echoing the sentiment that Elvis "stayed loyal" to his working-class roots—and his working-class fans.

These fan constructions of Elvis's and their own working-class loyalties correlate to their perceptions of his patriotism. At the peak of his popularity in the 1950s, Elvis was drafted. Trained as a tank driver, he was assigned to Company D, First Medium Tank Battalion, Thirty-second Armor, Third Armored Division, stationed with the U.S. Seventh Army at Friedberg, West Germany. For two years, from 1958 to 1960, he drove a jeep. Almost overnight, Elvis the Pelvis became Elvis the G.I., a responsible citizen, a regular Joe who could stand up to military discipline. For many fans, Elvis's image as a draftee who rose only to the rank of buck sergeant is central to their understanding of Elvis as a working-class American. Many recount that Elvis "served his country with honor" and "did his duty," rejecting (for whatever reasons) offers of special status and military privilege. For those fans who likewise "did their duty" in Vietnam or the Gulf, Elvis's army stint (reluctant though he apparently was, according to biographer Peter Guralnick) is claimed as proof of his, and their own, allegiance to America.[13] Elvis as a soldier dignifies them as soldiers; Elvis's image as a soldier braces the image of working-class Americans as virtuous, loyal, and self-sacrificing folk who countenance no special favors.

Elvis's image as a soldier broke John Lennon's heart; his remark "Elvis died the day he went into the Army," which he made when he heard of Elvis's death, was Lennon's way of explaining how the revolutionary potential of rock and roll had fizzled into the benign schmaltz of pop by the late 1950s. But New York newspaper columnist Hy Gardner captured both the rah-rah spirit of Cold War patriotism and the class consciousness of many contemporary Elvis fans when he boasted in 1958, as Elvis shipped out for Germany, "in what other nation in the world would such a rich and famous man serve alongside you other draftees without trying to use influence to buy his way out? In my book this is American democracy at its best."[14]

Elvis's image as a working-class guy who never really strayed from his down-home roots corresponds to his image, too, as a philanthro-

Image of Elvis as a G.I., Days Inn Motel window decoration during Elvis Week 1995, Memphis.

pist. Reconciling Elvis's material success with how much he "gave," fans especially relish the image of Elvis the "great humanitarian," a rock-and-roll Rockefeller who gave the gift of music, gave himself to his country, gave away scarves, cars, and expensive jewelry to friends and fans, and gave generously to charity. As the authors of a book on that topic proclaim, "Elvis was more than a performer. He was an inspiration, a man who achieved wealth and fame, but viewed his position as an opportunity to help others."[15] Throughout his career, Elvis did contribute to certain charities and in the 1970s, especially, made private donations to police departments and local hospitals, usually around Christmas and usually in the form of $1,000 checks. Most of his giving was, however, tightly controlled by his agent the Colonel, who went berserk when Elvis promised to perform free for charities in the 1950s and who never allowed Elvis to contribute at a level commensurate with his multimillionaire status. Still, fans see Elvis's impulsive giving of Cadillac Eldorados and diamond rings to "total strangers" as proof of his "regal generosity," and delight in recounting "how much he loved to give presents to people, how much he cared." As Albert Chrosto of Hortland, Wisconsin, comments, "Elvis was a warm, loving person who bought cars & houses for his bands' families and strangers. He always gave away things."

Finally, fans hold to the image of Elvis in pain. They often talk about how Elvis suffered, how despite his success he died alone, addicted to drugs, grossly overweight. One fan writes, "I read that Elvis once said, 'The three keys to happiness are: someone to love, something to do, and something to look forward to.' I don't think he had any of those things toward the end of his life." Another remarks, "I feel very sad at times for Elvis. Such talent, wealth, and everything going for him and to end up like he did." Some fans blame themselves for Elvis's suffering, feeling guilty that their demands were more than he could bear. "The fans who supposedly 'loved' him made his a very difficult life," writes one Michigan fan. "He was mobbed everywhere he went. He could not shop, take a walk, ride a motorcycle, or even go to an amusement park without elaborate security, secrecy and much planning. These restrictions, I feel, were probably the reason he resorted to alcohol and drugs." A fan from California says much the same thing: "They killed him with too much love. He had no private life. The pressure was too much."[16]

Intertwined images of talent, success, familiarity, sincerity, generosity, and suffering are all central to Elvis's abiding American presence and to the feelings fans have for him. Elvis's image is a model of hybridity: different images of Elvis, in other words, or different Elvises hold different meanings for different viewers. George Lipsitz describes the various ways his students "saw" Elvis when he showed them *Flaming Star* (1960), a Hollywood western in which Elvis plays a young, tanned, and mostly bare-chested mixed-blood Indian. One "working class white woman identified with Presley himself and his character as an emblem of upward mobility for her class. . . . A radical lesbian viewed Presley as an androgynous image, a heroic subject that was neither completely male nor female." The multiple ways Elvis is seen reveals the plurality of meanings that his image (or any image) can embody. Indeed, Elvis's "longevity as a cultural icon," as Kevin Quain puts it, "is largely due to his flexibility—his willingness to take the shape of what we most wanted to see. Whether our fantasies were psychic, sexual, cosmic, financial, or religious Elvis accommodated all of us."[17]

But if Elvis's iconic flexibility accounts for his abiding popularity, and if his sustenance as an American icon has largely depended on the unrestricted multiplicity of his image, the narrative instability of his image also reveals a number of tensions at work in American culture. Despite the fact that Elvis's music—if not his entire performance style—helped break down some of the barriers of race and class in post–World War II America, today some fans claim an image of Elvis that corresponds to their own racial and class prejudices. In their eyes, Elvis is the perfect symbol of a mostly middle-class white America getting what it feels it deserves: money, fame, a mansion in Memphis. These fans discount, or choose to ignore, how Elvis himself negotiated the nascent terrain of civil rights to participate in the creation of a more democratic popular culture in mid-1950s America.

Similarly, despite Elvis's obvious inability to "just say no" to drugs and doughnuts and sexual adventures with a vast number of female followers, many fans insist on a purer, practically sanctimonious image of Elvis. "Elvis was and is bigger than life," writes one fan from Chisholm, Minnesota. "To me, I saw the kind Elvis that was always giving to people and charities and helping when and where he could. He helped me get through tough times and still does." For these fans, Elvis is a clean-living, Bible-quoting family man who died because of an "enlarged heart," not from a massive overdose of some thirty-seven different prescription drugs.

But their image of Elvis clashes with the Elvis who has been conceptualized, analyzed, and stylized by scores of artists since he first burst on the American scene. Ray Johnson, Andy Warhol, Howard Finster, Keith Haring, Alexis Smith, and Patty Carroll, among many others, have used Elvis's image to explore issues ranging from mass adulation to celebrity sexuality, often taking artistic liberties that some fans find offensive. During Elvis Week 1997, for example, some fans took umbrage over an exhibition at the Memphis College of Art that included various depictions of an infant Elvis with the Virgin Mary, Elvis crucified, Elvis naked, and a photo collage titled *Elvis Eaten by Ants*. Memphis fan club president Mary Stonebraker complained that the pictures were in "very, very, very bad taste" and informed art college officials that she "would get every Elvis fan in town to picket and take down the building brick by brick and kick in every painting" unless they were removed. The college acquiesced, prompting local journalists and letter writers to a rousing discussion of Elvis's image and free speech. "The debacle over this little exhibition," exclaimed a columnist in the *Commercial Appeal*, "is one more chip away from the foundation of the importance of creativity, generosity, and tolerance in our culture."[18]

Alternative art-world images of Elvis, and the debates they inspire, accompany those of an eroticized Elvis who is claimed by certain fans—women and men, straight and gay—as a sexual fantasy. Some fans produce paintings, sculptures, and huge room-size installations centered around their sexual desires for Elvis; others write soft-core fiction about a loving, sensual, and intimate Elvis, a liberatory figure who insists on mutually pleasurable sexual encounters. A lesbian Elvis impersonator in Memphis relates that Elvis is the only male she's ever felt sexually attracted to; recent graffiti penciled on the fieldstone walls surrounding Graceland included words of devotion from "the world's only gay Elvis singer." Elvis is a profoundly ambiguous sexual icon, and perceptions of his androgyny have driven female and male responses from the mid-1950s to today.

Elvis Inc., though, claims a sanitized, drug-free, fat-free, and generally more one-dimensional Elvis. EPE is the legal proprietor of Elvis's "official" image and guards and promotes that image with its scripted tours at Graceland, its huge pool of Elvis merchandise, and its "Official Elvis Home Page," all of which conspicuously avoid attention to Elvis's fandom, his sexuality, his important relationships with black popular culture, and his demise. (EPE's "official" line on Elvis's death is that he died of cardiac arrhythmia.) Canny to the increasingly lucrative dimensions of Elvis's image, EPE is currently pursuing a number of new revenue streams, including restaurants, casinos, musicals, television specials, and advertising venues all about Elvis, yet it does so by holding to a relatively restrictive image of its primary product.

Taken all together, these multiple views of Elvis—along with many others—provide a compelling body of evidence to consider conflicted American attitudes about religion, sex, race, and celebrity, and the construction of postwar American identity. Struggles over Elvis's representation reveal the tensions that come into play when other people's images conflict with our own beliefs and when ownership of Elvis himself is claimed through ownership of his image. Conflicts over Elvis's image parallel those over knowledge itself, over how and what American history should be presented in public schools, over who is entitled to certain ideas and information. Knowledge isn't monolithic or static; there isn't one big seamless narrative of American history or one way of thinking about or seeing American culture. There is no single or fixed image of Elvis either, so our knowledge and understanding of what he represents and what he means are generally indeterminate and open to debate. Conflicts over Elvis's chimerical image articulate deeper questions about the personal politics of looking. Who do we *want* Elvis to be? Rock-and-roll rebel or Las Vegas superstar? Symbol of whiteness or sexual fantasy? Corporate logo or secular saint? If we admit that Elvis is all these images, and more, we recognize that his representation is mercurial and conflicted, making the meaning of the man and answers to the questions of his contemporary popularity extraordinarily complicated.

Much of this complexity revolves around Elvis's canonization in popular culture, and his conscious construction as a religious icon. Elvis shrines and altars abound, and the ritualized behaviors of his fans, especially during Elvis Week, seem to suggest his contemporary religious signification. Along with others, my initial response to the question "why Elvis?" was oriented toward a fairly superficial equation of Elvis with Jesus and of Elvis fans with religious fanatics. In my case, such reductive reasoning was stimulated especially by the specific circumstances in which I first really became interested in Elvis's image—by staring at a large portrait of Jesus Christ one Saturday in September 1992.

Sitting in the dark that afternoon, I listened to a lecture given by art historian David Morgan about the Protestant underpinnings and broader cultural importance of religious artist Warner Sallman's once enormously popular painting *The Head of Christ* (1940).[19] Suddenly, looking at the gigantic screen projection of Sallman's portrait of an ash-blond Jesus and reflecting on the estimated 8 billion or so reproductions of that picture that once dominated churches, homes,

Elvis shrine made by Margaret Martinez, Embudo, New Mexico,
photographed in 1996.

and public buildings across America and around the world, I thought,
"I know that image; I grew up with that image. But I don't 'see'
that image too much any more in America—and not just because
I've been a lapsed Episcopalian since about May 1974." As Morgan
segued into a persuasive explanation of how and why Sallman's image
of Jesus had lost a certain degree of credibility in a multicultural, post-

Warner Sallman, Head of Christ (1940). *Oil on canvas, 28¼ × 22⅛ inches. (Courtesy Jessie C. Wilson Galleries, Anderson University)*

Vietnam America, I asked myself what image, if any, may have taken its place: "Whose picture, whose face, do I see today, over and over, again and again, everywhere, commanding as much visual authority as that once held by Sallman's head of Jesus?" And in a flash, a weird sort of epiphanic rush, I thought of Elvis Presley.

I don't really know why I flashed on Elvis that academic afternoon, but the sudden obviousness of his extraordinary visual dominance made a strong, visceral impact. A sense of wonder, what Neil Evernden calls "radical astonishment," took over, with a kind of intensity and presentness that far exceeded any sort of rational registration.[20] I suppose I could have shrugged it off as a *National Enquirer* kind of moment ("Elvis Touches Prof from Beyond the Grave"). But if I was quite unexpectedly struck by this mysterious revelation of Elvis's visual omnipresence, I was even more curious about why and what it all meant. Provoked by the immediacy of my own intuition, I plunged into what has become this book's primary focus: to explore and analyze the meaning of Elvis Presley's image—his face and his body—in contemporary American culture.

I started by recognizing how removed I was from the whole topic. I had hardly even thought about Elvis Presley before, and I certainly hadn't grown up as an Elvis fan. I pledged allegiance to the Beatles and the Rolling Stones, hummed "Lovely Rita" at the dinner table, danced to a 45 of "Get Off My Cloud" in my bedroom. Like lots of other kids in the late 1960s and the 1970s, I put Elvis Presley in the past tense: 1950s, fat, finished, forgotten. Elvis wasn't hip. And some of us thought his efforts to "get [back] in touch with youth culture" were really pretty pathetic. I mean, Elvis was sort of sexy and snarly when he dressed up in black leather in 1968 for his so-called "comeback special," a TV variety show that had him twisting those still tantalizing hips with a whole crew of Nancy Sinatra wannabes. But Elvis was way too polite, too TV, too mainstream, for a generation more turned on by the truly subversive sexuality of crotch-grabbing, lip-smacking performers like Jim Morrison and Mick Jagger.

Elvis made a stab at decrying social injustice in AM-radio hits like "In the Ghetto" (1969), but his histrionic balladeering seemed sappy and insincere to those of us listening to the Temptations' "Ball of Confusion" or the underground FM-radio politics of Buffalo Springfield and Country Joe and the Fish. Elvis tried to outdo the greatest kitsch-meister of them all—Liberace—when he donned rhinestone-studded jumpsuits and twenty-pound superhero capes and karate-jabbed his way through hokey arena acts that had thousands of female fans mobbing the stage for one of his sweat-soaked scarves. But this sort of Las Vegas shtick was largely irrelevant to those of us who went to Woodstock (or wanted to).

I remember reading about Elvis's death ("in the bathroom?" "in his pajamas?") on the front page of the *Milwaukee Journal* on a hot afternoon in August 1977 and thinking, well, not really thinking much of anything. And I remember seeing Elvis's Memphis mansion for the first time one afternoon in 1982, when along with a busload of other American Studies types I gleefully abandoned the air-conditioned confines of our conference hotel and walked around Graceland's magnolia-planted grounds (the house wasn't open yet for tours). And I recall thinking, well, gee, Graceland's not that grand and Elvis's guitar-shaped swimming pool is awfully teeny and, besides, why would anyone want to live across the street from a strip mall, anyway? So flashing on Elvis on another afternoon years later really came as a surprise—a surprise because I'd never given this guitar-player-singer-entertainer-movie-star-has-been everyone else called "the King" more than about five seconds of attention and yet now I suddenly found myself, well, fascinated with Elvis Presley's omnipresent image.

I began sharing my Saturday afternoon revelation with anyone and everyone, finding Elvis's image everywhere—in ads, on stamps, decorating pot holders, glued to car deodorizers—and chatting up friends, family, colleagues, students, and complete strangers on the bus about what all those images might mean. What I found in all those conversations was how eager people were to talk about Elvis, to testify to how important he was in their lives and how long they had been fans. In my research, I learned about the hundreds of Elvis fan clubs, with tens of thousands of members, officially registered with Elvis Inc. I joined a few clubs myself, including one of the largest, the Elvis Presley Burning Love Fan Club, based in Streamwood, Illinois, and supported by more than a thousand members. I also joined Colorado Graceland, a smaller club in Denver, and began to receive fanzines from clubs all over the country: the Spirit of Elvis Fan Club, the Echo Will Never Fade Fan Club, the Snorkeling Elvises (based in Key West).

I made the pilgrimage to Graceland. I trekked to Tupelo and toured the shotgun shack where Elvis was born and lived as a baby, now a state park with a chapel, memorial garden, museum, and glitzy souvenir stand. Each summer from 1993 to 1997, I went to Memphis in the hellish humidity of August during Elvis Week. I participated in the Candlelight Vigil held on the anniversary of his death and watched fans reverently bearing glowing candles, small bouquets of flowers, handwritten poems, photos, and teddy bears slowly walk up Graceland's twisty driveway to Elvis's grave site for a brief, personal tribute.

I plowed through the books, essays, articles, editorials, graduate student theses, short stories, screenplays, and novels that make up the vast Elvis Culture industry, currently estimated at around 30,000 items, just on Elvis. (One writer argues that there's "a pressing need for someone, somewhere, to establish an encounter therapy group for all these emotionally disturbed authors unable to shake off the compulsion to write books about Elvis Presley."[21] I tend to agree.) I looked over hundreds of Elvis Web pages, both personal and "official," and eavesdropped on various online chat sites. I watched Elvis's movies (more than thirty, ranging from *Love Me Tender* [1956], in which Elvis plays a singing southern farmboy, to *Change of Habit* [1969], in which he plays an inner-city doctor and Mary Tyler Moore plays a nun). I watched multiple documentaries, docudramas, and bootleg concert videos. I listened to the music, from the mid-1950s rockabilly composites of black gospel and white country such as "That's All Right" (1954), to the jumpsuited revue schmaltz of "American Trilogy," a standard arena show closer at Elvis's 1970s concerts consisting of "Dixie," "All My Trials," and "The Battle Hymn of the Republic." I sat through hours and hours of Elvis impersonator contests, from regional tourneys at suburban dinner clubs to the most prestigious (and long-lived) gig of them all—the "Images of Elvis" contest held each August in Memphis.

I wrote to small-town and larger urban newspapers across America, from the *Ripon Commonwealth Press* to the *Denver Post*, asking editors to print my "Letter to Elvis Fans," which asked fans why they were fans and which Elvis image they liked the most. Hundreds of fans from all over the country generously and enthusiastically responded, many sending me photographs of themselves and their Elvis artwork, others mailing me fan club newsletters and various handmade Elvis items (including a shoe bag printed with tiny pictures of Elvis, sent by the mother of a Delta Airlines flight attendant), all relating their deepest and most passionate feelings about Elvis. Admittedly, my inquiries also prompted a handful of cantankerous responses from those questioning the validity of the entire project. "As a teacher I am sure you could find a more moral and uplifting subject to write a book about than the drug addicted, womanizing, pelvis thrusting, sorry specimen of manhood, ELVIS PRESLEY," wrote one woman from Tennessee, offering yet another image of Elvis.

Most of all, I talked with Elvis fans, especially those who collect Elvis stuff (their term) and make Elvis art (mine). In long conversations in homes and hotel rooms, in coffee shops and family-style restaurants (like the Shoney's near Graceland, on Elvis Presley Boulevard), in studios and galleries, on airplanes and in bus stations, we talked about what Elvis means to them and why they are fans. I asked "why Elvis?" and they shared their ideas and observations, many providing an exact date for when they first saw him on TV, or first heard him in concert, or bought their first Elvis record. I explained my own fascination with the image of Elvis everywhere and they nodded and invited me into their houses and apartments, into formerly ordinary spaces transformed into special places that they call Elvis Rooms. Proudly displaying their vast collections of Elvisiana, each treasure and trophy embodying in some fashion his face or his body or his name, fans told me about their personal relationship with Elvis Presley.

Centered around those images, objects, and relationships, this book responds to the question "why Elvis?" by looking at and thinking about the wide-ranging ways in which Elvis is everywhere as an icon, how people—particularly his fans—acknowledge those images, and what they mean in contemporary America. It is ultimately less about Elvis himself, his music, or his critics, than about the visual glut of Elvisiana everywhere and the legion of fans for whom the image of Elvis is especially meaningful. In part, this book is about fandom, about how and why people become fans and what being a fan means in terms of personal identity. But mostly, it is a book about the power of pictures in a predominantly visual culture, about the levels of appeal that images of Elvis have for his fans, and for outsiders like myself. Initiated by an epiphanic flash and my own curiosity about compelling images, this book is even more specifically centered around my questions about Elvis's image, and my search for answers. And while I aim to give representation and voice to Elvis fans, I also recognize the problems and tensions inherent in speaking for others.

Some fans, for example, responded to my queries—particularly those about sex, religion, and race—with hostility. Angered by an outsider attempting to understand Elvis's omnipresent image in ways other than theirs, they were understandably paranoid about the appearance of yet another snotty swipe at what some have called their "fanatical" and "cultist" behaviors. As one Ohio fan put it, "I assume you are not an Elvis Fan or you don't know much about Elvis. If you are not a true Elvis Fan, it may be hard to understand our Love for Elvis." Other fans threatened to undermine my project when I made it clear that I didn't necessarily share their particular ideas about Elvis Culture.

During Elvis Week 1994, for example, I had the opportunity to discuss my interest in Elvis's abiding popularity with several longtime fans over a meal at the Gridiron (Elvis's favorite Memphis hamburger joint). Our conversation turned to the topic of "negative" images of Elvis. One fan commented that she, like many fans, was "angry and insulted" that Elvis was often the subject of tasteless jokes about obesity and drugs on late-night TV talk shows. In her opinion, "disrespectful" images of Elvis, including the infamous *National Enquirer* cover photo of Elvis in his coffin, should be "banned." I countered with a defense of free speech, arguing for unlimited and self-determined expressions of Elvis. The next day, she pulled me aside at a fan club auction to tell me that she was upset with "the points I was making" and had decided to "tell other Elvis fans to stay away" from me. She did, in fact, "warn" some fans about me, and they, in turn, were wary about my presence in Elvis Culture.

Obviously, there were certain class and power relationships at work in my conversations and meetings with Elvis fans; ethnographic encounters are never free of these tensions. I am a middle-class, highly educated, and highly opinionated college professor. Perhaps more important, I'm not an Elvis fan—which I explained in conversations with fans when they asked me who I was and what I was doing. Or rather, if I like some of his music and I'm fascinated by Elvis's multifaceted image, this book aims for analysis, not adoration. My own biases in terms of class, race, and gender equity, and in favor of free speech, conflicted with those held by some (although hardly all) of the Elvis fans I talked with during the course of this project; my status as an Elvis Culture outsider meant that my inquiries about Elvis's image were occasionally met with angry responses from fans who were suspicious of the questions and the questioner.

By self-consciously foregrounding the conflicts and contradictions evident in Elvis Culture, where competition among many fans (and others) about Elvis's "correct" image doesn't engender much tolerance for those who see him differently, I've hopefully invited "judgment, evaluation, even disagreement" about my own interpretations of the ethnographic and visual evidence—and emphasized that they are my own interpretations. Hopefully, too, I've avoided completely falling into the "voxpop style" of audience-based cultural studies scholarship, whereby academic writers breathlessly construct the native intelligence, consumer savvy, and heroic oppositional politics of "the people" and, by so doing, narcissistically celebrate *their* discovery of living, breathing, postmodern revolutionaries.[22]

For some writers, Elvis Culture, as a key part of the "culture of celebrity" and mass commercial culture in general, is evidence of a profound pathology in contemporary America. Marxist and neoconservative critics alike see much of contemporary American culture "as ugly or dangerous, a symptom of the American decline into decadence, ignorance, and triviality."[23] Theorists ranging from Stuart Ewen and Neil Postman to Irving Kristol and Norman Podhoretz argue that public life has been sapped and gutted because Americans have transferred their allegiances to commercial culture; have, in turn, inappropriately imposed consumer values onto such a sphere as politics; and have shown themselves incapable of distinguishing between them. Commercial culture is perceived as an opiate of illusory satisfactions, an ideological tool that, as Theodor Adorno and Max Horkheimer and more recent Frankfurt School descendants argue, distracts, pacifies, and controls the masses.[24]

Following that view, Elvis fans are seen as the unempowered recipients of trivial images and numbing ideologies provided by a dominant commercial culture—especially by Elvis Inc., which aims to control the ubiquitous amount of stuff that circulates in Elvis Culture.

Surface, not substance, dominates; image has overtaken reality; imitation has replaced originality; passivity has replaced personal and civic activism. Jean Baudrillard posits that Americans have entered an "age of simulation" where "signs of the real" are understood as "the real itself."[25] All of which raises profound questions about the public sphere and American culture: What happens to meaningful public discourse and civic participation if commercialism dominates as the mode of reference? How can a democratic culture be sustained if authenticity and reality are no longer discernible but are mimicked, stylized, and marketed?

The primary assumption made by these critics is that images control human behavior in unmediated, direct, and closed ways. The prescription suggested by some is to insist that the "empty image" be overthrown and demystified, that the manipulative operations of commercial culture be exposed so that consumers will recognize and, it is then supposed, challenge and oppose them. Michael Parenti demands: "Resist we must. The public is not able to exercise much democratic control over image manipulation unless it is aware of the manipulation. The first step, then, is to develop a critical perspective. When it comes to the media, criticism is a form of defense."[26] An ameliorative offered by more puritanical critics is to shape resistance into abstinence, thus creating a cleaner and essentially monolithic culture that censors or excludes that which is deemed imitative or decadent.

I don't completely disagree with those who see commercial culture as illusory, empty, and trite; I, too, am often disgusted, or more generally bored, with the vacuity of a lot of contemporary American culture (like *Baywatch*). But the hand-wringing critiques just noted tend to treat people as helpless half-wits completely manipulated by "the media" and their own abnormal desires. They also tend to treat visual culture as something shallow and superficial, "empty" of real significance because it is too full of contradictions and confusion. Stuart Hall, John Fiske, and Janice Radway, among others, challenge these assumptions of an all-powerful mass culture by considering how audiences interpret—or negotiate—texts, images, and objects. In her study of the mostly female readership of contemporary romance novels, Radway explains how women "resist, alter, and reappropriate the materials designed elsewhere for their purchase."[27]

Such critiques call for an understanding of audience reception in the sociology of culture. By and large, however, and mostly because of its roots in literary criticism, reception and response theory remains focused on how audiences *derive* meaning from texts, especially written sources. It tends to ignore the fact that people understand images in very different ways. Visual culture is very much the product of response, the result of active and subjective relationships that take place between ourselves and the things we look at. Its ongoing construction consists of images and objects, their makers and viewers, and the spaces in between—physical and psychological spaces where we "behold" and respond to pictures and things. The real significance of visual culture is not that it is empty, but that it is overflowing with images that are multifaceted and ambivalent, that fluctuate in meaning because of our own fluctuating responses, and that refuse to be oversimplified into any all-encompassing theoretical construct. The power of images is not that they control us in unmediated ways (if they control us at all), but that they tease certain kinds of emotive responses (desire, hatred, faith, empathy) and that out of our reactions, and commingled with lots of other cultural baggage, we produce meaning. The work of art, writes Wendy Steiner, is "a virtual reality which we invest with value. . . . Alert to meaning and to pleasure, we go to art for an enlightened beguilement, exercising our freedom throughout."[28]

Most accounts of visual culture concentrate on its form and content: the shapes and subjects of paintings and sculptures, the way they look, the stories they tell. The context of art—who painted a picture and why, when it was exhibited, how much it is worth—has steadily become the primary scholarly focus of art history over the past several decades. Attention to the commercial and social institutions that promote and distribute art, to the interplay between the fine arts and popular culture, and to the ways that art reinforces or resists racism and sexism importantly situate the value and power of images and objects. But only rarely do art historians and critics consider what visual culture means to people, and how they use it in meaningful ways. Without ignoring any of these approaches, this book concen-

Jennifer Hoffecker, Elvis Plate *(1993). Porcelain, 12 inches round.*
(Collection of the author)

trates on Elvis fans and considers the intensity of their response to
his image. It looks at their visual choices and analyzes them in terms
of individual agency. It aims to show how visual culture is embedded
in everyday social practice and how, by understanding how and
why people look at pictures of Elvis, we can learn a lot about the
links and gaps between images and identity and making and looking,
thereby speculating about why Elvis's image is so dominant in contemporary America.

The social practices of Elvis fans include collecting, arranging, and displaying Elvis images and objects—stuff that is both handmade and mass-marketed—in specially designated Elvis Rooms or Elvis shrines. They include making Elvis artworks. They include making Elvis over through imitation or impersonation. They include participating in the ritual activities of Elvis Week each August. Most of all, they include the aesthetic experience—the sheer pleasure—of looking at images of Elvis. By engaging in any or all of these acts, Elvis fans continually revitalize his popularity, reworking, reimagining, and reinventing Elvis to mesh with their personal and social preferences. Fans do not simply derive meaning from Elvis's image, but actually "make" Elvis in dramatic and deeply emotional ways. These acts of cultural production are significant and charged and, I argue, key to the dominance that Elvis's image holds in contemporary American culture.

If Elvis's best biographer, Peter Guralnick, aims to "rescue" Elvis "from the dreary bondage of myth, from the oppressive aftershock of cultural significance," this book is explicitly focused on contemporary myth and cultural meaning. And if critic Greil Marcus argues that the key to understanding the cultural symbolism of "a dead but evanescent Elvis Presley" lies in his music, the music alone doesn't explain the abiding visual dominance of Elvis's image.[79] That can be understood only by looking carefully and thoughtfully at Elvis pictures and objects, by talking with Elvis artists and fans, and by seriously reflecting on the power—religious, political, personal—of popular culture imagery in late-twentieth-century America.

Seeing and saying that Elvis is everywhere, that Elvis is iconic, that Elvis is a saint, and that Elvis fans have constructed what may amount to a quasi-religion is fairly obvious. A more profound issue remains how and why certain popular culture figures become American icons, and how and why Elvis is such an icon. Looking at images of Elvis and reflecting on their origins, their audiences, their appeal, and their authority, this book aims to unravel the tangle of meanings that Elvis has and holds in contemporary American culture.

Paying Homage to ELVIS

GracelandToo, the Holly Springs, Mississippi, habitat of Paul MacLeod and his son, Elvis Aaron Presley MacLeod, is plastered from floor to ceiling with "everything Elvis." Elvis posters and film stills fill the entrance hallway. Elvis liquor decanters, dolls, and license plates parade up the risers leading to the second floor ("The Stairway to Elvis"). Elvis pictures encased inside fussy pink frames

Paul MacLeod leading a tour of Elvis fans from Japan, interior of GracelandToo, 1996, Holly Springs, Mississippi.

adorn the living room. Plastic shopping bags from the Memphis gift shops Elvisly Yours and Souvenirs of Elvis droop along the parlor walls. A portrait of Elvis in an ornate gilt frame, attended by a shiny metallic crown-shaped car deodorizer and two fancy brass candle-holders, is displayed over the mantle of the dining room fireplace.

Cases of Elvis memorabilia, trunks of carpet samples from his mansion in Memphis, stacks of newspapers from the date of his death, and bouquets of dried flowers from his grave clutter a narrow passageway leading from the bathroom (full of Elvis books and magazines) to the front door. Tributes to Elvis printed on multicolored sheets of paper are taped to the kitchen ceiling. Even the main floor bedroom of Paul MacLeod's elderly mother is decked out in full-blown Elvisiana: a quilt embellished with pictures of Elvis's best-selling 45s, windows draped in plush blue and shiny gold curtains, walls completely lined in rows and rows of Elvis album covers and black vinyl disks, all arranged in an infinite pattern of high-shine squares and circles.

(overleaf) *"Stairway to Elvis," interior of GracelandToo, 1996, Holly Springs, Mississippi.*

Midway between Memphis and Tupelo, Holly Springs (population 7,500) is flush with hundreds of huge baronial estates built from nineteenth-century cotton fortunes. Tours of antebellum houses, Rust College (a historically black liberal arts school), light industry, and a brand-new minimum-security prison drive the local economy, but lately, most visitors to Holly Springs seem to arrive with just one goal in mind: GracelandToo. It's the MacLeods' home and livelihood, a roadside attraction open 24 hours a day, 365 days a year, to anyone who knocks on the door. Since the MacLeods planted their hot-pink WEL-COME sign on the front lawn in 1991, some 100,000 folks have dropped by to take a peak at the "somewhere in the range of ten million" Elvis items that the MacLeods claim GracelandToo currently contains. After three tours, visitors become Lifetime GracelandToo Members, and the $5 entrance fee is waived. As a further bonus, each Lifer has his or her photo taken dressed up in one of Elvis's black leather jackets, which Paul MacLeod says he bought from one of Elvis's relatives in the early 1970s.

The MacLeods call themselves "The World's #1 Elvis Fans." Their entire antebellum home—a rather dilapidated white clapboard affair dating to 1853, flanked by two miniature cement lions and fronted (just like Graceland) with a jutting portico, a few columns, and green indoor/outdoor carpeting—is a tribute to Elvis and a monument to their lives as Elvis fans. Their cyberspace home page makes this especially clear: "While you are taking a tour of GracelandToo, you are reliving his [Elvis's] life, you also see what has made our lives complete, in doing what we love to do. Paul and Elvis Aaron Presley MacLeod have given up all they had in life to find their passion and live out their dreams daily by being surrounded by the image, voice, and the eternal flame of Elvis Aaron Presley. ELVIS WILL NEVER LEAVE THIS BUILDING AS HE WILL NEVER LEAVE OUR HEARTS!!!"[1]

Born in Detroit in 1942, Paul MacLeod became enamored with Elvis in 1956, after seeing him perform "Heartbreak Hotel" on CBS's *Stage Show* and "hearing Jackie Gleason say Elvis was just a 'flash in the pan.' But I figured anybody who moved like that, and looked like that, and combed his hair like that, well, he was somebody special." Hooked by Elvis's image, Paul began dressing like him in pegged pants and two-tone shoes, slicking his hair back in a duck-tail

Author wearing Elvis's black leather jacket, collection of Paul and Elvis Aaron MacLeod, GracelandToo, 1996, Holly Springs, Mississippi.

pompadour, growing sideburns. Over the past forty years, he hasn't changed much; he still sports slashing sideburns and a head of thickly pomaded black hair, and greets GracelandToo visitors in fancy ruffled shirts that (he admits) are a little tight around the waist. He likes to show off the gold lamé suit (an exact replica of the one Elvis wowed audiences with during concerts in 1957) that he swears he'll be buried in, if he loses a little weight.

Elvis MacLeod, born in 1973, is a bigger version of his dad (he

Exterior, GracelandToo, 1996, Holly Springs, Mississippi.

played football at Holly Springs High) and likes to wear black leather jackets and black pants—his approximation of Elvis's 1968 "comeback special" costume. Dismissing insinuations that he was "forced" to become a fan by his father, he says, "I had a normal childhood and live my life the way that I want." Recounting pleasurable early memories of listening to Elvis on the radio and seeing him in concert (he saw him four times before he was four years old), Elvis MacLeod sees himself as a member of "Generation E," a younger crowd of eighteen-to thirty-year-old fans who aim to "make the endless legacy of Elvis grow for a new generation of people, no matter what category of race, creed, or background." Both men describe themselves as "diehard Elvis fans" who have "lived, breathed, slept Elvis Presley." As Elvis MacLeod writes, "My father and I have dedicated our lives to preserving the legacy of Elvis Presley in the occurrences of our daily lives. This is our way of paying tribute to a man who has given so much to us."[2]

The MacLeods pay tribute to Elvis through imitation and possession, by dressing like him and collecting as much Elvis stuff as they can get their hands on. Paul began their collection by buying 1950s Elvis juvenilia: school binders, pencils, plastic belts, and billfolds all emblazoned with pictures of a sneering, gyrating, rockabilly Elvis. He "just kept collecting things," from Elvis's 1951 report card ("he flunked music, you can see it right there") and a 1953 program for a Memphis high-school talent show (Humes High Annual Minstrel, where Elvis played guitar), to rare Elvis bootleg records, autographed pictures, Elvis tapestries, Elvis busts, Vegas-era rhinestone-studded belts, tell-all biographies long out of print, tickets to several post-death arena shows.

Collecting Elvis extended to every possible contact Paul could have with him, too. He attended more than 120 Elvis concerts and "came close to meeting him eight times." Vacations in Holly Springs, where his mother had family, let him see Elvis perform all over the South in the 1950s, and after he quit his job at Detroit's Cadillac Motors ("Elvis's favorite car was a Cadillac") in the early 1970s, Paul followed Elvis all over the rest of the country. His wife, Serita, whom he married in 1968, often joined him. One faded photograph prominently displayed in GracelandToo's parlor shows the two of them, Paul outfitted in Elvis-esque sideburns and a baby-blue leisure suit, and a bouffant-coifed Serita looking a lot like Priscilla in the late 1960s, lounging in the backseat of a Las Vegas limo after catching Elvis's act at the International Hotel. Another photo, taken when Elvis MacLeod was a toddler, shows father and son standing in front of Graceland's Melody Gates.

Paul MacLeod moved to Holly Springs in 1973 and used to drive to

Graceland (about an hour away) "every night, around 11:00, to wait and see Elvis." Often he would take his young son, and the two of them became well known to Elvis's security guards and his uncle Vester Presley, who manned Graceland's gates and sometimes would invite them to take a walk around the grounds. One night, they chanced upon Elvis recording "Hurt" in Graceland's Jungle Room, an over-the-top den that Elvis had outfitted in green shag carpeting and quasi-Hawaiian furniture, sort of a material culture version of David Lindley's oft-performed tune "Tiki Tortures by Twilight." During the early hours of August 16, 1977, Paul says he shot "the last film of Elvis alive," a clip (now "locked up in a bank vault") featuring Elvis and his fiancée, Ginger Alden, gunning a Harley-Davidson down Graceland's twisty driveway.

Shattered by Elvis's death later that morning, the MacLeods joined some 60,000 other fans in mournful vigil outside Graceland's gates. An AP wire photo printed in newspapers across America a few days later showed the forlorn family—Paul, Serita, and four-year-old Elvis Aaron MacLeod—sitting on the lawn at Forest Hill Cemetery, watching Elvis Presley's funeral procession pass them by. The night of the funeral, Paul and a reporter "got locked up for 4½ hours in the mausoleum where Elvis was buried. I just kept banging on the doors until a guard let us out." In the early 1990s, Paul says his wife asked him "to make a decision: her or the Elvis collection, and well, you can see what happened. We were married 23 years." After Serita left and Elvis graduated from high school, the MacLeods opened their Holly Springs house to the world.

There is little furniture in GracelandToo, and some basic appliances were tossed out years ago to create more space for the MacLeods' ever-increasing collection of Elvis ephemera. But the MacLeods don't seem to need such creature comforts, spending most of their time collecting more and more Elvis stuff, conducting house tours, selling "I've Been to GracelandToo" T-shirts, and monitoring Elvis's mass-media appearances. The younger MacLeod, who leads most of the house tours and works the crowd with an auctioneer's pace and an impressive command of Elvis lore and legend, describes GracelandToo as "the world's largest Elvis archive," explaining that he and his father have filled more than 1,000 plastic notebooks with newspaper, radio, and TV references to Elvis—for example, "on September ninth [1993], at six forty-three Central time, on *Entertainment Tonight*, CBS, the actor Christian Slater talked about how he became a big Elvis fan while filming the movie *True Romance*. In the movie Val Kilmer plays Elvis's ghost and gives Slater advice."[3] Mass-media central is GracelandToo's living room, equipped with stacks of full-console TVs and a few VCRs, always turned on and tuned in to the slightest mention of Elvis. The fact that the MacLeods don't have cable TV or a satellite dish or a short-wave radio or access to every newspaper and journal in the world doesn't deter them from their earnest vow to footnote Elvis. Their archives are simply another version of how fans remember and revere Elvis through the stuff of material culture.

To outsiders, GracelandToo might seem trashy. More than a few who've trooped through the MacLeods' museum gawk and giggle at GracelandToo's low-life density: its fake fireplace, its blood-red shag carpets, its swags of gold rayon drapes trimmed in dingle-balls, its latticed mahogany-veneer wood-grain hutches, its liberal scattering of heart-shaped satin pillowcases, smoked-glass mirrors, freestanding brass ashtrays, plaster-of-paris eagles, flocked lampshades fringed in sparkly bric-a-brac—all interspersed amid an overwhelming array of Elvis images and objects. Others poke fun at the 40,000 newspaper clippings and the 11,000 video tapes and audio cassettes amassed over the years, pointing out—and the MacLeods are the first to agree—that even all of that doesn't come close to capturing Elvis's phenomenal presence in information culture over the past four decades. But GracelandToo isn't about good taste and it isn't about the thorough acquisition of a complete archive. GracelandToo is about how one family of fans pays homage to Elvis. The MacLeods may seem obsessive and extreme, but their ways of collecting and displaying Elvis stuff make Elvis meaningful and help shape their own identities.

Fandom is a way that men and women express their authority in popular culture. That isn't to say that fans don't also recognize how they are often manipulated by the mass-mediated commercialism and commodification of popular culture and that often, quite aware of this irony, they encourage that manipulation. Elvis fans have never been, in other words, simply or only the gullible victims of a manipulative culture industry but active and enthusiastic participants in the creation of a deeply materialist Elvis Culture. The two positions tend to exist simultaneously, with fans both helping to produce Elvis's celebrity and being caught up in the consumerist orientation of mass culture. Neither position has ever been exactly figured: culture industry analysts still don't have any real clues about the "precise ingredients of a bestseller formula."[4] Still, Elvis's abiding popular culture presence for the past forty years has largely depended on the ways that audiences, particularly his fans, have negotiated and understood his music and, especially, his image. Fans are essential to Elvis Culture, and the valorized Elvis stuff that fans like the MacLeods collect plays an instrumental role in shaping his larger cultural significance.

Material culture has always served both utilitarian and symbolic purposes, and the material culture that has flourished in Elvis Culture since the mid-1950s is no different. From its beginnings, Elvis Culture has been thoroughly involved with stuff: its fandom thoroughly saturated in commerce and consumerism; Elvis's meaning thoroughly attached to the images and objects, the pictures and things, the material goods that have replicated his body and his face. Ranging from the prosaic to the priceless, the artifacts of Elvis Culture—like things in general, as Mihaly Csikszentmihalyi has argued—display power and social status, provide a sense of historical continuity, and help fans assert and maintain their identities as fans.[5] None of this is particularly straightforward: circuitous and often conflicted relationships between fans and material culture are central to Elvis Culture, as are abiding struggles over who "owns" and can profit from Elvis's image. Importantly, Elvis's image has always been the stuff of enormous profit, symbolic and financial. Those profits depend on his fandom. Understanding the dense interplay among fandom, material culture, mass media, and commerce provides further insights into the fluid and dynamic relationships that exist between cultural production and consumption in Elvis Culture.

In the 1950s, fans like Paul MacLeod became fans, and stayed fans, because of what they saw as much as what they heard: Elvis's rhythmic and sexy body, his drop-dead image, his charismatic intimacy, his iconic presence. They viewed Elvis's Greek god good looks and "grunt and groin" performance style with desire, and articulated their desire through imitation and possession. Elvis's image personified liberation and pleasure and openness, and being a fan was a way of paying homage to that image and that openness, of claiming a body that refused containment and made them move, of becoming their own performance artists, of indulging emotions that were unpredictable and uncontrolled.

Of course, in 1950s consumer culture, as much as today's, all of that was easily commodified: powerful images that embody pleasure and freedom have always been seized as the stuff of profit in modern capitalism. And Elvis's image proved to be particularly profitable, marketed into a multimillion-dollar merchandising industry by 1956. The Colonel had been personally hawking souvenir programs and color photos at every Elvis show ever since he signed on as manager in 1955, and he also ran Elvis Presley Enterprises, the first business outfit (and forerunner of Elvis Inc.) to copyright Elvis's name and likeness in anticipation of merchandising royalties. After Elvis's exposure on national TV, Parker hit pay dirt by enlisting the retail-sales genius of Henry G. Saperstein, a Beverly Hills promoter who handled accounts for Lassie, the Lone Ranger, and Kellogg's Corn Flakes. Linking personalities with products was "nothing new," said Saperstein. "It happened with Valentino, Theda Bara, and Clara Bow. We are each of us insecure in our way. We like to identify ourselves with people who are somebody." What was new was tapping into a thriving 1950s youth market with Elvis products geared toward teen tastes and postwar prosperity. The 1956 census, after all, included 13 million teenagers, most earning more than $10 a week in spending money and all together contributing some $7 billion a year to the U.S. economy.[6]

Saperstein started a full-blown Elvis exploitation in the fall of 1956. Ascertaining that the average "insecure" teenager identified most with Elvis's twenty-one-year-old body and his flashy clothes, Saperstein began marketing Elvis-style jeans (black denim with emerald-green stitching, $2.98 a pair), T-shirts, skirts, sneakers, socks, belts, scarves, caps, pajamas, and sideburns (black plastic paste-on rectangles purchased for $1 from dime-store vending machines). Presley promotions quickly expanded to include products aimed especially at Elvis's female fans, including lipsticks (in six shades, including Hound Dog Orange and Heartbreak Pink), charm bracelets, brooches, necklaces,

Examples of Elvis exploitation, 1956. (Collection of William J. DeNight, Streamwood, Illinois)

rings, purses, patent-leather pumps (tooled with images of Elvis), dolls, and "Teddy Bear" eau de parfum.

Must-have teen fashion accessories were accompanied by the sort of school supplies that Paul MacLeod and thousands of other 1950s fans collected, and by Elvis board games, comic books, statuettes, busts, toy guitars, bookends, picture frames, scrapbooks, overnight cases, pillows, phonographs, ashtrays, plates, glasses, paint-by-number sets, bubble-gum cards, and glow-in-the-dark photographs. Saperstein and Parker's promotion of Elvis products, advertised in teen magazines like *Dig* and sold at Sears and Woolworth's, was one of the most successful merchandising schemes in modern history. There were other, "unofficial" purveyors of Elvis stuff in the 1950s, too, but their efforts, once discovered by the Colonel, were legally challenged and generally repressed on the grounds of copyright infringement. By the end of 1956, Elvis Presley Enterprises' sales of Elvis stuff reached $22 million, and Elvis's image easily matched that of Mickey Mouse and Jesus Christ in terms of mass reproduction. Saperstein predicted that the "Great Elvis Presley Industry" might top $55 million by 1958, a figure entirely exclusive of the millions simultaneously being made from the sales of Elvis's singles and albums and of tickets to his movies.[7]

Such optimism stemmed in large part from the phenomenal number of fans that Elvis had already attracted in his brief career. Both Parker and Saperstein, who had based their entire professional lives on promoting talents and products, were absolutely astounded by the "sustained, hysterical, frenzied roar" of fan reactions to Elvis. They also couldn't help but notice, long before their own Elvis exploitations took off, the number of fan clubs mushrooming across America, offering members photos and fanzines at nominal fees. Texas probably spawned the first Elvis fan club, organized in Dallas in 1954, and club members were seen all over the South during Elvis's mid-1950s concert tours, waving big signs with his name hand-lettered in glossy pink lipstick. At one concert, club president Kay Wheeler told a reporter: "He's the most fascinating human being I've ever known. Elvis is a living denial of the notion teenagers should be seen and not heard." By 1956, the Dallas club ("the biggest and most obnoxious Elvis Presley Fan Club in the world," griped one journalist) had 7,000 members.[8] Before being blatantly mass-marketed into a teen commodity, in other words, Elvis's image had attracted the unbridled devotion of a huge number of regional fans. Their response snowballed Elvis's success and spurred his exploitation; indeed, Saperstein chose Dallas to test-market those $1 tubes of Elvis Presley lipstick.

But the fans' response wasn't completely unmediated. Elvis was first heard on Memphis radio stations in July 1954, and appeared more

Elvis with fans, 1957. (Photo collection of William J. DeNight, Streamwood, Illinois)

than fifty times on the *Louisiana Hayride* (Shreveport's rival to the *Grand Ole Opry*) from 1954 to 1956, because of his own talents and ambitions—and because the culture industry sniffed success. Sun Records, Elvis's first record company, pushed him, his popular potential, and their own profits by cutting as many 45s and arranging as many stage shows and interviews as possible. Marion Keisker, the secretary at Sun and a Memphis radio personality well versed in public relations, organized the first "official" (or industry-related) fan club in the fall of 1954, when Elvis was still known primarily as the lead singer of a rockabilly combo called the Blue Moon Boys. Still, if Elvis's image was produced right from the start, that production took place only because a lot of teenagers had already emotionally and physically invested themselves in that image. It has remained fixed in American popular culture for more than four decades because Elvis fans like the MacLeods continue to center their lives around "the image, voice, and the eternal flame of Elvis Aaron Presley"—and because the culture industry continues to fan the flames of their devotion.

After Elvis left Sun and signed with RCA (in November 1955), and the Colonel took hold of his career, the club Keisker started was renamed the Elvis Presley National Fan Club and was headquartered in Madison, Tennessee, near Nashville (where Parker had previously promoted country music stars Eddy Arnold and Hank Snow). Elvis exploitation now became a full-time operation: by September 1956, more than 350 clubs had signed on with the national organization, which reported receiving "20,000 cards and letters" from fans every week. Fan club members were sent membership cards, autographed glossies, Elvis updates ("ELVIS is currently making his first picture! Wow! From all reports it sure will be terrific!"), and "personal" notes from Elvis himself, chatty form letters that emphasized his appeal ("just being near girls makes me kinda nervous and tingly all over, like getting shocked, but I like it!") and encouraged them to push his music ("drop your local disc jockey a card and ask him to spin one of my songs for you. . . . [R]emember that I'll be singing it just *for you!!*").[9] Later in 1956, Saperstein took over the club with the express purpose of selling Elvis merchandise to its conservatively estimated 200,000 members.

Presleymania had plenty of detractors in the 1950s, too. One popular ditty of the day was

Love me tender
love me quick
Elvis Presley
makes me sick

Parker, always alert to the vagaries of popular taste, sold "I Hate Elvis" buttons right alongside those that professed undying love. The mainstream press mostly belittled Elvis's exploitation and the voracious appetites of his teenage fans, hugely underestimating youth culture, and rock and roll especially, as a fad that wouldn't last long and wouldn't play a serious and sustainable economic role. Even Saperstein doubted Elvis could carry more than two years of heavy marketing: "He's too hot. He can't be sustained at the maximum level."[10]

Other popular culture observers drew on Elvis's meteoric rise to fame and cult-like following, and the success of the Elvis industry, as inspiration for their own sweeping critiques of Cold War America. In 1957, Tennessee Williams staged *Orpheus Descending*, in which a sexy southern singer named Valentine Xavier (played by Cliff Robertson), sporting an outlandish snakeskin jacket and a twelve-string guitar, is hotly pursued by every woman he meets ("She thought I had a sign 'Male at Stud' hung on me," he remarks) and ultimately succumbs to the jealousy and fanaticism of a small-town lynch mob.[11] Provoked, perhaps, by newspaper accounts of 14,000 fans tearing at Elvis's clothes during a 1955 concert in Jacksonville, Florida, Williams used *Orpheus Descending* to work out a cautionary tale about sexuality, desire, and postwar intolerance with a distinctly Elvis-esque character playing center stage.

Hollywood director Elia Kazan appropriated a similar Elvis icon in his bitter analysis of mass adulation and media manipulation, *A Face in the Crowd* (1957). Based on a screenplay by Budd Schulberg, the film focused on the rise—and fall—of Lonesome Rhodes, a hillbilly guitarist played by Andy Griffith. Before playing the television sheriff of Mayberry, Griffith had been a comical country-music star, sort of a postwar version of Will Rogers. He even headlined a few 1955 concerts in which Elvis's preshow appearance incited near riot conditions, and the two sang together on *The Steve Allen Show* in July 1956. In Kazan's movie, Griffith's character is "discovered" in an Arkansas jail and becomes a phenomenal television star, welcomed into the living rooms of "sixty-five million people" every week. Mobbed by female fans and mass-marketed in a slew of commercial gimmicks, Lonesome tries to turn his down-home, one-of-the-folks TV persona into political authority, but the film closes with his exposure as a fraud and a phony, a "Demagogue in Denim." A pointed critique about "the power of television" and the "mule-stupid" masses, *A Face in the Crowd* was filmed at exactly the same time Elvis was soaring to success.[12] Certain scenes eerily resemble newsreels of Elvis playing before hordes of screaming teenage fans, matching the ways his image was exploited as the stuff of mass consumerism.

For postwar intellectuals, Elvis Presley—a.k.a. "Valentine Xavier" and "Lonesome Rhodes"—symbolized the allure and evil of mass culture, damned as a seductive fiend that corrupted innocents and made the masses into irrational mobs. Their anxieties were shared by the popular press of the 1950s, which in a postwar climate of enthusiastic American pseudo-individualism tended to equate mass taste with political and social perversion. One critic at the *Los Angeles Mirror-News* saw Elvis's concerts as the stuff of dangerous totalitarianism, writing that his performance style resembled "one of those screeching, uninhibited party rallies which the Nazis used to hold for Hitler." Only a decade removed from World War II, Cold War critics held fast to the idea that the masses, and their popular culture, could easily become the basis for the kind of political deviance recently repelled in Nazi Germany and fascist Italy, and still strong behind Communism's iron curtain. Excitable and excessive, easily persuaded by image and invitation, Elvis's teenage fans personified the much feared masses. Their "idol worship" of Elvis was held out for particular contempt.[13]

Castigated for their cultish conduct, Elvis fans were also stamped as nonconformists who refused to channel their individualism into "acceptable outlets." A spokesman for the Midwestern Psychological Association warned that Elvis "worshippers" and "hardened criminals" were similarly social "misfits." A 1957 survey, based on interviews with 100 teens, described Elvis fans as "rabid" rebels "who can't face [the] adult world." Compared with the devotees of Frank Sinatra, Pat Boone, and Perry Como, the survey found that Elvis fans got lower grades, didn't like to join clubs "operated by their school, church or community," and were "shockingly unconcerned about the future." According to this study, irresponsible and "unadjusted" teens were drawn to Elvis because he mocked parental authority: "Through an alliance of the spirit with Presley, the teenager is able to act out his infantile desires of striving for power through the destruction of adult standards and symbols. He can satisfy his need to belong by uniting with other youngsters of similar aims."[14]

Perceptions of a rising tide of juvenile delinquency obsessed many postwar Americans, and Elvis (along with James Dean and Marlon Brando) came to symbolize a maladjusted youth culture. Some of this concern stemmed from anxiety about the menacing energies of rock and roll itself, consistently demonized in the 1950s for its overtures to social and sexual deviancy. Sinatra, watching his popular culture authority slip among America's teenagers, likened Elvis to a "sideburned delinquent" and damned "his kind of music" as "phony and false" and "deplorable, a rancid-smelling aphrodisiac."[15] As though his own slick crooning never aroused any teenage lust, Sinatra's agitation about rock and roll's rhythmic affinity to sex was widespread in a Cold War America as obsessed with illicit teenage sex, especially among girls, as it was with teenage delinquency.

Much of the postwar critique of Elvis's fans was, in fact, a thinly veiled attack on teenage girls, steadily maligned throughout 1950s America for profoundly violating social norms by having babies out of wedlock (the illegitimacy rate tripled between 1940 and 1957). Sexual panic possessed postwar Americans, and never more so than in the mid-1950s, when teenage pregnancy hit all-time highs and Elvis first appeared on the national stage. Elvis's eroticism was thought to dangerously spur the sexual deviancy of his female fans, seemingly aroused to a rutting frenzy by his "grunt and groin" performance art, and to threaten social order. Nasty sketches of those female fans betray the overall misogyny and sexual repression of 1950s culture: *Look* called them "half-grown females with half-baked ideas," and *Life* frequently printed photographs of "hysterical" adolescent girls brought "to the breaking point" by Elvis's gyrating suggestiveness.[16] Condescending reporters repeatedly described how "silly" girls squealed, screamed, shrieked, sobbed, and swooned during Elvis's concerts, emphasizing their irrationality and animalism, their sexual heat.

These 1950s critiques may explain why, forty years later, Elvis's fans—still predominantly female in the thriving Elvis fan clubs—continue to be ridiculed. The word "fan" comes from *fanum*, what the Romans called the temples of the various religious cults they encountered around the classical world. Shortened from the Latin *fanaticus*, an adjective describing the lunatic devotions of those temple cultists, the word "fan" has always been linked with over-the-top enthusiasm and excess. *Mondo Elvis* (1984), Tom Corboy's "documentary style" video, perfectly captures how Elvis fans continue to be viewed as fixated freaks.[17] The film focuses on a select handful of Elvis devotees, including teenage twins Jenny and Judy Carroll, who say they "would like to see Elvis Presley become the first Protestant saint" and explain that Elvis is their "real father" because they look just like him: "We have his features, we have his eyes, we even have his little cut-off lips." Elvis impersonator Artie Mentz talks about how he "was chosen" to imitate Elvis ("an impersonator like myself to Elvis is like a priest to the church") and is grooming his five-year-old son to do the same. And forty-something New Jersey housewife Frankie Horrocks tells of leaving her children in order to live near Graceland—prior to which her husband filed for divorce on the grounds of "excessive devotion to Elvis Presley."

Infatuated and outrageous, *Mondo Elvis*'s subjects come across as wild-eyed wackos. Abiding cultural uneasiness about excessive emotionalism partially accounts for how Elvis fans are viewed in this film (and elsewhere), but not entirely. It's perfectly acceptable, for example, to be a rabid sports fan—to paint your entire body green and scream your guts out in below-zero weather at Lambeau Field in adulation of the Green Bay Packers. Starting in the late nineteenth century, it became the norm to call American baseball enthusiasts "fans," and no particular deviance was attached to that description. The contemporary sports world is big business and mostly male (Howard Cosell said it had the "roughhouse aura of a stag party"), and both factors account for the social acceptance, or at least the spotty criticism, of its fans.[18] Elvis Culture, on the contrary, doesn't rate high as an economic agent (although the annual net at Elvis Inc. ought to suggest otherwise) and is generally thought to consist mainly of female fans—the grownup girls of the 1950s. An increasing number of sports fans are women, of course, and many Elvis fans are men, but gendered assumptions about each category of fans permit their particular social positioning: screaming for Packers quarterback Brett Favre is acceptable; screaming for Elvis isn't.

Sports fans aside, fans are typically viewed on pathological terms as obsessed loners and deranged psychotics (like Mark Chapman, who shot John Lennon, or Yolanda Saldivar, who murdered Latina pop star Selena) or as hysterics and hooligans (teenage girls screaming for the Beatles, teenage boys at heavy-metal concerts). Fans are perceived as irrational, uncontrollable, and insecure social deviants, abnormal "others" who are absurdly enthralled with celebrities, dead or alive. Even though opera buffs, antique-doll collectors, and Shakespeare scholars may be equally infatuated and obsessed, they are respected as discriminating aficionados, not fans. The inherent deviance of fandom, in other words, is related to cultural biases about taste and class: a connoisseur is someone who collects Picasso prints; a fan is someone who collects Elvis liquor decanters. Fandom's deviance further stems from anxieties about the sociopolitical threat of the disaffected masses. Stereotyped as uneducated and lower-class, with unreasonable (and perhaps politically dangerous) attachments to "unworthy cultural figures and forms," fans are dehumanized as passive pawns, seen as easy prey to what many believe is the hypnotic power of an all-consuming mass culture.[19]

Assumptions about their pathological character may account for the fact that fans of all kinds have been pretty much ignored as serious cultural and historical subjects. The few studies that exist tend to be gaga compilations of fan fantasies (such as the book *Starlust* [1985], which collages the sexual obsessions of David Bowie and Barry Manilow fans), exuberant insider recollections of performances and parties (such as several recent books on Deadheads, followers of the Grateful Dead), or the few academic accounts analyzing fandom primarily from ethnographic and mass-media perspectives.[20] Concentrating on either the special talents of the star or the psychosis of the fan, most studies ignore how the provocation of performers and the responses of fans work together to produce popularity and fandom.

Fans do not simply take in what they see and hear; they make it meaningful for themselves, for others, and for performers. Whatever that meaning may be and however Elvis fans shape it—from waving signs at concerts and pinning pictures of him on their bedroom walls in the 1950s, to forming fan clubs, collecting Elvis stuff, and going to Graceland in the 1990s—it activated Elvis's importance forty years ago and continues to motivate his fans today. There are different kinds of Elvis fans, of course, with different degrees of devotion. Some fans, like the folks in *Mondo Elvis* and like Paul MacLeod—who chased Elvis around the country, hung out in front of his home, copied his clothes and his hairdo, and now fills GracelandToo with all possible traces of his image—are obviously more "into" Elvis than others. Whatever the depth of their devotion, their investment in Elvis simultaneously forges their own identity and creates Elvis's meaning; fandom has an "affective sensibility" that makes for a circuitous relationship between audiences and performers.[21]

There is, in other words, a definite "codependency" between fans and the figures they adore. An insecure Elvis, made even more so by 1950s critics who obsessed on the physical affect he had on his audience and tended to ignore his talents as a singer or his contributions to the emergent culture of rock and roll, came to especially realize himself in terms of his fans. As early as October 1956, he was telling reporters, "Teen-agers are my life and my triumph. I'd be nowhere without them." In September 1958, just before he shipped out to Germany for his two-year stint in the army, Elvis asked reporters to send a "special message" to his fans: "I'd like to say that in spite of the fact that I'm going away and will be out of their eyes for some time, I hope I'm not out of their minds."[22]

Elvis's image changed during the two decades his fans eyed him in the flesh—from flashy rocker to sleek soldier, from tanned B-movie star to slick Las Vegas showman. Still, despite his own complexity and his profound musical presence, Elvis remains an outsider, largely because he is still "seen" mostly in terms of fandom, and fandom is suspect. Elvis refuses, as Greil Marcus writes, to "go away," but today's Elvis dissections focus especially on his white-trash roots, his "simple" southern ways, and his degraded death—in short, deflections from Elvis's aesthetic contributions that tend to deny his autonomy, talent, and larger cultural importance. As Marcus comments, "it is the impossibility of Elvis Presley as a conscious cultural agent that now buries him beneath his culture, the culture he inherited, the culture he made, and the culture that then to such a great degree remade itself according to his promises, complexities, contradictions, and defeats."[23]

A similar sort of refusal informs contemporary profiles of Elvis fans, generally dismissed as fat and fanatical females, usually southern, rural, uneducated, middle-aged, and lower-class. They, too, refuse to "go away" and, like Elvis, are rarely taken seriously. Now in their fifties or older, the original fans persist, but today's fans also include many who became fans only in the 1960s or after Elvis's death in 1977. They range from lawyers who hang velvet Elvises (black velvet paintings featuring a Vegas-era Elvis clutching a microphone) on their office walls as a modest token of middle-age rebellion, to elementary-school kids who "make Elvis things" in art class and wear Elvis costumes for Halloween; from heads of colleges (University of Colorado president John Buechner is "a big Elvis fan"), to heads of state (Bill Clinton made repeated overtures to Elvis Culture during the 1992 presidential campaign, even playing "Heartbreak Hotel" on *The Arsenio Hall Show*).

They include fans who make the pilgrimage to Graceland several times a year and those who stay home and fill special rooms with Elvis stuff; fans who maintain Elvis adoration Web sites and those who insist he's still alive. Some belong to fan clubs, and many don't. Elvis fans are everywhere and anyone, and can't be categorized into any geographic region, race, or class; their feelings for Elvis are complicated and can't be reduced to any simple sound bite. As Janelle McComb, a retired schoolteacher who turned her private collection of Elvis memorabilia into the Elvis Presley Museum in Tupelo, Mississippi, remarks, "You're not talking about people with two heads here. These are very intelligent people bonded together by admiration of a man with a usable past. I often wonder why the media take pictures of the people who wear all these Elvis buttons and take it to excess but bypass the professor of law who's also an Elvis fan."[24]

McComb's remarks are revealing: in Elvis fandom, Elvis's meaning is tightly bound to his—and his fans'—cultural vilification. Sniggering stereotypes about an obese pill-addicted Elvis, and those that stigmatize his fans as delusional middle-aged devotees, dominate public opinion and the popular press. How Elvis fans are understood has a lot to do with how they behave as fans and how they understand themselves. Believing, like many people, that an all-powerful entity called "the media" significantly constructs identity, Elvis fans struggle against negative stereotypes of Elvis and themselves. Paying homage to Elvis by defending his image—by "taking care of Elvis"—has motivated the surge in fan club growth in recent years.

In 1997, according to Patsy Anderson, head of fan relations at Elvis Presley Enterprises, Inc., there were approximately 525 Elvis fan clubs in forty-four countries and all but three states (North Dakota, Idaho, and Wyoming). These are only the clubs registered with Elvis Inc.; in all likelihood, there are hundreds of other, "unofficial" fan clubs around the globe. In the late 1950s, there were thousands of Elvis fan clubs; by the time of his death, there were fewer than 65. Today, about 50 new clubs are formed each year, with the fastest growth taking place in the United States, which has around 280 clubs. Some clubs take their names from song titles (the Jailhouse Rockers, Blue Hawaiians for Elvis, the Suspicious Minds Fan Club, Elvis Now or Never) or regional in-jokes (The Snorkeling Elvises: His Southernmost Fan Club). Most name themselves after what they're all about: All for the Love of Elvis (Missouri), Because of Elvis (Texas), Elvis Friendship Circle (Louisiana), Elvis Memories (California), Reflections of Elvis (Indiana), True Fans for Elvis (Maine).

Fan clubs in general have boomed in the past decade: desktop publishing and the Internet have made it easier to form booster groups for movie stars like Marilyn Monroe and performance artists like Laurie Anderson, and also for lesser celebs like Norma Zimmer (Lawrence Welk's champagne lady) and Mr. Ed (the talking horse). Engelbert Humperdinck is supported by 9 fan clubs; Gumby has 12,000 official fans; untold thousands are involved in clubs that honor TV series like Star Trek and Dark Shadows.[25] But Elvis leads them all with more clubs, more fanzines, more annual conventions, more merchandise and memorabilia, and more followers than any other figure in fandom.

Elvis fan clubs vary in size from a handful to hundreds; in 1995, the Elvis Presley Burning Love Fan Club listed 1,200 members. There is some variance, too, in terms of age, gender, and race, but my own informal survey, based on an analysis of three different clubs, suggests that a majority of Elvis fan club members in the United States are white, between thirty-five and fifty-five years old, and female. A 1990 survey by Direct Image Concepts, which was hired to help Elvis Inc.

with various direct-marketing campaigns and which obtained data from some 7,000 shoppers at Graceland's gift shops, found that most Elvis fans are white women between the ages of forty-five and fifty-five who live in small towns or edge-city suburbs. Similarly, a study of thirty fans done in Memphis during Elvis Week 1993 showed that most were female (twenty-five of thirty respondents), middle-aged (over twenty were between the ages of thirty-five and sixty-four), and middle-class (most had an annual income between $25,000 and $50,000).[26] These statistics, of course, provide information only about fans who join clubs, shop at Graceland, and/or attend Elvis Week; they do not delineate "the" Elvis fan.

Anderson's office helps facilitate the clubs, sending out packets of information on what Elvis Inc. expects ("dignity and honesty in your dealings"), mailing the latest "Elvis news" to fan club presidents (anticipated record releases, events at Graceland, updates about "Elvis people" like his backup musicians and his family), and inviting them to special Graceland get-togethers each August during Elvis Week and each January for his birthday celebration. Cognizant of the culture industry's long-standing contempt for fans, yet its eagerness to exploit them, Anderson sees her role as Elvis fan champion. "A lot of the company doesn't understand the fans," she observes, "and it's my job to tell them how important they are. We certainly know the importance of the fans in terms of record sales, merchandising, and marketing. We have obligations to the fan clubs, especially since they do so much for Elvis and his name."

Grassroots clubs, like the first Elvis fan club started in Dallas in 1954, form because of shared interests and collective admiration. Centered around Elvis appreciation, fan clubs in the 1950s were information outlets and social venues through which members kept track of Elvis's concert dates, TV appearances, and record releases, and built relationships with other fans. They were also marketing channels for the "official" club run by the Colonel. Fan clubs in the 1990s are similarly sociable and the target of today's Elvis merchandising industry. Some serve as little more than conduits for the Elvis collectibles market. Some try to reconstruct the social setting, the collectivity and emotional release, of Elvis's concerts by supporting Elvis impersonators. Colorado Graceland, a Denver club with about eighty members, helps promote the professional career of Charles King, a twenty-six-year-old entertainer who was judged "the closest thing to the one, true Elvis Presley" at the American International Elvis Competition (Memphis) in 1992.[27]

But contemporary fan clubs especially focus on "taking care" of Elvis by defending his image. Testifying to the "true" Elvis, telling the world who Elvis "really" was, and correcting media "errors" is the mission of most clubs. As Florida fan Mary Cartaya writes, "It disturbs me to realize that in his final years, he was lonely and felt betrayed by those closest to him, who continued to mar his image. This is why we, the fans, MUST UNITE, and show these FOOLS that NOTHING will EVER CHANGE OUR FEELINGS FOR ELVIS." The "club goal" of Expressly Elvis (Colorado) echoes Cartaya's passionate declaration of purpose: "to further his memory and the love, compassion and music ELVIS PRESLEY left to all of us."

Motivated by Elvis's gift-giving image ("just carrying on where Elvis left off" is a widely held fan club motto), about 80 percent of today's clubs pay homage to Elvis through fund raising. Many sponsor conventions, auctions, and benefits to support the charities that Elvis himself supported, like Le Bonheur Children's Medical Center and St. Jude Children's Research Hospital in Memphis. Over a twelve-year period ending in 1995, the Burning Love Fan Club raised $130,000 (the largest amount to date raised by any single club), and Anderson estimates that over the past twenty years, Elvis fan clubs have generated close to $2 million for Memphis charities. She applauds their efforts, but also encourages them "to work with the charities in their own home towns. The charities in Memphis might be mad to hear that, but it's one way of keeping Elvis important all over, not just in Memphis."

Fund raising gives the clubs a sense of mission beyond their own primarily social, and selfish, interests in Elvis. It mitigates the guilt some fans feel about how much Elvis gave when he was alive, and how much more they always wanted. It assuages worries about the surfeit of stuff, the conspicuous consumption, and the profoundly materialist orientation of Elvis Culture. It also helps fans construct a better public image for the man they adore. "Elvis was so warm and caring," remarks Renton, Washington, fan Alice Schlichte, who sponsors the annual Elvis Lives On Fan Convention to raise money for several Seattle charities. "The public should never forget this. In Elvis's name I give."[28] Of course, if charitable giving broadcasts Elvis's humanitarian image, it also helps fans construct their own. Several Memphis medical centers have "Elvis Walls" filled with engraved plaques noting the names of their Elvis fan club donors and how much they gave; in 1995, Burning Love had more than 100 plaques on display at the Elvis Presley Memorial Trauma Center and another Memphis hospital. In fact, despite Anderson's advice, most clubs seem to direct their charity efforts toward Memphis's medical centers rather than the homeless shelters, food banks, or rehab clinics in their own communities. Perhaps fans feel that Memphis's hospitals are the only places where they can reconcile "taking care" of Elvis with "taking care" of those in need. But then again, those "Elvis Walls" may have more appeal than America's underclass.

If defending Elvis's image, and their own, drives fan club fund raising, it also accounts for the restrictions that clubs frequently place on that image. The Looking for Elvis Fan Club in Mobile, Alabama, urges fans to boycott the tabloid *Star* because it has "belittled Elvis by referring to him as a gaudy drug addict worth more dead than alive." Similarly, Elvis Memphis Style encourages its members to "make phone calls and write letters in opposition to false and slanderous articles and statements made about Elvis Presley on television, the radio, or in print." In 1991, a Memphis chapter of the Jaycees (which had named Elvis "one of the ten most outstanding young men in America" twenty years earlier) sponsored a highly successful Halloween fund raiser whose haunted house display featured an Elvis impersonator lying in a coffin, who mumbled "Thank yuh very much" whenever someone entered the room. Surrounded by jelly doughnuts, empty pizza boxes, bottles of pills, and a toilet, the Dead Elvis Display was more comical than terrifying, but many fans didn't like the joke. Memphis Style's members flooded the Jaycees' phone lines with irate calls about this "show of disrespect to Elvis."

For these fans, Elvis's image is narrowly defined in terms of talent and generosity. They readily admit that Elvis was "no saint," but their image of him as a great entertainer and humanitarian outweighs his "human sins." Images of Elvis that smack of irreverence—from the

Jaycees' Halloween display to Albert Goldman's lurid biography of Elvis (consistently held out by many fans as "the worst of all the bad things" produced about Elvis)—are heatedly denounced. These fans have "rules" about Elvis's "right" image, and, free speech aside, jokes about that image are simply not tolerated. Wearing an "Elvis Shot J.F.K." T-shirt (a big seller in used-record stores) is tantamount to heresy, expressions of interest in seeing the "secret Elvis autopsy videotape" can be met with blows, and exhibiting "offensive" Elvis artwork—as the Memphis College of Art did in 1997—is prohibited. Determining which image of Elvis is the "true" Elvis can lead to fierce rivalry between clubs, too. Some side with Elvis's persona as a rock-and-roll rebel, while others tend to support the Jesus-in-a-jumpsuit image Elvis cultivated in later years; some support Elvis impersonators, while others condemn them as aberrant imposters. Elvis Culture newcomers, many of whom bring different ideas about his image into the mix, are often suspected of inauthenticity by older, longtime fans. "It's kind of like different churches," observes Fred Whobrey, a fan from Decatur, Illinois, who is also president of the International Federation of Elvis Presley Fan Clubs. "Schisms occur. The new club will say the old one wasn't putting Elvis first."[29]

Claims to Elvis's "correct" image especially correspond to how fans themselves want to be seen. For many, Elvis's image closely mirrors their own, and struggles to "keep Elvis important" relate to their own struggles for public legitimacy and autonomy. The fact that so many of the clubs consist primarily of female members bears comparison with the many voluntary associations that American women created after the Civil War and into the twentieth century. The Women's Christian Temperance Union and the League of Women Voters provided women with opportunities to work together and to learn how to organize and administer groups with significant social and political influence. Social clubs like the Junior League urged women toward self-improvement and "municipal housekeeping."[30] Elvis fan clubs provide similar kinds of collective opportunities for women, many of whom are deeply involved in fund raising and charity drives. Ostensibly organized to defend Elvis's name and reputation, today's fan clubs can also be seen as energizing and supportive communities set apart from a hostile society, sisterhoods brought together through shared interest in Elvis. They validate Elvis and affirm his female fans, many of whom use the clubs to carefully construct what they feel is Elvis's— and their own—appropriate public image.

Paying homage to Elvis extends beyond the collective, public world of the fan clubs, of course. Neither Paul nor Elvis MacLeod—"The World's #1 Elvis Fans"—belongs to any Elvis fan clubs, preferring to "take care of Elvis" on their own, at GracelandToo. Their house isn't a Mississippi knockoff of the Memphis original, either (it isn't called Graceland 2), but a personalized tribute to what Paul MacLeod (and lots of other fans) remembers most about Elvis's beloved mansion in the 1970s, before he died. GracelandToo's cluttered bordello ambience resembles Graceland's "red phase," a decorating scheme Elvis pursued when he redid his house in crimson shag carpets, valentine-red drapes, and layers of veneered and gilt furnishings—a look that disgusted Priscilla Presley and one she largely eliminated before re-opening Graceland to the public in 1982.[31] The MacLeods are sure Elvis "would feel more at home" at GracelandToo than at today's Graceland. In some ways, their house is all about making Elvis comfortable, about indulging him in a material culture they feel best embodies his "real" image.

Material culture practices are among the most cogent indicators of Elvis's contemporary significance. Elvis stuff has always been plentiful, but the memorabilia market has boomed since his death. Elvis collectibles from the 1950s (like postwar collectibles in general) have skyrocketed in price, with an Elvis doll that retailed in 1957 for $3.98 now selling for $3,000, and those $1 Elvis lipsticks now going for around $700 each. More important, collecting Elvis stuff continues to be a primary, if not an essential, activity in Elvis Culture. As Fred Whobrey remarked while perusing tables of stuff for sale in Memphis during Elvis Week 1997, "I buy and sell things to support my collecting habit. It's a good habit and a natural high." Collecting Elvis stuff, he added, helps create Elvis fandom: "Let's face it. The main reason we're here is gone. But even in death Elvis is doing the same he did in life, bringing people together."[32]

Fandom in general thrives on stuff, especially stuff that bears some

Elvis collection owned by William J. DeNight, 1993, Streamwood, Illinois.

trace (literally) of the figure that fans adore: the pap smear from Madonna that is treasured by one of the kids in the movie *Slackers*; the reliquary-like "Abba Turd" that is the prized possession of one of the characters in *Priscilla, Queen of the Desert*; the black leather jacket worn by Elvis that is lovingly highlighted at GracelandToo. Like many fans, the MacLeods rely on visual, touchable stuff to signal Elvis's special status and stake their claims on him. They dress like him, to be sure, but the ways they collect and display their Elvis stuff also conveys the responsibility they feel for Elvis. The stuff itself ranges from the mundane (the plastic shopping bags hung in GracelandToo's parlor) to the absurd (a toilet from one of the German homes Elvis lived in during his army service), from the valuable (his jumpsuits fetch tens of thousands of dollars) to the trivial (Elvis fly swatters). It doesn't

Elvis Aaron MacLeod with Elvis stuff, interior, Graceland Too, 1996, Holly Springs, Mississippi.

matter. Inscribed with his image or his name or touched by him in some way, it all embodies Elvis and, as such, is very, very powerful. "We know he's gone," says Paul MacLeod. "These things keep him alive in our hearts."

Elvis, after all, liked to collect stuff, too. In the mid-1950s, extra bedrooms in the first Memphis house he bought were filled with carloads of carnival kitsch, with gigantic stuffed animals won at county fairs and hundreds of others mailed to him by fans (especially after "Teddy Bear" was released in 1957). Elvis loved furniture, writes Karal Ann Marling, and he filled his homes with the latest model tables, sofas, lamps, ashtrays, mirrors, telephones, and TV sets. In the 1960s, Elvis started collecting guns and badges, now prominently displayed in blue velvet frames along one wall of Graceland's Trophy Room (itself outfitted with the gold records, industry awards, and personal memorabilia that Elvis collected). His insatiable appetite for more even led to a fervid encounter in late 1970 at the Nixon White House, where Elvis out and out asked the bewildered president to help him "get" a federal narcotics agent badge. As a gift of his own, Elvis gave Nixon a wood-handled, silver-barreled .45 pistol (complete with ammo) and promised to help him out with America's "drug problem."[33]

Elvis's own collecting obsessions, particularly toward the latter part of his life, showed him struggling to restore some kind of security and order in his life—collecting guns to fend off the fans he depended on and yet also feared (death threats were apparently not uncommon), collecting badges to somehow reassert his popular culture authority when the British invasion increasingly topped the charts. The collecting mania of his fans is equally autobiographical. One fan remarks that "real fans do need Elvis items around their houses," explaining how fans construct personal relationships with Elvis through their Elvis stuff and implying that fans who don't have a lot of that stuff aren't true-blue fans.[34]

Collecting Elvis, in other words, authenticates the loyalty of his fans. The rarity, completeness, and sheer quantity of their Elvis stuff establish the depth of their devotion: the fan who possesses a ticket stub from his last performance (in Indianapolis on June 26, 1977), a copy of his Humes High School Yearbook (1953), a sweat-stained scarf tossed from the stage of his "Aloha from Hawaii" concert (1973), or the full set of Elvis liquor decanter music boxes made by the McCormick Distilling Company in the 1980s, is deemed an especially true—meaning truly devoted—fan. Similarly, the fan who builds a 3,000-square-foot addition onto his or her home in order to accommodate Elvis stuff, which is what Australian fan Reg Pendergast did in the mid-1990s, is deemed a true fan.[35] By these standards, Paul and Elvis MacLeod are truly "The World's #1 Elvis Fans."

Collecting Elvis is mainly a private and independent activity, but it can form the basis of relationships with other fans. Record collectors, for example, like to check out other collections, saying things like "I've got this" or "Wow, it's really been a long time since I saw a copy of this," sharing insights, circulating knowledge, passing judgment, and generally establishing themselves in this particular cultural sphere. It's no different in Elvis Culture. Elvis collections are mirrors of identity, ways in which fans define themselves as fans, distance themselves from those who aren't, and connect with others. Elvis stuff is compared and traded, giving fans a common language and something to

Paul MacLeod with Elvis stuff ranging from collectibles to bubble-gum cards, interior, GracelandToo, 1996, Holly Springs, Mississippi.

talk about. It is also the source of a good deal of rivalry, envy, and bitterness among many fans, some of whom say they "can hardly afford" to be fans and to show how much they love Elvis because prices have been "jacked up by rich collectors." Collecting Elvis is as deeply imbricated in issues of class and taste as is collecting art.[36]

Still, as much as Elvis collectibles have risen in price over the past decade, few fans seem to cache their Elvis stuff or buy it strictly for investment purposes. And few seem to use what they buy in anticipated institutional ways. Most fans, and the MacLeods are good examples, displace the intended economic value of their Elvis stuff by collecting both rare and mundane Elvis items and displaying them together. GracelandToo features countless instances of the juxtaposition of coveted collectibles (Elvis's report cards and rare bootleg records) with completely banal Elvis ephemera (bubble-gum cards, buttons, bumper stickers). Each is treasured. This erasure of cultural hierarchy suggests how Elvis fans, like consumers in general, often subvert the stuff of mass culture and use it toward their own ends; GracelandToo is testimony to how fans make use of the vast amount of stuff available in Elvis Culture, applying diverse "tactics of consumption" to make it all meaningful—to themselves.[37]

The MacLeods may not actually make their Elvis stuff, but the ways they collect it and organize it inside GracelandToo make it significant. Collecting Elvis helps fans control his image, defending and displaying it the way *they* want—as opposed to the ways a malevolent "media" or cynical outsiders might image Elvis. Fan desires to tell the story of Elvis's importance and their own roles in Elvis Culture, to guide and direct the narrative of his and their own histories, are relevant here. Speaking at a fan get-together during Elvis Week 1993, George Klein (a high-school classmate of Elvis who became a member of his "Memphis Mafia") stated that Elvis fans are "all historians." Recalling a plaque at Baylor University, Klein remarked that "the preservers of history are more courageous than its makers," and added: "Well, you fans are those preservers of history, you with your scrapbooks and with your Elvis impersonators." For many fans, collecting Elvis is a means of preserving and controlling Elvis's history, of revising and redeeming his historical memory.

Walter Benjamin argued that the "aura" of a work of art declines with its mechanical reproduction, but for fans like the MacLeods, the seductive authority of Elvis's image increases through repetition, mass circulation, and steady consumption.[38] Elvisiana is never the equivalent of Elvis himself, of course, and most fans say they would happily give up all their stuff if he were to return. As one South Carolina fan remarks, "The important Elvis memorabilia is not for sale at any price. His music and the memories that live with us is what is most important." Still, however inadequate, Elvis images, and even those talismans simply blazoned with his name or the letters "TCB" ("Taking Care of Business," the logo Elvis adopted in the 1970s), embody his aura—and it is for this reason that so much of this stuff is consumed and collected by fans. Rather than diminishing, Elvis's power flourishes through the mass-reproduction of his image. GracelandToo is especially powerful because it is thoroughly saturated in Elvis stuff.

The stuff inside GracelandToo is not intrinsic in and of itself, but is activated through the meaningful relationships that Paul and Elvis MacLeod have with it all. Meaning intensifies and notions of loyalty and sacrifice are linked as fans assess their personal commitment to

Elvis (and that of other fans) on the basis of how much time, space, and money they are willing to dedicate to Elvis. Such altruism often takes the form of owning, and refusing to relinquish, items sanctioned by the Elvis collectibles market. As Bill DeNight, the president of the Burning Love Fan Club, remarked in 1993, "In my basement, I have about three-quarters of a million dollars' worth of Elvis memorabilia: all 38 liquor decanters, all 117 Elvis plates, all the coins, all in 17 glass show-cases. I've had offers but I'd never give it up, it means too much to me." The MacLeods are much the same, repeatedly refusing "cash offers" for their Elvis stuff and spending most of their income acquiring more.

Fully aware of how much their collections are "worth" and how much they've spent on them, fans sacrifice market value for private pleasure, often describing their Elvis collections as "labors of love." This stems, in part, from their souvenir origins. As stuff purchased, for example, from Graceland's gift shops, Elvis memorabilia evokes the personal experience of visiting Elvis's home. Re-collected in their own homes, these souvenirs help fans not only return to that experience, but also re-create Graceland's aura. (GracelandToo is more compact, combining both the ambience of Elvis's Memphis mansion *and* the souvenir stands across the street.) It isn't surprising, then, that the MacLeods and other fans tend to treat mass-produced Elvis items with more reverence than those that are handmade, that commemorative plates are more highly valued in Elvis Culture than are individual Elvis paintings by artists like Joni Mabe and Howard Finster. This is the reverse of most patterns of art collecting, of course, in which connoisseurs vie for unique masterpieces by well-known artists. But then Elvis fans aren't collecting art; they're assembling stuff that articulates their feelings for Elvis.

It's not enough to simply listen to Elvis's music; fans want to see and feel and be with Elvis, and most do so through material culture. By collecting Elvis stuff and displaying it in their homes—or by turning their homes into Elvis museums, like GracelandToo—fans say they are taking care of Elvis, keeping his memory alive, rescuing him from historical oblivion. Their explanations might seem to simply justify conspicuous consumption, giving them permission to indulge, and even wallow, in the crass materialism of Elvis Culture. But Elvis

Elvis stuff, interior, GracelandToo, 1996, Holly Springs, Mississippi.

collections "transcend mere accumulation" because of Elvis's absence.[39] Most fans believe Elvis is dead, but by collecting and displaying Elvis stuff they construct his immortality. Highly charged and passionately loved, Elvis images and objects are antidotes to Elvis's absence, fetishistic substitutes for Elvis himself.

Elvis's hybridity as a "God-given gift" and a gift-giver especially figures in fan collections. In fact, notions of Elvis's generosity, coupled with anger and remorse—anger because the gifts Elvis bestowed (himself, his music, his money) go unrecognized or are ridiculed in the larger culture, and remorse because fans think their demands may have contributed to his demise—are as central in these material culture practices as they are in the fan clubs. A "cycle of giving and indebtedness" is embodied in Elvis collections, whereby individual fans try to redress critical indifference, media mockery, and their own complicity in Elvis's pain by amassing and arranging Elvis stuff— paying him back with their own gifts, their time, their money, their gaze.[40] It's an endless cycle because what fans give Elvis can never really match what he gives them; Elvis gives them pleasure and purpose and all they can really give back is their thanks, their guilt, and their promises of eternal adulation. Still, if Elvis collections are about compensation and atonement and figure prominently in a consideration of his religious or spiritual importance, they are also about the continuity of the bonds between Elvis and his fans.

GracelandToo personifies how some contemporary fans pay homage to Elvis. By copying the "look" of Graceland when Elvis lived there and by imitating Elvis's own collecting passions, the MacLeods celebrate Elvis through the stuff of material culture and construct their own identities. For the past forty years, fans like these and fan clubs have shaped Elvis's presence in America and contributed to the widespread dominance of his image. Yet, while clearly fixed in our national consciousness, there is no consensus about what Elvis's mercurial image really represents. The multifaceted dimensions of Elvis's image—as a religious icon, a sexual fantasy, an emblem of "whiteness," and a legally copyrighted commodity—provide the core of analysis in the following chapters, which further speculate about the ways Elvis is seen and the meaning of his image in contemporary America.

Saint elvis

Every inch of Kiki Apostolakos's Memphis apartment is covered with images of Elvis: Elvis pictures cut from magazines and
pasted onto aluminum foil and cellophane backdrops, Elvis posters,
album covers, and tapestries arranged from floor to ceiling. In her
bedroom a large picture of Elvis hangs next to one of Jesus. In 1985,
Apostolakos, a language and psychology teacher in Athens, married a

Greek-American and emigrated to Memphis in order to "be closer" to Elvis; she now works as a waitress in a restaurant near Graceland. She calls her apartment a "shrine to Elvis" and calls herself an "Elvis artist." "The day he passed away, it hit me like lightning," she remembers. "That very day I started making my arrangements, using the gold foil from cigarette packages, and decorating Elvis pictures. I feel so blessed that I can live in Memphis and do this. Elvis, his image, is so alive inside me." Apostolakos spends every spare moment she can at Elvis's grave, tending it and honoring him with votive offerings—angels, hearts, tokens, small portable shrines—all handmade and all featuring his image. Sometimes she will spend an entire evening in Graceland's Meditation Gardens, engrossed in an all-night vigil of prayer and remembrance.

Her image making and grave-site rituals symbolize her deeply spiritual relationship with Elvis. A devout Catholic (raised Greek Orthodox), Apostolakos does not worship Elvis, but sees him as a man sent by God "to wake us up, to shake us, to ask us, what are we doing, where are we going?" Elvis is a mediator, an intercessor between herself, and other fans, and God. As she says, "There is a distance between human beings and God. That is why we are close to Elvis. He is like a bridge between us and God."[1] If, along with other fans, Apostolakos imagines Elvis as a saint, she also sees him as a redemptive figure. "I believe in Jesus Christ and I believe in God," she remarks, "but Elvis was special. Elvis was in our times, he was given to us to remind us to be good." Servant of God and Christ-like savior, Elvis brings Apostolakos joy, intensity, pleasure, and purpose. "I don't go to church much now. I don't ask for anything else from God, my prayers have been answered," she says, acknowledging that her personal relationship with Elvis, as well as the artworks that she makes and the rituals that she performs that express that relationship, are the most meaningful cultural and social practices in her life.

Like Apostolakos's apartment, every inch of Elayne Goodman's six-foot-tall *Altar to Elvis* (1990) is covered with images of Elvis, many bordered by beads, buttons, or bric-a-brac; some glued onto frilly

(overleaf) *Elvis shrine made by Kiki Apostolakos, on view in Meditation Gardens, Graceland, during Elvis Week 1993.*

Elayne Goodman, Altar to Elvis *(1990). Mixed media installation, 72 × 48 inches. (Collection of the artist, Columbus, Mississippi)*

valentines or mounted in elaborate gold and silver frames; still others revealed on the altar's wings and in its secret niches. Elvis pictures are accompanied by Elvis busts and Elvis statues, and by what Goodman calls "Genuine Fake Relics," simulated bits and pieces of Elvis's hair and fingernails captured and displayed in tiny vials and little boxes. A "self-taught" artist who has lived most of her life in Columbus, Mississippi, a small town only ninety miles from Tupelo, Elvis's birthplace, Goodman has made Elvis angels, shrines, and altars for the past two decades, all fashioned from stuff she finds in flea markets and garage sales.

Visually resplendent in reds and blacks and golds, the high holy colors of religious cultures from Byzantine to Buddhist, Goodman's *Altar to Elvis* is fun, funny, and tricky. Encrusted with pictures of Elvis, it draws attention to the vast number of Elvis images that exist—everywhere—in everyday vernacular culture. But it also cleverly points out how Elvis's image is frequently received and experienced, poking fun at his contemporary iconic status and at those who put Elvis's image, body, and even body parts on such a holy pedestal. Recycling altar-like conventions common to religions all over the globe, Goodman's Elvis shrine clearly invests the secular Elvis with sacred importance and broadly addresses the ways in which Elvis is increasingly perceived, desired, and constructed on religious terms.

In fact, comments like "it's a religious thing" tend to dominate the discourse surrounding Elvis's abiding cultural presence in contemporary America and around the world. Eager to explain, and especially to debunk, the preponderance of Elvis imagery and the emotional and collective behavior of his fans, many of the mainstream journalists and academic critics attendant in Elvis Culture relate how "culture" has become "cult." Some point out that Elvis's rags-to-riches life story, his rock culture marginalization, and his tragic death neatly parallel the secular/sacred narrative of Jesus and hint at the contemporary possibility of Elvis's own eponymous cult foundation. Several hilarious spoofs of these Elvis-as-Messiah analogies have emerged in recent years, including *The Two Kings* (1994), which contrasts "the bizarre parallels and strange similarities" between Jesus and Elvis ("Jesus was baptized in the River Jordan," "Elvis' backup group was the Jordanaires"), and the piously tongue-in-cheek *Gospel of Elvis* (1996), which tells how "a boy from the poorest village of the land of Plenty became the Priest-King of the Whole World."[2]

Others cite a long list of quasi-religious factors and conditions that seem to confirm Elvis's contemporary deification: how in the years since his death, a veritable Elvis religion has emerged, replete with prophets (Elvis impersonators), sacred texts (Elvis records), disciples (Elvis fans), relics (the scarves, Cadillacs, and diamond rings that Elvis lavished on fans and friends), pilgrimages (to Tupelo and Graceland), shrines (his Graceland grave site), churches (such as the 24-Hour Church of Elvis in Portland, Oregon), and all the appearances of a resurrection (with reported Elvis sightings at, among other places, a Burger King in Kalamazoo, Michigan). Ritual activities that occur in Memphis each August during Elvis Week (nicknamed "Death Week" by more sarcastic observers) are cited as further evidence of Elvis's cult status.

"The worship, adoration and the perpetuation of the memory of Elvis today, closely resembles a religious cult," boldly states Ted Harrison, a former religious affairs correspondent with the BBC. It is, he proclaims, "nothing less than a religion in embryo." Writer Ron Rosenbaum agrees, arguing in a 1995 *New York Times* article that Elvis's popularity has "transcended the familiar contours of a dead celebrity cult and has begun to assume the dimensions of a redemptive faith." A host of scholars have probed the Elvis cult's Celtic, Gnostic, Hindi, and vodun derivations, contemplated Graceland's status as "sacred space"; and considered how and why some insist that Elvis, like Jesus, defeated death. Less charitable writers cynically attribute the entire phenomenon to the incredibly successful mass-marketing techniques of Elvis Inc. and to the susceptibility of an apparently passive public bent on escaping from the real world through, especially, the "transformative" ideology of consumerism. "Explicit manifestations of 'Elvis Christ' did not exactly evolve," carps British journalist John Windsor. "They were cunningly contrived for a mass market."[3]

Easy explanations that Elvis's omnipresence and the devotion of his fans embodies a cult or religion bring up all sorts of questions, including the issue of religious essentialism. What is it about the revered images, ritual practices, and devotional behaviors within Elvis Culture that is essentially religious? And do these images and practices constitute the making of a discrete and legitimate religion? Why is it that *images* of Elvis, unlike those of most other popular contemporary figures, seem to have taken on the dimensions of faith and devotion, viewed by many Elvis fans as links between themselves and God, as ex-votos for expressing and giving thanks, as empowered objects that can fulfill wishes and desires?

These questions are complicated by the fact that most fans quickly dismiss intimations that Elvis is a religious figure or that Elvis images and Elvis-centered practices constitute any sort of Elvis religion. "Elvis did not die for our sins, nor is he Jesus Christ and it is very wrong to even try and draw comparisons," writes one fan. "It's only the media who seem to be obsessed with turning Elvis into a religion, you don't hear normal fans discuss it," says another, who adds: "You only have to see the number of books published on the topic in recent years to see it's yet another way to make yet more money out of Elvis. This topic makes Elvis fans look foolish and I'm sure Elvis would be deeply offended."

Such protestations may confuse Elvis's cult status: What does it mean when adherents deny the religiosity of something that looks so much like a religion? Yet their resistance begs consideration. Some fans object in order to avoid charges of heresy or iconoclasm, because their religion forbids sacred status for secular figures, because seeing Elvis as a saint violates, for example, Protestant dogma. But most do so to avoid being ridiculed as religious fanatics. Consider the glee with which journalists exposed the sex and money scandals of Jim and Tammy Faye Bakker's PTL (Praise the Lord) television ministry in 1987. If religion was "respectable and respected" at the close of the 1950s, today it is spoofed or under constant surveillance by a popular press that is generally uneasy with displays of religious emotionalism and obsessed more with religious misconduct than with genuine, deeply felt human needs for intimations of the divine.[4]

Fringe religions, moreover, are almost always held up against the standards and values of mainstream religions, so most media accounts of Elvis's "cult" status frame his fans as abnormal outsiders whose faith doesn't follow institutionalized spiritual practices. Further disenfranchised as the lemming-like addicts of Elvis Inc. merchandising schemes, fans are consistently consigned to lower social and religious categories, stereotyped as lower-class, uneducated, and hence disreputable and irrational worshipers of a "fat, pill-filled Vegas singer." Unflattering pictures of unnamed Elvis fans in Rosenbaum's article, for example, including a shot taken in Memphis by James Hamilton during Elvis Week 1995 of an older couple wearing Elvis T-shirts, Elvis buttons, Elvis rings, and admission badges to the "Elvis Presley Fan Club President's Lunch," caricature "Elvisians" as the delusional devoted and work to reassure *New York Times* readers of the alien and aberrant dimensions of such fringe fanaticism.[5] Aware of their marginalization by the media, it isn't surprising that many fans hotly deny fidelity to any sort of Elvis cult or religion, suspicious of facile analyses that come close to equating them with the Branch Davidians or the Japanese followers of Aum Supreme Truth.

Without discounting their objections, however, it is important to recognize that from its "city on the hill" creation myth to the present-day proliferation of New Age spirituality and the growth of fundamentalism, religiosity—mainstream and fringe—remains central to American identity and experience. As a profoundly religious

AMONG THE BELIEVERS

"Among the Believers," © 1999 by Ron Rosenbaum, originally appeared in the
September 24, 1995, issue of the New York Times Magazine. (Reprinted by
permission of the author.) The unnamed fans are Diane and Bert MacArthur of
Little Rock, Arkansas.

people, Americans tend to treat things on religious terms, apply religious categories, and generally make a religion out of much of what
is touched and understood. According to a 1980 Gallup poll, Americans "value religion" and maintain "strong religious beliefs" to far
greater degrees than do the citizens of any other Western industrial
nation.[6]

Yet Americans tend to be predominantly private and diverse in their
religious beliefs and practices. Indeed, much of America's "ongoing
religious vitality" can be attributed to the long-standing democratic,
or populist, orientation of American Christianity: as "custodians of
their own beliefs," Americans traditionally have shaped and accommodated their religious practices to mesh with individual, rather than
strictly institutional, desires. Contemporary Americans continue to
mix and match religious beliefs and practices, creating and claiming
their own spiritual convictions out of that amalgamation.[7] It may be
that when Elvis fans protest that their devotion to Elvis is not "religious," they are really objecting to an institutional definition of the
term. In fact, their privatizing veneration of Elvis is one strong historical form of American religiosity.

My references here to "religion" are not meant as metaphorical flourishes, nor do I want to mitigate the reverence that many fans have for Elvis as a "kind of" religion. Religion constitutes those practices and attitudes that imbue a person's life with meaning by linking him or her to a transcendent reality: that which is beyond purely immanent, or secular, experience and understanding. Assertions of affinity between religion and the generally privatized spiritual beliefs and practices of Elvis fans stem from their similarly supernatural, and inexplicable, character and authority. Collecting Elvis stuff, creating Elvis shrines, and going to Graceland are not, in and of themselves, religious acts and practices. But they can become religious if they affect a transcendent and all-powerful order that can influence human affairs and is not inherently apprehensible.

The issue of Elvis's place in America's democratic, diverse, and individually synthesized religious realm may best be considered by asking why so many Americans have come to place their faith in an image of Elvis. Why is Elvis an icon, and what does this reveal about how contemporary Americans visualize faith? What is it about images of Elvis that arouse powerful emotional responses and behaviors? Examining how and why his fans have made him a figure of popular culture canonization, and how his iconic dominance is actually embedded in and extended from their religious beliefs and practices, may provide some answers.

Elvis was, of course—and remains—a profoundly charismatic figure, which clearly contributes to his popular, and perhaps religious, status. Mainstream religions tend to be fronted by charismatic types (Jesus, Confucius, Buddha, Muhammad, Joseph Smith), as do their cult counterparts (most recently, Jim Jones, David Koresh, Shoko Ashahara). And the diversity of Elvis's extraordinarily magnetic image, whether sexually provocative teen idol or jumpsuited superstar, has certainly generated his appeal on many different levels for many different fans. But being charismatic doesn't automatically translate into reverential status; plenty of contemporary rock stars and sports figures are objects of adoration, but few sustain religious veneration. Contrary to presumptions about "the religion of the stars," the cult of celebrity and the religious beliefs and practices cultivated by Elvis fans are not exactly the same. Elvis's religious import hinges on his multifaceted image, which is for many fans imbued with a certain mystical greatness and looked on for access to a transcendent reality. It is long-standing, too: as early as 1957, some fans were trying to start an "Elvis Presley Church"; as recently as 1995, a St. Louis group (the Congregation for Causes of Saints) sought his canonization.[8] Most fans, however, prefer to commune with Elvis privately, in their homes.

Whether or not they believe Elvis is a "religion," fans do believe in Elvis and often express it most tellingly in their own homes. The domestic sphere is a safe haven far away from an unfriendly outside world, a sanctuary where fans can be with Elvis without drawing attention. Many Elvis fans have special rooms or areas in their homes especially dedicated to Elvis. Fans describe them as "quiet places" where they can think about and "be really close to Elvis." Barb Bennett, a fan from Kentucky, observes that "seeing Graceland as a shrine to Elvis" helped her make the decision to turn an empty bedroom in her home "into my own shrine where I think about Elvis and about his family."

Many fans tell how they spend hours each day in their Elvis Rooms, listening to Elvis's music, watching his movies, looking at pictures of him in books and magazines. "I like to go to my Elvis Room, down in the basement, after supper," remarks Kim Epperly of Roanoke, Virginia. "It's a quiet space and time for me." Filled with Elvis stuff that she has collected since the 1950s, Epperly's room "helps to keep memories of Elvis alive." As places where secular thoughts and tasks are suspended, Elvis Rooms allow personal and private moments of contemplation and solitude. As places where fans spotlight their collections of Elvisiana, they also speak to the ways in which material culture plays a major role in sanctifying and legitimizing Elvis as a special, important entity.

This combination of religious and commercial sensibilities in the American home is nothing new; in the nineteenth century, Protestants and Catholics alike linked religiosity with domesticity, creating a sanctified hominess with parlor organs, Bibles, religious pictures, and plaster statues of the Madonna and Child. While this changed somewhat in the twentieth century, many post–World War II Christian homes remained reverential, largely through the widespread consumption of mass-produced images and religio-commercial objects, such as Warner Sallman's painting *The Head of Christ*.[9] Filling special rooms, and sometimes whole houses, with Elvis paintings, collector's plates, trading cards, limited-edition lithographs, watches, dolls, framed needlepoint projects, and all sorts of other mass-produced and handmade items, Elvis fans sacralize their contemporary American homes in similar sorts of ways, using images and objects to declare their deeply felt devotion to Elvis.

The ways that fans organize their Elvis Rooms reveal how they freely appropriate the look and feel of domestic religiosity in order to cultivate a reverential atmosphere in a secular realm. Whatever their religious affiliation, or lack thereof, Elvis fans tend to choose patterns of visual piety that closely correspond to the home shrines that have long been a "vital part of domestic Christianity" for Americans of African, Irish, Italian, Latino, Polish, Portuguese, and many other backgrounds. From the modest grouping of a framed religious motto and a few family photographs on top of a living room piano or TV set, to more elaborate assemblages of holy cards, votive candles, religious prints, school photos, party favors, dried flowers, and private mementos, home shrines sacralize domestic interiors. Furthermore, they demonstrate the spiritual possibilities of popular and material culture, familiarizing "transcendental experience by creating a personal universe from mainly domestic resources." In this regard, they are closely linked to what Tomás Ybarra-Frausto calls *rasquachismo*, a Chicano aesthetic of resilience, resourcefulness, and adaptability that invests ordinary things with special significance.[10] Uniquely coded by their primarily female makers, home altars integrate personal and sentimental items with more purely devotional offerings, thus blurring distinctions between the domestic and the divine.

The circulation of Judeo-Christian visual and material traditions within Elvis Culture is clearly evident in the homes of many fans. Stepping into Mary Cartaya's Florida home, for example, is like walking into a private Catholic chapel, but in place of crucifixes, religious pictures, and reliquaries there are dense rows of neatly displayed Elvis posters, decanters, pennants, spoons, and plates. Chock-a-block Elvis images and objects compete for attention amid etched mirrors, small gilded wall decorations, hanging lamps made of glass and brass, ar-

Interior, home of Mary Cartaya, 1995, Florida.

rangements of plastic, silk, and metallic flowers, scented candles, personal photographs in small ceramic frames, miniature vases, and a variety of other brightly colored bric-a-brac. On one wall hangs a tiny plastic package of Elvis's hair, swept up during one of his appointments with an army barber in 1958.

Cartaya calls her home a "memorial to Elvis" and calls Elvis her "guardian angel." She is a practicing Catholic and has special allegiance to Our Lady of the Miraculous Medal (a group founded in 1830 after the Virgin Mary appeared to a Parisian nun and instructed her to make a special medal in her honor), but there are few Catholic religious items displayed in her home. Born in 1942, she describes her father as an "abuser" who beat his wife and three children, and kicked Mary out of their South Miami home at the age of fifteen. "All I had was my record player and my Elvis records," she recalls, "and I listened to them over and over." Cartaya married in 1967, and her only child died at birth in the early 1970s; her second marriage, in 1982, lasted for only six months. In the early 1980s, she became a "serious" collector of the Elvis images and objects that now fill her home. "I was alone and

Elvis was there for me," she remarks. "He gives me the boost to overcome the hurdles. Through him I know that things can be done."

She adds:

> I believe that everything stems from God. Elvis was an instrument of God. He was God's gift to me, to help me survive everything I went through. I could have done drugs, I could have been a prostitute, but God put him on the earth and he got me through the worst times in my life. Elvis's music and his movies have brought so much to me, and when he died I wanted to make sure his image wasn't mutilated.

Cartaya's comments reveal the meaning and power that Elvis has in her life. Her private faith in Elvis has helped her through hard times, and she venerates him by reinventing her home as a shrine in his honor.

In the opening pages of her novel *Graced Land* (1992), Laura Kalpakian describes another altar to Elvis, this one on a fan's front porch:

> Nailed up across the two front porch windows there was an American flag and a Confederate flag and below them, a picnic table covered in a sheet. . . . The table reverently displayed a Gideon Bible at either end. A wreath of plastic daisies lay before a poster-sized picture of the mature Elvis wearing a white spangled bodysuit with a flaring cape. The picture was framed in quilted black satin with four satin rosettes at each corner and long mourning ribbons. . . . A huge hand-lettered sign read: Sacred to the Memory of This Prince Among Men. Elvis Aron Presley. 1935–1977. Long Live the King. His Truth Goes Marching On.[11]

Collaging an icon of the Vegas Elvis with various symbols of America's civil religion (U.S. and Confederate flags) and Christian culture (Gideon Bibles), Kalpakian's shrine maker posits transcendent communion with American patriotism and Elvis Presley. For her, and for Elvis fans like Kiki Apostolakos, Elayne Goodman, and Mary Cartaya, the religiosity of Elvis's image lies in its iconic authority and emotive power, in the ways it embodies, and perhaps satisfies, spiritual needs and personal notions of contemporary piety.

The overwhelming visual abundance and intensity of feeling of

Cartaya's home shrine are analogous. Seen from the outside, her surburban brick ranch house is completely ordinary and indistinguishable from those up and down the predominantly middle-class block. But "full of Elvis treasures," as she proudly says, "from beginning to end" and visually saturated with the cut glass, polished metals, and bright colors of contemporary American interior decoration, the insides of Cartaya's home shimmer and radiate with an altar-like sensibility. By blending Elvis with familiar household furnishings including photographs of family and friends, Cartaya claims him as part of her everyday reality; by concentrating almost exclusively on his image she elevates him as a revered, supernatural figure. Her lavish home shrine evokes the intimacy, affection, and responsibility she feels for Elvis: hidden from a hostile outside world that might "mutilate" his image, Elvis is safe inside Cartaya's home. Generating an emotional immediacy and directness, and accentuating her sincere devotion to the man she calls "the love of my life," it also speaks to the ways in which the combined resources of domesticity and material culture can be reworked to express an Elvis fan's personal piety.

For such fans, Elvis Rooms are creative means to help them cope with the difficulties and needs in their lives, refuges where they experience the depth of their feelings for Elvis privately, on their own terms. Judeo-Christian home shrines are similarly powerful forms of domestic piety, especially for the women who have traditionally made them. Generally excluded from public forms of religious expression and leadership, Christian women often use the domestic sphere to communicate their spiritual needs and desires. Home altars are one of these manifestations, both private religious endeavors and visibly conscious expressions of family relationships, traditions, and memories. By making them, women strengthen those relationships and traditions, their religious beliefs, and their own identities.[12] By blending the domestic and the divine, home altars nurture female and family spirituality and transform the private sphere into a powerful locus of religiosity.

Not all Elvis Rooms are made by women, of course, but their home altar aesthetics bear kinship to these female-centered expressions of Judeo-Christian domesticity. GracelandToo, for example, the Holly Springs habitat of Paul and Elvis MacLeod, is an extraordinary

Interior, home of Mary Cartaya, 1995, Florida.

representation of the devotional acts and behaviors of two male Elvis fans. Visually and physically powerful (practically to the point of claustrophobia) and privately coded with a blend of Elvis stuff and the MacLeods' own family memorabilia, GracelandToo is a fantastic, dramatic, and otherworldly space that parallels the intensity of the MacLeods' devotion to Elvis. Neither Paul MacLeod nor his son belongs to any church or calls himself "religious." Yet the look and feel of

GracelandToo suggest that various Judeo-Christian traditions of domestic religiosity that allow believers to decorate their homes and venerate their chosen deities or holy figures in highly personalized ways appear to have been absorbed by many Elvis fans. The public is invited to vicariously experience the iconographic universe of the MacLeods' home shrine, but GracelandToo remains essentially the private, altar-like domain of two devout fans.

Some suggest that densely cluttered, vividly textured, and highly colored domestic spaces, such as those inhabited by the MacLeods, are typical style choices made by poor and working-class people in order to counter the oppressively bleak conditions of their everyday lives.[13] Empowerment is certainly key to the making and meaning of home altars, from Christian to Elvis. But assumptions about class don't completely account for the look and feel of Elvis Rooms and home shrines. Like GracelandToo, Mary Cartaya's home and Kiki Apostolakos's apartment are dazzling, exaggerated environments that glorify Elvis. Yet neither woman can be said to occupy a low socioeconomic sphere. Cartaya, for example, is a single woman in her mid-fifties who owns her own home, has worked some twenty-five years as a civil servant, and makes an annual salary close to $50,000. Apostolakos is also middle-aged and single (her husband died in 1986) and, although she now works in a restaurant, comes from a middle-class background. Both women could choose other, perhaps more restrained or "tasteful" modes of visual display. But "good" taste does not drive their devotion to Elvis. The extravagance of their home shrines stems from self-conscious decisions to venerate Elvis in dramatic, sentimental, and highly sensory modes of recycled religious materialism. By utilizing altar-like styles and conventions, these Elvis fans turn their Elvis Rooms into sacred spaces.

Seen by outsiders simply as Elvis Rooms, packed full of Elvis stuff, these spaces have their own secret meanings among Elvis fans: they provide a common language and something to talk about, they allow private moments of solitude and communion with Elvis, and they are highly intensified physical settings where fans make Elvis into a passionately loved and revered figure. If many of today's religious institutions are racked by theological disputation and sectarian splintering, the domestic sphere may provide a spiritual ameliorative. Certainly for many Elvis fans, the making of Elvis Rooms suggests how their homes have become spiritual sanctuaries in which they freely express the devotional nature of their relationship with Elvis. They also suggest how Americans continue to adapt and reorder various religious practices in order to accommodate their personal spiritual beliefs. While distancing themselves from the real-life problems of contemporary mainstream religions, Elvis fans subvert and appropriate religious styles and sensibilities to construct special private spaces where Elvis holds center stage.

Elvis Rooms are also places where fans rehearse public expressions of devotion. The home, after all, mediates between the private and the public sphere. Likewise, the home shrines of Elvis fans, while separate from the outside world, help permeate that world with Elvis's presence. Shrines, as William Christian comments in his study of relationships to the divine between communities and individuals in a Spanish village, "are energy transformation stations—the loci for the transformation of divine energy for human purposes and the transformation of human energy for divine purposes."[14] Many of the images, effects, and rituals that fans use in their homes to articulate their devotion to Elvis are repeated in the public sphere, especially at Graceland each August, during Elvis Week.

North Carolina photographer Ralph Burns recalls listening to the radio in mid-August 1978 and hearing reports that thousands of Elvis fans were converging on Memphis on the first anniversary of Elvis's death. Their journeys were entirely spontaneous and consisted mainly of paying tribute to Elvis's image and his body, at his home and at his grave, at Graceland. Jumping into his car, Burns drove all night and joined them. For the past two decades, he has documented Graceland's pilgrims in an exhaustive series of starkly compelling black-and-white prints. As he explains:

> Each return is my last, but when I miss two or three in a row I began to feel disconnected. So I go back and stand by the grave and watch people, some of whom are now my friends, and talk with them about their lives and inevitably wonder about them and about me and about us and wish that I had answers and that I know more about this incredible love and pain and worship spread so easily before me.[15]

Ralph Burns, Untitled (from Graceland Series, 1977–93). Six photographic silver prints, 11 × 14 inches each. (Photograph © Ralph Burns. All rights reserved)

Increasingly, Elvis fan pilgrimages have become more popular and more institutionalized, such that today specific rituals and practices occur at Graceland and throughout Memphis during Elvis Week, from August 8 through August 16 (and also, to a lesser degree, on January 8, Elvis's birthday).

Pilgrims make their way to shrines, the sites of saints, sacred relics, or miracles. Generally enclosed and set apart from the secular world, shrines are located wherever the special qualities of a holy person, thing, or event are "believed to be more concentrated" than anywhere else. In their study of contemporary Christian pilgrimages in Europe, Mary Lee Nolan and Sidney Nolan argue that a place becomes a shrine "if people think of it in that way and behave accordingly." Pilgrims visit shrines "in order to commune more intimately" with who-ever (or whatever) is thought to be sanctified there. And, as the Nolans further determined, pilgrimage sites are commonly marked by two conflicted features: centrally located, in order to attract and benefit the largest number of devotees, they are also often found in places that are uncomfortable and hard to reach.[16] A shrine's special or sacred charac-ter is enhanced, in other words, by the difficulties of pilgrimage.

Religious terms like "pilgrimage" and "shrine" are generally not part of the average Graceland visitor's vocabulary, and many fans might be offended if they heard these words used in relation to their visits to the site. Still, Elvis's estate has become the object of venera-tion for thousands of fans who visit it every year, and for thousands more who wish that they, too, could go to Graceland. As Ricardo Massa, a thirty-five-year-old Elvis fan from Bayonne, New Jersey, ex-claims: "Graceland is like the worshipping ground for all Elvis fans." The homes and graves of other American icons and celebrities can't compete with the powerful, magisterial, and transcendent image that fans give to Graceland, an image that plays a central role in Elvis's contemporary iconic status.

Set back on a hill and surrounded by fieldstone walls and white picket fences, Graceland is conceptualized by thousands of Elvis fans as an especially hallowed place whose every surface is charged with the spirit of Elvis. Going there, much more so than visiting Elvis's humble childhood home in Tupelo or taking a peek at the cramped Lauderdale Courts Apartments in Memphis, where the Presley family moved in the late 1940s, is a deeply significant and generally formida-ble act for most fans. Graceland itself is easily accessible, just a few miles from Memphis International Airport and near the crossroads of several major interstates. But the blistering heat and paint-stripping humidity of August make Memphis a hellhole during Elvis Week. And going to Graceland is expensive: the average fan spends hundreds of dollars on travel, car rental, motel room, meals, admission to the mansion, and souvenirs. Rarely impulsive, fan pilgrimages to Grace-land are carefully planned journeys that usually entail months, if not years, of scrimping and saving.

Despite these pilgrimage hardships, going to Graceland is the deepest desire of most Elvis fans. "My dream was to see him in concert

Exterior, Graceland, Memphis. Elvis's home, at 3764 Elvis Presley Boulevard, Memphis, was originally built in 1938 and 1939. Elvis bought it in 1957.

and see Graceland," writes Debra Hannan of Chisholm, Minnesota. "Well," she adds, "one dream came true when my husband took me to Graceland on our honeymoon." Many fans try to go as many times as they can, hoping to partake of Graceland's spirit as often as possible. "My husband surprised me with a trip to Graceland and it was so special," says Betty Mendoza of San Leandro, California. "We have been back a second time and are planning to be there for the 20th anniversary of Elvis's death." Graceland's significance, in other words, depends on the meaning Elvis fans give it. As the focus of their pilgrimage, Graceland is special because they make it special: their beliefs and behaviors transform it from historic home to shrine. To be sure, Elvis Inc., facilitates their faith, eager to profit from Graceland's spiritual significance, but the fans themselves ensure its home shrine glory.

Of course, not everyone who goes to Graceland is an Elvis fan. As with any shrine, Graceland's audience is a blend of pilgrims and casual tourists—families on vacation, retirees in RVs, college students on the road. Still, however diverse this crowd might be, it is safe to say that most are drawn to Graceland, and drawn together, to try to come to terms with Elvis's abiding popularity. Their presence feeds the phenomenon; even the most ambivalent tourist, who goes to Graceland to see why everyone else goes, adds to Elvis's popular culture canonization.

That isn't to say they all share the same insights about Elvis. During Elvis Week, especially, Graceland draws a diverse crowd not only of fans but of journalists and documentary filmmakers in search of a good story about "the Elvis thing." Some fans humor the press, even making up stories about "when I met Elvis" or "when I dated Elvis." Most, however, resent the intrusion of "the media" and other outsiders into Elvis Culture and onto their turf. Some are even suspicious of recently declared fans making their first trip to Graceland, eyeing them as "fake fans," as inauthentic wannabes who haven't loved Elvis long enough. In other words, while Graceland brings a lot of different people together, it is not infrequently the site of conflict as fans, tourists, reporters, and lots of other people argue about who Elvis was, what his image represents, and what (and who) accounts for and profits from his contemporary popularity.

For most fans, the desire to see and experience Graceland is akin to the desire to see and feel Elvis. From 1957, when he bought the "big house on the hill," to 1977, when he died in it, Elvis withdrew from the outside world inside Graceland's fences, escaping from the pressures of performing (he gave few live concerts in the 1960s), from the repetitious B-movie sets of Hollywood, and from the rapacious appetites of his fans. Touted as the authentically preserved stomping grounds of the real-life Elvis (although most fans seem to know that Priscilla Presley had the main house "tastefully refurbished" before its public unveiling in 1982), Graceland lends authority to Elvis's real-time, 1957 to 1977, existence.[17]

"Seeing his home, Meditation Gardens, the planes and many of his personal belongings, I realized that he was a real person with a real life," writes one fan. "I was on cloud nine walking around there, seeing in person how Elvis lived and played," exclaims another. "It's so hard to describe the feelings when you're there," still another says. "To know you're in his home, walking where he has walked." Resonant with Elvis—his possessions, his body, his spirit—fans go to Graceland to walk in his mansion, gaze at his things, mourn at his grave site, and be that much closer to the man they adore. Some leave things for Elvis; a tour guide who worked at Graceland in the mid-1980s recalls finding slips of paper tucked under vases or hidden behind curtains with messages like "Elvis, we miss you. Love, Bob and Marge." Others can't resist the temptation to take a little of piece of Graceland home with them, pocketing leaves, pebbles, sticks, and pinches of dirt as tokens of their pilgrimage and their brush with Elvis. Once again, it is the stuff of material culture—here, Graceland and its relics—that is pivotal to the devotional practices and beliefs of Elvis's fans.

The house itself isn't that remarkable: a pseudo-Georgian structure of about 4,500 square feet and a teeny guitar-shaped pool. If it is ironic that this mundane mansion has now become the most public house shrine in America, drawing well over 750,000 visitors a year, the fact that Elvis died and is buried there has a lot to do with it. Elvis was originally interred at Forest Hill Cemetery in Memphis, but after numerous reports of tomb break-ins (such as that by Paul MacLeod), Vernon Presley had his son reburied at Graceland. It was a smart move. While cemeteries and Memorial Day celebrations generally seem to have declined in significance, contemporary Americans are increasingly drawn to the sites of tragic death—pinning mementos to the steel fence surrounding the bombed remains of the federal building in Oklahoma City, placing teddy bears and children's toys at the shore of the South Carolina lake where Susan Smith drowned her sons, tossing flowers into the waters off Long Island where TWA 800 went down in 1996.[18]

Mostly insulated from death and disaster, and discouraged from public displays of grief, people go to these places to see and touch real-life tragedy, to weep and mourn and *feel* in socially acceptable situations. As shrines, they memorialize not only the horrible events that occurred there, but the feelings of visitors. Ghoulish fascination with inexplicable death—the death of unfortunates, the death of innocents —is matched by feelings of guilt and gratitude, with worries about personal responsibility, with thanks that it wasn't us inside that federal building, inside that car, aboard that plane. Similarly, however morbid it might seem to make the pilgrimage to the grave of their favorite American icon, even on a honeymoon, Elvis fans go to Graceland to emotionally indulge themselves, to become overwhelmed by their feelings of love, loss, and loneliness for Elvis. Elated inside his house, many openly weep beside his grave.

Fans repeatedly talk about Graceland in terms of its emotional intensity. "I feel drawn there," comments Wanda Cole of Sumner, Texas, who writes that she goes to Graceland "*each* year" during Elvis Week. "I am not alone in this feeling," she explains. "I can feel his presence there and I want him to know his music still means so much to me and that because of him, I have so many wonderful friends." Or, as Jeanine Wickersham of Golden, Colorado, remarks, "A walk through the garden where he and his family are laid to rest. It's a chilling feeling and warm feeling all at once. It's like never wanting to leave, the other Elvis fans bond there with everyone. You can discuss your feelings with no regrets." For these fans, Graceland is the most visible public place where they can comfortably and collectively express their private feelings for Elvis.

As with other acts of pilgrimage, going to Graceland engages "the social self of its devotees." Fans come to Memphis as individuals but come together at Graceland, especially during Elvis Week, as public witnesses to Elvis, collectively engaged in a "kind of defiant testimony" to his greatness. There is immense emotive power in the transformative bond of *communitas* that going to Graceland generates among Elvis fans. The fans who gather there during Elvis Week tend to bond as a "community of admirers" and a "community of sorrow," brought together in their love for Elvis and their profound grief that he is gone.[19] United in their devotion to Elvis and allied against the jeers and jokes of those who don't share their faith, Graceland's pilgrims swap stories of difficult journeys, share memories of the "first time" they saw Elvis or when they became fans, discuss Elvis collections, compare Elvis Rooms, gossip about other fans, and generally articulate what their personal relationship with Elvis is all about. Their time together is more than just a week-long collective drama, but a process by which they renew their faith in Elvis. Strengthened in a community of other fans who share their love and feel their pain, Graceland's pilgrims return to their own homes revitalized in their private commitment to Elvis.

The pleasure of being inside Elvis's house and the pain experienced while standing at his tomb often give way to feelings of duty and responsibility. As Cara Striff, a member of the We Remember Elvis fan club of Gainesville, Florida, remarks, "I'm not sure why I and so many others keep returning to Graceland. It's just that feeling of dedication and devotion, almost an obligation to Elvis to keep returning to Graceland." If Elvis's estate is where his fans most conspicuously express themselves, it is also where they most publically pay homage, give thanks, and renew their vows to Elvis, and these essentially moralistic acts are not mutually exclusive. Elvis "was exploited and used by many people around him, but his fans never, never left him even in death," writes Judith Adams of Johnson City, Tennessee, adding: "All of those music magnates should thank Elvis for helping make the music industry the lucrative business it is today." At Graceland, fans atone for what they perceive as the injustice of Elvis's contemporary neglect and media ridicule by bearing witness to his greatness. As Mary Cartaya comments, "It makes my heart flutter when I sit quietly at the gardens and watch all the people from around the world paying respects to Elvis, and it is at this moment I know he is never going to be anything short of Number 1."

Graceland's shrine-like sensibility is particularly evident during Elvis Week, when the number of fans swells and the intensity of their devotion is most apparent. In 1993, for example, more than 45,000 Elvis fans converged on Graceland, filling every motel for miles around, especially those along Elvis Presley Boulevard, the fast-paced four-lane highway that fronts his estate. In 1997, on the twentieth anniversary of his death, some 60,000 fans—along with a huge number of journalists and photographers—descended on Graceland.

Fans engage in specific rituals during Elvis Week, although, again, most of them wouldn't see them as rituals. After taking the Graceland house tour, at least once, they typically spend their days at fan fests and auctions, engaging in charity work in Elvis's name, buying raffle

Days Inn Motel window decoration during Elvis Week 1995, Memphis.

tickets, and vying for Elvis collectibles. They go to benefit concerts for area hospitals, donate blood to the Elvis Presley Memorial Trauma Center, attend talks and memorial services, watch Elvis impersonator contests, visit Elvis's birthplace, high school, and karate studio, tag their names on Graceland's fieldstone walls, drink iced tea at Rockabilly's Diner in Graceland Plaza, and splurge on the $8.95 all-you-can-eat fried chicken buffet at the Shoney's Restaurant down the street from Elvis's house.

They spend a lot of their time buying Elvis stuff at the gift shops that surround Graceland. Many fans who stay at area motels such as the Days Inn or Wilson World participate in elaborate window-decorating competitions, while others submit handmade pictures and crafts to the Elvis Art Exhibit and Contest sponsored by Elvis Inc. and held at the Graceland Plaza Visitor Center. Ordinary spaces—motel rooms, school classrooms, health spas, fast-food restaurants—become sacred spaces during Elvis Week, because Elvis fans occupy them and fill them with images and objects that they deem to have special significance. Simultaneously a shrine and a shopping mall, Graceland's multiacre complex is no different from other pilgrimage sites: from Lourdes to the Basilica of the Virgin of Guadalupe in Mexico City, devotional practices, material culture, and commercialism are typically mixed.

As with other pilgrimages, an undercurrent of transgression is evident during Elvis Week. Traditional Christian pilgrimage, observes Stephen Wilson,

> cuts across geographical and social boundaries, takes people out of their established places, mixes social strata and the sexes, allows individuals to wander like vagabonds, and focuses, not on the Church's formal rituals though these may be present, but on a whole range of para-liturgical and unorthodox practices (such as touching tombs, kissing relics, making circuits and processions, bathing, imbibing, feasting).[20]

Going to Graceland, especially during Elvis Week, involves many of the same subversive and carnivalesque elements. Fans, for example, often declare their fidelity to Elvis Culture by wearing Elvis buttons, pins, and T-shirts that are handmade and unlicensed by Elvis Inc., the "official" owner of Elvis's image and subsequent merchandise. By wearing this sort of contraband Elvis stuff and engaging in various "unorthodox" public acts (such as writing graffiti on Graceland's walls, decorating motel windows, cheering for Elvis impersonators, and generally indulging their emotions), many fans willfully violate social norms and challenge Elvis Inc.'s authority.

One of the most important rituals during Elvis Week is visiting the Meditation Gardens, where Elvis, his mother, his father, and his paternal grandmother are buried, and where his stillborn twin brother, Jesse Garon (buried in a Tupelo cemetery), is memorialized with a bronze plaque. Each dawn throughout the year, the gardens are open free of charge. During Elvis Week, free visitation extends to evening hours as well and most fans take full advantage of these opportunities to walk up Graceland's twisty driveway and spend some time at Elvis's grave site. The ritual of taking photographs at Elvis's grave, of freezing and preserving the moment of their participation at the exact spot where Elvis is buried, is key to these fan moments in the Meditation Gardens.

Elvis fans in Meditation Gardens, Graceland, Elvis Week 1996.

In a 1994 newsletter, Burning Love Fan Club president Bill De-Night wrote:

SATURDAY AUGUST 13TH

As we have, each and EVERY day, since we arrived in Memphis, We are at the Graceland Gates, at about 5:30 AM, waiting for the Morning "WALK-UP" to start. 6:00 AM and the gates open. We walk up the L-O-N——G driveway, round the corner, at the top, and "HERE WE ARE AGAIN," in Meditation Gardens, the final resting place of the man we all "LOVE" SO VERY MUCH, "ELVIS." We pay our respects, say a few prayers, and sit on the steps, quietly, for a few minutes. WHAT A WONDERFUL PLACE IT IS!!!!

From prayerful meditation at his grave to souvenir bargaining at fan club auctions, Elvis Week rituals reinforce Graceland's special meaning. Layered and blended, sacred and secular behaviors alike enhance Graceland's reverential status.

Elvis Week culminates in the all-night Candlelight Vigil, held on the anniversary of Elvis's death. The Elvis Country Fan Club of Dallas started the vigil the year after Elvis's death, and it continues to organize the ritual. Beginning on the afternoon of August 15, fans gather in front of Graceland's Melody Gates. By evening, traffic is blocked off along the boulevard, and thousands of fans queue up in long lines along the mansion's stone wall. Most clasp candles, some held in plastic liter-bottles of Diet Coke, others fixed inside brightly colored holders embroidered in needlepoint or decorated with ribbons. For years, the Burning Love Fan Club gave away candles to vigil participants, protesting the $5 that Graceland Plaza stores were charging for a single taper. Elvis Inc. now provides "free candles to those newcomers who arrive at the vigil without knowing to bring their own" and, in recent years, has set up first aid stations with jugs of water, medical personnel, and ambulances outside Graceland's gates.

Around 9:00 P.M., Elvis Country Fan Club members officially start the ceremony with prayers, poems, and Elvis songs. A dignitary (usually a member of the Presley family or an executive from Elvis Inc.) lights a torch from the eternal flame at Elvis's grave and walks down to Graceland's gates. Shortly thereafter, the gates open and the single-file procession to the Meditation Gardens begins. Standing at attention, feet planted, hands clasped, heads bowed, members of the Elvis Country Fan Club and fan club presidents from around the world line Graceland's driveway, often wearing matching vestments— Elvis Week T-shirts, for example, or red, white, and blue jackets. Between this gauntlet of sentries and acolytes, fans snake their way up the mansion's steep pathway to the Meditation Gardens for a brief, private tribute to Elvis. Each solemnly bears a glowing candle, lit from the torch at the start of the procession. Once back down the driveway and outside Graceland's gates, they snuff it out.

The tone of this ritual is clearly borrowed from traditional religious practices, from the ceremonial ambience of midnight mass services at Christmas to the precisely timed vigils at the Shrine of St. Jude in Chicago, where candle lighting marks the beginning and the end of each pilgrim's devotional encounter.[21] It also resembles secular-realm rituals, from the Bic-flicking encore summons at rock concerts to the lighting of the Olympic Torch. For those who aren't familiar with sacred or secular ceremonies, Elvis Inc. provides some "special guidelines": "Please avoid loud talking or laughter or any behavior that might be offensive to, or unappreciated by those who take this tribute

Elvis fan Nicholas Russell from Perth, Australia, during Candlelight Vigil, Meditation Gardens, Graceland, Elvis Week 1994.

seriously. The Candlelight Vigil is intended to be a solemn, respectful tribute." The procession up and down the driveway goes on all night, until every fan has had a chance to visit Elvis's grave. Knowing that Elvis died some time in the morning of August 16, 1977, some fans don't take their "walk-up" to his tomb until dawn.

For most Elvis fans, the Candlelight Vigil is a hushed and somber ceremony, the cathartic moment of a highly emotional week. If rituals have special meaning because of their tangible and sensual qualities, this one is a particularly sensational ceremony. The sounds of cicadas, low murmurs, hushed cries, and Elvis's music broadcast over strategically placed loudspeakers all over the mansion grounds; the visual spectacle of Graceland lit up at night, of flickering candles and a seemingly endless line of fans slowly parading up and then down Graceland's serpentine driveway; the smells of wax, perfume, flowering magnolias, mounds of roses, and sweat; and, of course, the damp and steamy heat, made even more oppressive from standing in line pressed against tens of thousands of other fans for hours on end— all combine to make the Candlelight Vigil an especially spectacular ritual.

Its special character is enhanced by the offerings that fans leave at Elvis's tomb, especially the flowers. Flowers have played a big role in Elvis Culture fandom since his death: so many arrangements were sent by grieving fans that his father orchestrated a "flower-grab" at Forest Hill Cemetery following Elvis's funeral. Brenda Davidson of Dallas, visiting Elvis's grave that morning, recalls, "People rushed into the cemetery in incredible numbers. Since there were so many arrangements, there were thousands and thousands of individual flowers, plenty for everybody. But people came in and began behaving like they were insane."[22] The "flower-grab" at the cemetery was similar to the buying and selling of Elvis stuff that occurred simultaneously: within hours of the announcement of Elvis's death, vendors across the street from Graceland set up makeshift stands and began to sell T-shirts, pennants, bumper stickers, and other stuff featuring Elvis's image.

Decades later, this sort of stuff remains essential in Elvis Culture. During the Candlelight Vigil procession, many fans carry single roses or small bouquets that they lay at the graves of Elvis and his family. At

"Florals" and other gifts left at Elvis's grave during Elvis Week 1995.

the grave site, on the white wooden fence nearby, and strewn throughout the poolside gardens are hundreds of floral arrangements from fans and fan clubs all over the world. "His grave was piled high with roses and flowers two feet thick," one fan recounts. "The air was so sweet it brought tears to my eyes." Although ephemeral, flowers are traditional grave-site offerings, so replenishing them at the Presley family burial grounds is one way that fans continually renew their devotion to Elvis. Fan clubs ask members to "take care of Elvis" by donating to flower funds and making sure that fresh flower arrangements (average cost $65) always venerate Elvis's grave. These are always, too, clearly marked with who and where they're from, and the clubs are fiercely competitive about where their "florals" get positioned: during Elvis Week, especially, there is far more prestige in having an arrangement right at Elvis's grave, rather than along the fence near the Meditation Gardens.

Flowers, pins, ribbons, candles, incense, money, jewelry, horseshoes, clothing, paintings, statues, letters, livestock, canes, crutches, chains, wheelchairs, ex-votos made of wax, silver, or gold, and promises of land, buildings, and human services are among the traditional gifts left at religious shrines. Flowers, photographs, pictures, dolls, toys, records, handwritten messages, and, occasionally, crutches, women's panties, and poems (such as "From Graceland to the Promise Land / We followed you here / We will follow you there") are among the items found at Graceland's Meditation Gardens.[23] Kiki Apostolakos's self-appointed role as graveyard handmaiden might also be seen as an offering to Elvis. Oddly enough, the teddy bear has become the ubiquitous symbol of contemporary grief—found in front of the Vietnam Veterans Memorial in Washington D.C., along the chain-link fence surrounding what's left of the federal building in Oklahoma City, beside the South Carolina lake where the Smith boys died, and, especially, at Elvis's tomb. Teddy bears by the hundreds, in every imaginable shape, size, and color, blanket Elvis's grave in furry acrylic on the anniversary of his death, evoking for fans both his hit song "Teddy Bear" and the intimacy of a beloved companion.

Some of the gifts left at Graceland, especially those that feature images of Elvis, are like ex-votos, or *milagros*, made of tin and shaped like body parts (hearts, hands, feet). Commonly left at the shrines of saints or holy figures, ex-votos act as petitions or thanks for cures and healing. An ex-voto of a leg might be left at Lourdes, for example, to thank the Virgin Mary for mending a broken bone. Offerings of Elvis dolls and Elvis pictures, which simulate Elvis's body or his face and are placed in close physical contact with the spot where he is buried, seem to have similarly powerful connotations for the fans who leave

"Floral" sent by *Los Angeles Fans for Elvis Fan Club, placed along the white picket fence next to Meditation Gardens, Graceland, Elvis Week 1996.*

Gifts left by fans at Elvis's grave during Elvis Week 1996.

them at the Meditation Gardens. Some offerings more specifically request Elvis's intervention: a gift left at his grave during Elvis Week 1996, for example, featured a school photo and a hand-printed letter that read: "Dear Elvis: Miss Yoko was here at Graceland last summer but can't make it this time because she died in a car accident in September last year. You don't know how much she loved you but we hope she is with you in the heaven. Her friends from Japan."

Other fans simply offer homemade gifts. During Elvis Week 1995, the Love 4 Elvis Fan Club of Clifton, New Jersey, left an intricately bejeweled box featuring the letters "T" and "C" ("taking" and "care") sculpted in semiprecious stones. Fans from Colorado Graceland left a wooden plaque decorated with a picture of the Presley home in Tupelo and embossed with the slogan "Elvis Lives In Our Hearts." Ilse Ouellette, a fan from Fort Leonard, Missouri, often leaves tableaus at Elvis's grave, usually incorporating letters or mementos from fans who can't make the trip to Graceland. One, sculpted out of tinfoil, gift wrap, and plastic flowers, included a pledge of devotion from Ralf, a disabled fifteen-year-old fan from Beckmann, Germany. Another combined Elvis images with pages from Kahlil Gibran's poem *The Prophet*, one of Elvis's favorite books. Kiki Apostolakos's portable

Close-up view of gifts, including votive candles, photographs, and numerous teddy bears, left by fans at Elvis's grave during Elvis Week 1996.

dioramas are frequently present in the gardens; one, recycled from traditional cemetery practices in Europe and Latin America, consisted of a plywood maquette of a Graceland-like mansion and an oval photo of Elvis, and changed with the seasons. On Valentine's Day, her house shrine featured roses and a heart-shaped candy box; on the Fourth of July, it was covered with red carnations, blue bunting, and an American flag.

These grave-site gifts are expressions of gratitude—thank yous to Elvis from his fans. In a culture where mourning often takes material form—including placing flowers on graves, leaving dogtags at the Vietnam Veterans Memorial, and making panels for the NAMES Quilt (the huge public art project commemorating those who have died of AIDS)—the offerings left at Graceland, especially during Elvis Week, help fans express their profound grief about Elvis's death. The images and objects that they place on Elvis's grave are the physically expressive focal points of their tributes to both his greatness and his absence, and help them atone for the pleasure he gives them, for the pain of his death, and for the sorrow of their loss. The fact that few fans even think of asking to have their gifts returned (and Graceland staff generally throw them away, uninterested in suggestions that they col-

Elvis gift made by Ilse Ouellette, featuring Kahlil Gibran's The Prophet, *left at Meditation Gardens, Graceland, during Elvis Week 1993.*

lect and catalog them, as the National Park Service does at the Vietnam Veterans Memorial) suggests that they are most important as offerings to Elvis.

The gifts that fans leave at Elvis's grave especially attest to the personal relationships that fans have with him. They do so in a most public manner, however. While the "gift of their presence is the most essential offering" that fans make in maintaining Graceland, and Elvis's, special status, the tokens that they leave also commemorate their identity as fans. Fans, and fan clubs, insist that the offerings they place at Elvis's grave are gestures of thanksgiving, yet if this were wholly true they wouldn't have their names so prominently displayed on them or feel so territorial about their placement. Graceland's gift exchange, in other words, is reciprocal: fans offer tokens of admiration that testify to Elvis's importance and further propel his celebrity; in return, they receive a heightened sense of self-importance about being Elvis fans. What is given is not, however, equal to what is owed; gifts are not debts, which, when paid off, bring an obligation to a close.[24] Rather, the gifts that fans leave at Elvis's grave are part of an ongoing relationship that they have with him, a relationship that is continually being replenished and renewed with images and objects, with the stuff of material culture.

There are other quasi-religious manifestations within Elvis Culture, too, such as the Elvis "churches" that have sprouted up over the past few years: the First Church of Elvis ("pastored" by Doug Isaacks of Austin, Texas, since 1991), the Greater Las Vegas Church of Elvis, and the 24-Hour Church of Elvis (a storefront "artomat" in Portland, Oregon, whose "holy trinity" consists of plastic, Styrofoam, and Elvis). In 1996, the Reverend Mort Farndu (a.k.a. Marty Rush of Denver) and Dr. Karl Edwards (a.k.a. Ed Karlin of Hoboken), the founders of the First Presleyterian Church of Elvis the Divine, staged a widely publicized two-day "Elvis Revival" bent on "E-vangelizing" students at Lehigh University, in Bethlehem, Pennsylvania. The First Presleyterian, like most of these manifestations of Elvis divine, is mostly realized online—a click-in church of the cyberspace, says Lotus software founder Mitch Kapor, that is the "great new spiritual frontier."[25]

Primarily the products of Gen X fans who've cottoned on to Elvis's vast spiritual appeal or, as in the case of the Presleyterians, contemporary versions of 1960s guerrilla theater, these Elvis churches are certainly more cynical than the home shrines and Graceland rituals of "authentic" Elvis fans. But those kinds of distinctions don't really work, especially since the tricksters who organize these campy parodies of an institutionalized Elvis faith say that they're Elvis fans, too. Silly and sardonic, to be sure, they make a definite commitment to debunking the "secret" religious underpinnings of Elvis Culture and to generally demystifying Elvis's iconic status. A lot of time and energy is invested in producing "sacred" cyberspace Elvis texts and shrines—from Farndu and Edwards's online "sermons" (with weekly topics like "How to Be Spiritually Correct" and "The Contract with Elvis"), to the home page of "The Oracle of the Plywood Elvis" (a holiday lawn decoration in Belgrade, Montana, that features an Elvis Elf "who provides guidance" and "wards off the adverse effects of deep fried food"). "Although I see all this as satire," says Isaacks, "Elvis may actually evolve into a major religion some day. Let's face it, it's no sillier than any other religion." Or as Norm Girardot, a professor of religious studies, comments, "The Presleyterians remind us [that] the seriousness of religion can only be rediscovered in relation to all of its glorious absurdity."[26] Humor and jokes and derision, after all, are all forms of participation, ways of mocking and celebrating at the same time. Embedded in all the quasi-religious revelations of Elvis along the electronic highway there lurks a real contemporary yearning for spiritual intensity and belonging.

People build shrines and make pilgrimages for religious reasons, because of deeply felt needs for meaning and enlightenment, in hopes of salvation or expectations of spiritual satisfaction, as tributes to special, sacred figures, things, or places. The burgeoning of Elvis home shrines, Elvis Week rituals, and Elvis cyberspace temples and texts suggests that Elvis Culture has taken on the dimensions of religious faith and belief. The central component in this quasi-religious construction is, of course, Elvis himself and the ways he is imagined as a special, wondrous, virtuous, transcendent, and even miraculous figure. "Elvis was no god," his fans say again and again, but the ways many of them revere him suggest that he is often perceived as a saint and a savior, an intercessor and a redeemer.

Still, fearful of accusations of cultism or heresy, fans are careful to distinguish between their beliefs in God and their feelings for Elvis. As Bill DeNight remarks, "God gave us two great men, Jesus Christ and Elvis. I don't look at Elvis in the same way as Jesus but both were special men." Or as Cara Striff says, "I don't think of Elvis as a God but I do think he had a rare, God-given power over people." Cathy Lester of Bellingham, Washington, writes that "there is something beyond human about him, as if he were a step above the rest of us," and Monica Natzel of Superior, Wisconsin, simply states: "His image is bigger than life." Gloria Winters of Elizabethon, Tennessee, comments, "I think that God looked down on him and saw the unselfish heart and smiled on him, making him the ultimate king of all time, except for Jesus Christ himself." And Piqua, Ohio, fan Ron Graham writes: "Elvis has done so much for so many, he has brought joy where there was sadness, those that were sick he has helped feel better, he has helped so many of us thru some bad times. I feel that God blessed Elvis in a very special way." Elvis, as all of these fans explain, was great, rare, beyond human, a step above, unselfish, bigger than life, blessed. Elvis and Jesus were different, but both were powerful and important —"special"—men. And if fans revere Elvis separately from Jesus, they do revere him and do so in remarkably "religious" ways.

Perceptions of the religiosity of Elvis Culture generally rest on assumptions of its *challenge* to mainstream Christianity. But as historian Laurence Moore points out, "The contemporary religious scene in the United States is no longer completely accessible by perusal of the annual *Yearbook of American and Canadian Churches*."[27] Infiltrated by evangelical and New Age manifestations of spirituality and therapy, of metaphysics, healing, miracles, and meditation, today's Judeo-Christian religions are awash in a blend of mysticism and millennialism, and today's faith in Christian redemption is often accompanied by dabblings in a variety of other spiritual strains. Devotion to Elvis dovetails with this contemporary religious blending, particularly among Americans who have long made a habit of spiritual synthesis and reconfiguration. Elvis's own acts of institutional defiance—his hip-swaying sexuality on television, for example, and his introduction of African-American blues and southern gospel to mainstream radio— hold great weight among his fans. Their personal treatment of Elvis as a quasi-mystical mediator and a redemptive Christ-like figure is less the suggestion of heresy or alienation with religious orthodoxy than a typically American pattern of privatized spiritual assimilation. As Mary Cartaya remarks, "I've got Elvis sitting on my left shoulder and God on my right and with that combination, I cannot fail."

Not surprisingly, fan understandings of Elvis's religiosity generally correspond to their own particular religious persuasions. Fundamentalist Christian fans say Elvis was "very religious" and cite his Pentecostal upbringing (the Presleys attended various First Assembly of God churches in Tupelo and Memphis), his religious faith ("All good things come from God," said Elvis in 1956), and his various gospel albums (including *His Hand in Mine* [1960], *How Great Thou Art* [1967], and *You'll Never Walk Alone* [1971]). They know that one of the first things Elvis bought for his mother when his music royalties started to come in was a picture of Jesus, which she hung in her bedroom. They like to say Elvis "would have been a preacher" if he hadn't become the King of Rock and Roll.[28] As one fan states, Elvis "knew the Bible better than most ministers do and studied many different religions although he only practiced Christianity."

Others see Elvis more as a New Age spiritualist, recounting his interest in alternative religions, mysticism, channeling, and the occult, pointing out that the book he was reading in the bathroom when he died was *A Scientific Search for the Face of Jesus* (about the Shroud of Turin). A few quote the fantastic accounts detailed in various books by Larry Geller, Elvis's hairdresser and self-proclaimed "spiritual advisor," who turned Elvis on to Eastern religions, parapsychology, and New Age proselytizers like Linda Goodman and Edgar Cayce before being fired by Colonel Parker. In one book, Geller describes Elvis's "healing" hands and his miraculous ability to move clouds, and quotes Elvis saying, "Think back when I had that experience in the desert. I didn't only see Jesus' picture in the clouds—Jesus Christ literally exploded in me. Larry, it *was* me! I *was* Christ!"[29]

Recently, a lot of fans have imaged Elvis as an angel—not a teen angel, but a radiant personality appointed for spiritual service. He was the cherub of the month for a 1995 issue of *Angel Times*, a glossy magazine with the publishing philosophy that "God's angels appear to all peoples of the world regardless of religion, race, culture." Inside that issue, Maia Shamayyim, author of *Magii from the Blue Star: The*

Spiritual Drama and Mystical Heritage of Elvis Aaron Presley, described Elvis as a spiritual leader "bestowed with special angelic grace" and asserted that sightings of Elvis since his death are, in fact, "beautiful visitations" of his angelic being. Southern fundamentalist preacher, supernatural New Ager, or rock-and-roll angel, fans make Elvis into the religious icon they want him to be. As one remarks, "Although I am not a religious person I am drawn to Elvis almost as though he was a disciple of God. I suppose it is as close to religion as I will ever get."[30]

Understanding the faith that fans have in Elvis does not lend itself easily to deterministic models of cultural or historical analysis. Fans talk about the "wonder" and "mystique" of Elvis and repeatedly describe him as a "miracle." As one "forty-something year old white female" fan writes: "Elvis is an emotion that entails everything we are capable of feeling. It cannot be captured. It cannot be bought. You cannot draw it. You cannot write it. You cannot take a photograph of it. You can't even explain it. YOU HAVE TO FEEL IT—IT MUST BE FELT BECAUSE IT COMES STRAIGHT FROM THE HEART!!" There are "popular ways of knowing" that are emotive, irrational, superstitious, and revelatory, and these are the ways that fans feel about Elvis and how they see him as a special and transcendent figure in their lives.[31] Their faith in him is made real through the tangible stuff of material culture, through Elvis's image.

Some argue that these materialist forms of Elvis's "deification" are only a facet of the American obsession with transformative consumerism. Elvis is indeed an intercessor in this scenario, but he mediates only between his fans and their faith in consumption; collecting Elvis stuff and making Elvis shrines, in other words, may help fans construct meaning in their everyday lives, but it mainly keeps them addicted to an ideology of buying things to feel better. Obviously, Elvis Culture is thoroughly drenched in the world of consumerism, and fans readily admit that they "need" Elvis stuff in order to "take care" of Elvis and participate in his fandom. But such a view fails to take into consideration the ways in which fans rely on Elvis's image as an all-powerful, nonreferential, and largely incomprehensible transcendence. As such, Elvis's image doesn't simply prop fundamental beliefs in consumerism but raises the issue, as art historian David Freedberg writes, of the "deep cognitive potential that arises from the relations between looking—looking hard—and figured material object[s]."[32]

Looking plays a large role in the formation and practice of religious belief; there is the "identification of the *seen* with what is to be *believed*," Michel de Certeau argues. There is a plurality of visual pieties, as well, and different fans see Elvis in different religious roles.[33] Some view him as an especially integrative spiritual figure. One fan remarks, "Although I am a Christian, I have never experienced such unity in any form of worship. Elvis bonds us between nations, religions, and across all age ranges."[34] Perceptions of fellowship are enhanced by the visual memories that fans have of Elvis's stage style or by videos that capture him in concert.

Elvis was raised in the performative religion of Pentecostalism, in churches that encouraged physically expressive movement and the use of percussive musical instruments, such as guitars, drums, and pianos. Drawing on this religious culture and that of African-American gospel, Elvis turned his own performances into veritable rock-and-roll revivals, replete with apparently automatist behavior (his body twitching, his left leg jerking), frenzied stimuli, and ecstatic release.[35] The joyful and exuberant community of feeling that fans experienced during those concerts still visibly flourishes long after Elvis's death. It is bolstered somewhat by the legions of impersonators who seek to physically replace Elvis's dynamic body and rejuvenate the bonds he created between himself and his audience. It is extended even more through the behaviors of the fans themselves, whose fan club get-togethers and Elvis Week rituals create a unity of fellowship held together by Elvis's image.

Many female fans image Elvis as a loving, intimate, and merciful figure, imagining him in much the same way that antebellum American Christian women imagined Jesus as a warmer and more affectionate spiritual authority.[36] He was a "gentle man," writes Mary Cartaya, who "never hurt us, but instead, left so much for us to enjoy." Elvis was "about love and happiness," says Kiki Apostolakos. "The way Elvis did his songs goes along with the ways women feel," says Ilse Ouellette, who provides this gendered perspective: "Men and women have different perceptions. Women are usually much more sensitive to Elvis's music, his charisma. Men have a harder time relating to Elvis emotionally. I think that's why men spend their time as collectors and women fans spend time expressing their emotions about Elvis with their art and the florals."

Others see Elvis as a healer. Some fans talk about listening to Elvis's music "to get through many painful situations"; one says that her recovery from a triple-bypass operation came from "Elvis's voice." Still more fans talk about Elvis's image as the most important source of comfort in times of need. An English fan comments that when she sees a picture of Elvis "hanging on the wall," she often says, "Oh Elvis, I wish you could sort my life out. . . . [A]nd sometimes it comes right." A fan from Pennsylvania remarks that when she looks at Elvis's "beautiful face with his white teeth & *eyes* that sparkle & his high cheekbones—my emotions *feel frozen*. I can only feel happy & good. I count myself lucky to have found Elvis as my answer to problems and *not* alcohol or medication. He's a great part of my life daily."[37] And in an especially poignant memoir, a fan from Duluth writes that her mother's long and painful bout with cancer was eased by her vast collection of Elvis memorabilia:

> The velvet Elvis was in her bedroom. The bronze plaque was hanging above the stove in the kitchen. The 26 inch statue that could play Elvis songs on mini cassettes was on the T.V. set. There was even a painting in the bathroom. In the final stages of illness, when she was heavily medicated on morphine, she often commented that the various Elvis's around the house were talking to her, comforting her.

Most religions distinguish between a higher god (or gods) and lesser divines. In the Christian world, saints are seen as advocates, as mediators between believers and the divine. Only Christ is viewed as a savior, a redeemer, a figure of salvation. Based on their comments and behaviors and on the way they look at Elvis, it appears that many Christian Elvis fans, and even those who aren't Christian but whose sense of what is religious stems from living in America's overwhelmingly Judeo-Christian milieu, see Elvis as both a saintly mediator and a redemptive, Christ-like figure. Blending religious archetypes, or simply mixing them up, many fans liken Elvis to a spiritual intercessor whom they produce and personalize—in art and in ritual practices—as an instrument of therapeutic relief.

Admittedly, some fans say Elvis "was no saint," but these are often Catholic fans for whom the word "saint" strictly connotes a canonized figure who performed miracles and behaved in an especially virtuous manner during his or her lifetime—which Elvis, most fans agree, did not. Others argue that there are differences between religious beings and contemporary celebrities, but they tend to ignore the way secular figures (from Eva Peron to Che Guevara) can become saints by way of shrines, pilgrimages, and popular veneration. Saints, as Stephen Wilson remarks, "belong to and reflect the societies which produce and honour them, and no one would expect late twentieth-century believers or non-believers to have the same saints necessarily as the contemporaries of St. Simeon Stylites."[38] The fact that so many fans look on Elvis's image as a source of protection and relief, and think of him as a special man who was "beyond human" and "bigger than life," certainly suggests that they have extended sanctity to include the King of Rock and Roll.

Whether viewed as Saint Elvis or "alter Christus," Elvis is venerated and admired by many—more so than any other popular culture figure in contemporary America. Fan understandings of Elvis as saint and savior follow from their imaging of him as a legendary entertainer, a down-home southern gentleman, a patriot, a philanthropist, and a sad man who died alone—each image an amalgamation of Elvis fact and Elvis apocrypha. Some suggest Elvis is especially seen as a "permissive savior" who encourages his followers to indulge and consume and enjoy themselves. But as much as fans find pleasure in Elvis's image and music, it is pain, and the sense that through their devotion to him they can somehow ease that pain, that is most evident in their ritualistic behaviors during Elvis Week. Aside from assassinated political figures (Lincoln, J.F.K., Martin Luther King, Jr.), Americans have historically embraced few secular-realm martyrs. Elvis's pain and suffering, his drug-addict death in a gilded bathroom, his failure to find happiness *despite* achieving the American dream, may be what attract so many of his fans, who likewise are caught up in pursuing the myth of the American dream. They identify Elvis as a fellow sufferer, which may explain why the image of Elvis most loved by contemporary American fans, and most frequently evoked by his impersonators, is that of the Vegas Elvis, the "Late, Fat, Pain-Racked, Self-Destructive Elvis."[39] That image of Elvis embodies the pleasure *and* the pain of his devotees.

Elvis Rooms and Elvis Week rituals testify to the profound manner in which Elvis is understood by many fans as a revered figure of enormous capacity who mediates between themselves and their particular theological constructs. Images of Elvis, by extension, are understood by fans as icons with the explicit power to intercede between themselves and a higher power (god). This works because images of Elvis are multifaceted, mercurial, and mysterious, and because American religiosity is essentially flexible and democratic. On one level, then, fans place their faith in images of Elvis because they correspond to the personal mores and ecclesiastical self-image they desire. On another level, fans place their faith in images of Elvis because he provides a kind of "secular spiritual succor," because he both shares and can minister to their pleasure and their pain.[40]

For many fans, the authority of Elvis's image lies in its iconic ability to satisfy spiritual needs and respond to *personal* notions of contemporary piety. Many critics lump these essentially private constellations of belief and practice together, eager to construct cultish apparitions of an Elvis Religion. But there is no totalizing institutional religious paradigm at work in Elvis Culture. Instead, Elvis fans independently construct a series of cultural and social practices that both foster a sense of belonging (which is largely what the fan clubs are all about) and allow room for individual beliefs. Faith in Elvis neatly corresponds to abiding American needs for spiritual community and spiritual solitude, which makes Elvis a profoundly democratic American icon.

Admittedly, Elvis Inc. aims to institutionalize the beliefs and practices of Elvis fans. Sensing that profits may be maximized by fostering a reverential atmosphere at Graceland, Elvis Inc. has reshaped Elvis's home on pseudo-monastic terms, complete with immaculate outside landscaping, a ritualized house tour, and the sanitized treatment of Elvis's image. But lately, more than a few fans appear to have abandoned Elvis Week and their annual August pilgrimage to Graceland.

While numbers were high at the Twentieth Annual Elvis International Tribute Week, attendees at the 1996 ceremonies were estimated at only 8,000. Those who attended in 1998 numbered fewer than 6,000. As Mary Cartaya remarks, "I don't need to go back to Graceland. I've got Elvis in my heart." The religious import of Elvis, then, may be less about place than image, and less about an official image than the images that the fans themselves create and construct. As their home shrines and ritual practices reveal, Elvis fans challenge a limited, marketplace utility of Elvis by making his image mesh with their own spiritual needs. Their faith in Elvis demonstrates the important links among popular culture, cultural production, and religiosity in America's contemporary public sphere.

Sexing elvis

In 1988, Georgia artist Joni Mabe began touring her *Travelling Panoramic Encyclopedia of Everything Elvis*, an elaborate exhibit of Elvisiana showcased in a series of room-size installations. The floor-to-ceiling display consists of some 30,000 Elvis artifacts, from the usual Elvis stuff like posters, ashtrays, clocks, snow domes, and liquor decanters to rarer relics like the *Maybe Elvis Toenail* (which Mabe stumbled upon in the shag carpet of Graceland's Jungle Room in 1983) and the *Elvis Wart* (which, removed from Elvis's right wrist in 1958, is "as big as a black eyed pea"). Nestled among her arty assemblage of cherished Elvis ephemera are Mabe's own Elvis pictures, including *Love Letter to Elvis*.

Composed on August 16, 1983, the sixth anniversary of Elvis's death, the collage "is about Elvis as a sexual fantasy and is totally sincere," according to Mabe. Framed in frilly pink lace, *Love Letter* features a little picture of a bare-chested Elvis pulling on his pants and other little pictures of a bare-breasted Mabe smooching and posing, à la sex kitten and pseudo-softcore-porn queen, with a life-size bust of Elvis. The handwritten letter reads, in part:

Dear Elvis,
You don't know how many times I've dreamt and wished that you were my lover—or father. . . . I worship you. My sleep is filled with longing for you. . . . I lie here now thinking, agonizing—in other words masturbating. . . . Other men in their fleshly selves could never measure up to your perfection. When making love to you in the later years, I still could sense your throbbing manliness. You really touched the woman in me. . . . No matter who I'm with, it's always you. Elvis, I have a confession to make: I'm carrying your child. The last Elvis imitator I fucked was carrying your sacred seed. Please send money. Enclosed are the photographs of myself and the earthly messenger you sent.
Love-sick for you, Baby . . . Joni

(overleaf) *Joni Mabe*, Traveling Panoramic Encyclopedia of Everything Elvis, 1988. *Mixed media installation, 1,600 square feet. (Collection of the artist, Athens, Georgia)*

Joni Mabe, Love Letter to Elvis (1983). Mixed media, 21 × 14 inches. Composed on August 16, 1983. (Collection of Randall Morris, New York)

Mabe became an Elvis fan on the day he died: "I was outside washing and waxing my car when I heard the news of Elvis's death on the radio. I started thinking about him, about how he's absolutely beautiful. I became this obsessed person—I dreamed about him, I had sex with him in my dreams." Born in Atlanta in 1957 and raised in the

Georgia town of Mt. Airy (where her dad was mayor for nineteen years), Mabe had been "mostly a Southern boogie, Allman Brothers, Lynyrd Skynyrd, Bad Company kind of fan." But when Elvis died, her life changed. She began collecting Elvis stuff and making Elvis art, using Elvis's image to explore "notions about America, the South, sex, religion, death and whatever else took my fancy."[1] In 1983, fulfilling requirements for a graduate degree in printmaking at the University of Georgia, Mabe exhibited *The Elvis Room*, an installation of her Elvis memorabilia and Elvis lithographs—huge, multicolored icons of Elvis's face adorned with glitter and sequins, accompanied by texts declaring: "Elvis called his penis 'Little Elvis' " and "Elvis gave millions of women orgasms by gyrating."

Elvis's eroticism is widely assumed to hold the key to his 1950s popularity. Mabe's contemporary imaging of Elvis shows that his sexuality continues to be a major draw for today's fans. And as blatant as Mabe is about her sexual obsession for Elvis, she's not alone. In 1995, Lucy Lee, a freelance writer from Virginia attending a conference on Elvis at the University of Mississippi, made the comment: "I think they need to explore his sexuality more. If a fifty-two-year-old woman like me still gets chills up and down her spine every time she hears Elvis, there's something more to the man than just a singer." Cindy Beatty, a thirty-two-year-old elementary-school teacher from Los Angeles who went to the same get-together, said much the same: "He always looked like he just rolled out of bed, and you want to just grab his arm and roll him back in. Sex is a big part of Elvis."[2]

It certainly is for fans like Frankie Horrocks of *Mondo Elvis* fame, who fell in love with Elvis on her honeymoon in 1966, watching him in the movie *Blue Hawaii*. "Any normal, red-blooded American woman that loves him is a liar if she said she would not want to go to bed with Elvis Presley," said the forty-something Horrocks in the early 1980s (by then divorced because of her "excessive devotion to Elvis"). "No, I take that back. I met a woman who said if she was given the opportunity of making love to Elvis or having him sing to her, she would want him to sing to her. And I looked at her and said, 'You're sick.' I said, 'Personally, I'd want him to sing while he was making love but if I had the choice there's no way I'd choose the singing over the screwing, any day.' "

And it is for countless fans who have posters and tapestries of Elvis hung on their bedroom walls. In his short story "Elvis Bound" (1987), W. P. Kinsella tells the tale of Tyler Presley, whose "obsession with Elvis" nearly destroys her marriage.[3] Born in 1957, nine months after her sixteen-year-old mom saw Elvis in concert and had sex with another fan "in a 1953 Chevy Bel-Air with blue terrycloth seat covers," and named in memory of that liaison, Tyler insists on outfitting her marital chamber with a life-size "pink-haloed poster of Elvis," which she stares up at whenever she and her husband, Ben, make love. Ben objects ("it pissed me off that Elvis was getting credit for all my hard work in bed") and, one night, goes berserk—leaping out of bed, grabbing a roll of tape, and trussing up Elvis's picture "like a turkey goin' to market." Bound, but still prominently displayed (it even travels with them), the poster of Elvis satisfies them both: Tyler continues to fantasize about Elvis's erotic image, and Ben feels that he has restored his sexual authority. Elvis in the bedroom helps "perk things up" in their sex life.

Elvis in the bedroom is pretty much the focus of Mabe's *Everything Elvis*, where Elvis prints and paraphernalia surround a girly-girl bed decked out with Elvis pillows, Elvis teddy bears, and an Elvis bedspread. Hundreds of Elvis images—mostly of him alone, an isolated icon of desire—are framed in Valentine hearts and pink lace, embraced by bunches of plastic flowers and strings of colored lights. Bedside tables with matching Elvis lamps topped with frilly red shades share Mabe's boudoir ensemble of erotic anticipation. Like Tyler Presley, Mabe claims Elvis on romantic terms as a "pink-haloed" lover, a tactile and tender man. Her husband, Chuck Hawkins (her high-school sweetheart and a car dealer in Athens, Georgia, where they live), tends to ignore his wife's "feelings" for Elvis. "Chuck's real good," says Mabe. "He lives in his own little world and I live in mine. Besides, Elvis is a dead man, so I don't feel guilty. I wouldn't have an affair with a live man, I'd feel too guilty. A live man—they drain your energy. But when they're dead, you can pick your own time, your own fantasy. Elvis enters my world when I want him to. I'm in control."

Everything Elvis is a liberatory environment, a free space where Mabe attends to her private sexual fantasies about Elvis Presley. Like the Harlequin Romance novels read by millions of women, Mabe's Elvis artwork might be seen as an outlet from dissatisfying male–female relationships, a compensatory escape from real-life, real-time tensions.[4] That doesn't mean *Everything Elvis* (or the Harlequins) simply deflects or recontains those problematic relationships and tensions. In fact, it openly—and quite hilariously—critiques a patriarchal culture in which male pleasure has traditionally been dominant. Elvis may occupy center stage in Mabe's fantasy installation, but she drives the fantasy. The pleasure of the piece is very much her own— she's "in control."

Sexual control accounts for a variety of other depictions of an erotic Elvis, especially those by women who make practically pornographic pictures of Elvis for certain fanzines and Internet sites, and who write soft-core fiction about an intimate and lusty Elvis. Debby Wimer, a thirty-something fan from Escondido, California, sketches provocative pictures of Elvis and Ginger Alden, best known as Elvis's last girlfriend, and the last person to see him alive. Wimar has also penned the steamy novella *Spanish Eyes*, in which a young and beautiful Elvis fan helps him return to rock stardom (a decade after his "supposed death"), thrills to his "warm, firm, masculine" touch, and eventually bears his child. Similarly, in the "tragic and touching love story" *Are You Lonesome Tonight?* (1987), Lucy de Barbin recounts her "secret" twenty-five-year romance with a "wild, untamed, and incredibly sexy" Elvis, "a man beyond the image everyone saw," who "saves" her from a hellish marriage and awakens her to "gentle love." Describing their first sexual dalliance, de Barbin writes:

> I could see the silhouette of Elvis's frame against the dying light as I walked up the hill. He was like a magnet pulling me nearer. . . . When we touched, a soft breeze gently blew through my hair. . . . We lay down facing each other with our bodies together. Slowly Elvis began caressing each part of my body. He playfully nibbled my lips as he stroked my face, neck, and breasts with his hands. Under the bright stars of a cool Memphis night, we consummated our love. It was more than just making love.

Female fans who produce overtly sexualized images of Elvis often do so to make him the kind of fantasy lover *they* want: sensitive, soft, and unthreatening, a retooled male, a romantic ideal.[5]

Elvis isn't, however, just a sexual icon for straight women: many lesbian fans claim him as a figure of erotic fascination, too. Lesbian pin-up and chanteuse k.d. lang is sometimes even called "the first female Elvis." (She's not: RCA artist Janis Martin, billed as the "Female Elvis Presley," played the Grand Ole Opry in 1957, and so delighted Elvis that he sent his best wishes and a dozen red roses when she appeared at an RCA convention.) Lang pays homage to Elvis's loose-fitting rockabilly clothes, his leg-shaking performance style, his 1950s hairstyle, and his sneer, and often interjects how Elvis "has been a major influence" in her life during her concerts. "Elvis is alive—and she's beautiful," quipped Madonna, after meeting lang backstage at a 1993 concert. Toni Rae, an Elvis impersonator from Memphis who regularly performs in the "Images of Elvis" contest held each year during Elvis Week, remarks: "He's the only man I've ever felt sexually attracted to, I'll tell you that." And the book *Nothing But the Girl: The Blatant Lesbian Image* (1996) features several erotic photographs of gay women dressed à la Elvis, including a sexy shot of Elvis Herselvis (a.k.a. Leigh Crow), an impersonator from San Francisco who is a dead ringer for the 1956 Elvis.[6]

Men, of course, also find Elvis erotic—or at least describe him often enough on sexual terms. Male music critics, for example, have long idolized the 1950s Elvis as a virile stud, as the absolute model of rock-and-roll machismo. Lester Bangs, who once described looking at Elvis with "an erection of the heart," extolled how Elvis "kicked 'How Much is That Doggie in the Window' *out* the window and replaced it with 'Let's fuck.'" George Melly lauded Elvis as "the master of the sexual simile, treating his guitar as both phallus and girl, punctuating his lyrics with the animal grunts and groans of the male approaching an orgasm." Dave Marsh eulogized the "pure fuck-me splendor" of Elvis's mid-1950s performance style.[7]

Many male fans likewise celebrate Elvis as the first—"and still the best"—in a "cock-rocker" continuum that includes Jim Morrison and Robert Plant.[8] Favorite Elvis images in the homes of many male fans tend to be pictures of Elvis onstage, circa 1956, and posters of the leather-clad rock god of the 1968 "comeback special"—scenes where Elvis was surrounded by a rapturous audience. "I remember a highly educated man rhapsodizing about how phallic the black leather suit was that Elvis wore in his 1968 television appearance," writes Linda Ray Pratt.[9] While reticent to admit that they find these images of Elvis

Elvis performing during 1968 "comeback special."
(Reprinted with permission of Life Magazine. *Copyright Time Warner, Inc.)*

erotic, male fans sometimes betray themselves by using words like "sexy," "raw," and "hungry." Elvis is "an icon of masculinity, the Tutankhamen of American pop music," says Hank Schwemmer of Austin; Elvis is "a synonym for everything that is cool, wild and attractive in a man," echoes Jim Rosenfeld, another Texas fan. Wanting to *be* that most attractive, virile, studly, macho icon underlies these observations from male critics and fans, whose vicarious enjoyment of Elvis's sexuality often translates into their own desires to get the girls that Elvis got. Or as Jim Krohn of Longmont, Colorado, puts it, "the fact that Elvis held the girls' total attention" is what holds his attention, too.

Getting Elvis's girls doesn't inform all male responses to Elvis's eroticism, of course. Andy Warhol, whose privatized homosexuality apparently piqued his pop art imaging of scores of male sex stars, including Troy Donahue and Warren Beatty, repeatedly imaged Elvis as a sexually charged gunslinger in a series of early-1960s silkscreens based on publicity stills from *Flaming Star* (1960), the B-movie western in which Elvis played Pacer, a "half-breed Kiowa caught in the crossfire of a bloody strife between settlers and Indians" on the Texas frontier. Prints like *Elvis I and II* (1964) picture a pistol-pointing, spread legged Elvis as the object of homoerotic desire—dragged up in "Revlon Red" lipstick, heavy black mascara, and purple jeans in the left panel, evanescent in the monochromatic tones of a silver-screen cowboy on the right. Warhol's provocative insights about Elvis's own camp aesthetics continues in the fast-growing field of Elvis impersonation. Miming his songs, his moves, and his lover-like gestures, and costumed in rockabilly getups or, more commonly, skintight jumpsuits slashed to the waist, thousands of contemporary Elvis impersonators blatantly evoke his cross-gendered sexual appeal.

Sexing Elvis as a masturbatory fantasy, cuddly companion, cockrocker, and/or transgendered erotic idol corresponds to how fans construct their own narratives about pleasure, desire, erotica, and gender. Elvis's meaning as a sexual icon depends, too, on their understandings of Elvis's own sexual dynamics. Especially during his 1950s "rebel" years and then again in the 1970s, when he honed his image as a jumpsuited superstar, Elvis slipped "in and out of gender" in performance style and sartorial display, rupturing notions about masculinity

Andy Warhol, Elvis I and II *(1964). Left panel: silkscreen on acylic; right panel: silkscreen on aluminum; each panel, 82½ × 82½ inches. (Collection of the Art Gallery of Ontario, Toronto; gift from the Women's Committee Fund, 1966)*

and femininity, encouraging new models of visual pleasure. Elvis had a kind of "sexual mobility" that appealed to both men and women.[10] His performance style and gender-slippery sexuality outraged most critics (and set the pace for their critiques), but it meshed with other revolutions (most notably feminism) already in play. Today, Elvis is still imaged on erotic terms because of his sexual liquidity, and because many contemporary Americans seem to have largely rejected essentialist ideas about what it means to be a boy or a girl, a man or a woman. Not surprisingly, Elvis's contemporary cultural popularity is largely linked to the different ways that women and men, straights and queers, see him as a sexual icon.

Some fans, of course, don't *want* to see Elvis sexually and become absolutely outraged when the topic is even broached. More than a few say they are "disgusted" by the "vulgar and sick" renderings of an erotic Elvis made by other fans. The comment books for Mabe's *Everything Elvis,* for example, are sprinkled with incensed remarks like "I found this exhibit in poor taste and quite disrespectful to his memory" and "We hope people who are not Elvis fans do not get the wrong idea from your tacky, raunchy art." When Elvis Herselvis and her band, the Straight White Males, were booked to play at the Second Annual International Conference on Elvis at Ole Miss in 1996, both Elvis Inc. and the Tupelo Convention and Visitors Bureau withdrew their support. Jack Soden, the CEO of Elvis Inc., went on record: "We think those guys [the conference organizers at the University of Mississippi] have lost their minds." My own online inquiries of fans about Elvis's eroticism were met mostly with flames (mostly from men) such as "this whole thing is tasteless" and "get off this group and crawl back in your little hovel and leave us alone."

Obviously, cultural prohibitions about admissions of sexual desire and bigoted views about sexual difference are at work here; god forbid that heterosexual males, for example, openly admit to sexual fantasies about any man, even Elvis. (Although Christian Slater, in the 1993 movie *True Romance*, does offhandedly observe: "Man, Elvis looked good. Yeah, I ain't no fag, but Elvis, he was prettier than most women. I always said if I had to fuck a guy—had to if my life depended on it—I'd fuck Elvis.") Likewise, it is doubtful that the "official" keepers of Elvis's legend (Elvis Inc., for example, and those who manage his birthplace) will ever admit that Elvis is, in fact, an erotic image with sweeping, cross-gendered sexual fascination. And, too, competition among fans about Elvis's "correct" image doesn't engender much tolerance for those who "see" him differently—especially, those who claim him as a sexual icon.

Certainly, the sorts of passions or affections that Elvis arouses on a spiritual level are comparable; Elvis's image has always had a protean capacity for multiple understandings. The propensity to imagine Elvis on sexual terms stems from Elvis's own profoundly physical and eroticized sense of self. Elvis loved his body and he loved intimating what he could do with it, especially with the fans who wanted to do it with him, too. Fans never simply looked at Elvis; they touched him and consumed him, grabbing at his body and his clothes during concerts, fantasizing about his image in their bedrooms, treasuring his autograph and any other material artifact (the black leather jacket displayed at GracelandToo, the toenail and wart of *Everything Elvis*) that embodied his trace and their desires. And Elvis was ever eager to please; as any number of biographers report, he had a rapacious sexual appetite and according to some accounts, Elvis (and "little Elvis") had sex with at least 1,000 women before 1960. He carefully constructed his sexual image and their desire, appropriating any number of audience-arousing performance styles—from the physical posturing of Pentecostal preachers and black gospel and soul artists, to the magnetic body motifs of country music megastar Hank Williams, the South's most popular performer until his early death at age thirty in 1953. Elvis undoubtedly copied Williams's "sexually aggressive stage manner," which involved leaning intimately into the microphone, bending his knees, swinging his legs, and swaying with the music, and which, according to country music personality "Cousin" Minnie Pearl, completely "destroyed the women in the audience."[11]

Fully aware of the sex appeal that he worked hard to perfect, Elvis's construction of his own identity was almost completely tangled up in how others saw him as an erotic body. Throughout his career, critics consistently described him in terms of how he looked and how he moved, and the explosive "effect" that his body had on his audiences. Fans saw him and still see him as a physical specimen, a desirable object, a thing to collect and fantasize about. If Elvis was disappointed by their refusal to appreciate his musical talents, he never really moved very far beyond his own narcissism—pursuing movie stardom in the 1960s because, as he put it, "you can't build a whole career on just singing. Look at Frank Sinatra. Until he added acting to singing he found himself slipping downhill."[12] Sometimes Elvis lampooned his sexual magnetism—mocking his rockabilly sneer during the 1968 "comeback special" by mumbling "Wait a minute, my lips's stuck," clowning with a bra on his head at a 1972 concert in Chicago. But lacking the self-assurance (and support) to picture himself as anything but a sexually desirable body, Elvis's sense of self remained solidly fixed on his physical image.

Many other male entertainers, from Hank Williams and Johnnie Ray to Frank Sinatra and Dean Martin, were also seen as sex objects in the 1950s. But Elvis was always more of a transgendered sexual fantasy. That isn't to say that Elvis was gay, or even bisexual, but that he adopted mannerisms that said it was OK for men to celebrate the sensuality of their bodies in ways other than sports, and he courted ways of dressing that reconciled American manhood with mascara. Much like the silent film star Rudolph Valentino, Elvis helped destabilize conventional understandings of masculinity with "connotations of sexual ambiguity."[13] The degrees to which this was publicly visible, and broadly accepted, make his gender transgression all the more important in an analysis of postwar spectatorship and Elvis's abiding popularity.

In the 1950s and in the last years of his life, Elvis culled his sexual charisma with provocatively androgynous costumes and with particular attention to his face and his eyes—the parts of his body that many fans say they see as the most alluring, the most seductive. He selected uninhibiting clothes (baggy trousers and big, big jackets in the 1950s; pseudo-spandex ensembles twenty years later) that let his body rock and twist and kick, and invited fans to imagine what was inside, underneath. He wore ruffled pink shirts and black pants with pink stripes, deliberately claiming "girl" colors (pink being *the* female color of the 1950s) for himself; later recalling having seen Elvis decked out in such a costume, his guitarist Scottie Moore remarked, "I thought my wife was going out the back door." He painted himself in black mascara and royal-blue eyeshadow, too—so much so that country music star Chet Atkins, seeing Elvis perform at the Grand Ole Opry in 1954, was shocked into remarking, "It was like seein' a couple of guys kissin' in Key West."[14]

He had his nose fixed, surgically smoothed his formerly pimply skin, spent hours doing (and dyeing) his hair, and courted fashion designers like Nudie Cohen and Bill Belew to dress him up in glamorous gold lamé tuxedos or fringed and bejeweled jumpsuits emblazoned with eagles, tigers, peacocks, and sundials. In all of this personal transformation, Elvis violated the familiar: souping up the tailored man's suit in inappropriate colors and materials, appropriating the woman's world of cosmetics for his own look, satiating his apparent hunger for physical metamorphosis with styles and inflections that suggested sexual ambiguity. Andy Warhol picked up on Elvis's transgressive character early on: working as a commercial artist for the fashion industry in the mid-1950s, Warhol sketched imaginary footwear for American celebrities like James Dean, Truman Capote, and Julie Andrews, and drew a golden buccaneer boot for Elvis with a decidedly "foppish quality."[15]

Elvis's erotic ambiguity can especially be seen in two mid-1950s photographs: Alfred Wertheimer's 1956 picture of Elvis French-kissing with a perky blonde backstage at a Richmond theater, and *Parade* magazine photojournalist Lloyd Shearer's portrait of Elvis at home in

Alfred Wertheimer, The Kiss, 1956. Elvis and his date, backstage, Mosque Theatre, Richmond, Virginia, June 30, 1956. (Photograph © Alfred Wertheimer. All rights reserved/Dauman Pictures, New York)

Memphis, in his bedroom, taken a year earlier. Both focus on the seductiveness of Elvis's image, capturing an androgynous figure who is coy and playful in the one shot, melancholy and languid in the other. Years later, Shearer recalled that during the 1955 interview, Elvis told him that he had "made a study" of Marlon Brando, James Dean, and Gary Cooper—three male stars of equally ambivalent sexual imaging in the 1950s.[16] Appropriating their poses and personalities as he worked on developing his own, Elvis made himself over from poor white trash to gender-bending Memphis flash.

Elvis's gender slippage was problematic in a postwar America where heterosexuality was the accepted norm, homosexuality a closeted and mostly illicit deviance, and sex in general a taboo topic. The 1950s were profoundly conflicted about the body and sexual display: Playboy was first published in December 1953 (with the era's other sexual icon, Marilyn Monroe, as its first centerfold offering), but sex itself was viewed as something dangerous and explosive, best contained at home.[17] Sexy women were called "bombshells," but were expected to tame their fleshy bodies inside Bestform bras and Lovable latex girdles, and to unleash their sexual energies only within the

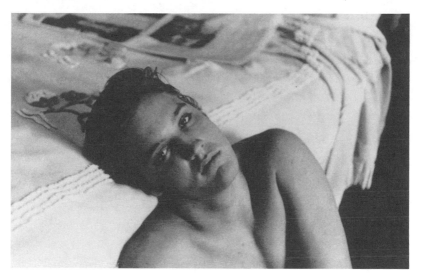

Lloyd Shearer, photograph of Elvis in his bedroom, 1955.

safe confines of the marital bedroom. In an anxious Cold War culture that demanded the demarcation of gender difference—gray-flanneled businessmen versus the Marilyns and Moms of American womanhood—Elvis clearly violated mainstream sexual roles. Openly inviting popular audiences to consider new, powerful forms of pleasure, Elvis opened himself up to patriarchal critiques that tried to displace his provocative entreaties to sexual empowerment.

His success as a sexual icon emasculated him in the eyes of critics who objectified him as *only* a body—a lesser role usually reserved for women and anyone else (blacks, homosexuals) deemed inferior in postwar America. Generally ignoring his rock-and-roll talents or questioning their validity because of what they assumed was his predominantly female-based popularity, mid-1950s reporters zeroed in on Elvis's physique and repeatedly likened his performance art to a kind of striptease: "his hips swing sensuously from side to side and his entire body takes on a frantic quiver, as if he had swallowed a jackhammer" (*Time*); "[his] gyrating pelvic motions are best described as a cross between an Apache war dance and a burlesque queen's old-fashioned bumps and grind" (*Dallas Morning News*); "what Elvis offers is not basically music but a sex show" (*Los Angeles Mirror-*

News).[18] In fact, drummer D. J. Fontana's previous experiences in burlesque bands did lend a certain Gypsy Rose Lee rhythm to Elvis's act. Still, it wasn't simply the music that 1950s critics objected to, but Elvis's subversion of what they considered to be conventional male behavior. There wouldn't have been so much browbeating about the "crisis" of postwar masculinity and femininity—the topic of popular books like *Modern Woman: The Lost Sex* (1947)—unless challenges to gendered difference and authority like Elvis's were in the works.[19]

Still worse was the fact that audiences, especially teenage girls and teenage boys, were clearly thrilled by Elvis's sexually provocative and gender-destabilizing performances. Amy Taubin recalls watching Elvis on TV in 1956 in terms of pure lust:

> It entered me via Elvis's voice and face (the close-up, rather than the wide-angle on his body, was the operative shot). . . . I must stress that I never desired Elvis nor did I identity with him. I simply could not help miming, at an all but invisible level of muscular contraction and release—after all, my parents were in the room— his rhythms, his breathing, and his facial expressions. And I was astonished to discover that when I dropped my lower lip, my clit twitched.[20]

Men tend to be more guarded in describing their physical response to Elvis's 1950s body, but they did respond—copying his looks and his moves, thrilled by his insolence and his open invitation to sensual exuberance. "His rebel appeal was the thing that grabbed my attention," writes Austin fan Edwin Richison. "Elvis was the first true rebel of rock and roll," echoes New Jersey fan Art Pfeiffer, who adds: "His style brought out pent-up passions that teenagers had yearned to release. He created new mores, a more sensual approach to love."

"Let's face it, Elvis gave us a heightened sense of our own sexuality, especially women," says one Wisconsin fan. More than a few female fans claim Elvis's eroticism as an important component in their own sexual liberation. "Hundreds of thousands of women and girls were physically aroused by his sexual gyrations," writes a fifty-two-year-old fan from Omaha who "drew and painted pictures of Elvis" when she was a teenager. She is quite explicit about how Elvis's "shaking-rocking dance aroused women" and challenged repressive postwar moralism. Comparing Elvis's erotic authority with that of Alfred Kinsey, whose studies of American sexuality were published in 1948 and 1953, she comments,

Presley rose to power on the heels of the Kinsey Report[s] which largely portrayed women as repulsed by men's bodies and sexually mutant. Kinsey told women it was unusual for them to be easily or rapidly sexually aroused. Presley showed them it wasn't. The sexual mutant lie couldn't work anymore. Kinsey was a false prophet of the Old Guard. Presley and the pill brought about Women's Liberation.[21]

In the 1950s, Elvis's powerful effect on audiences—and, particularly, his subversive appeal to female sexual emancipation—was sensationalized, and thus trivialized, in countless media exposés of the outrageous adulation of his fans. In addition to titillating coverage of young girls moaning, screaming, and weeping at his concerts, the press reveled in the spectacle of even more unthinkable female behavior: girls asking Elvis to autograph their bras—and breasts—and panties, women begging him to come away with them ("I've got my husband's Cadillac outside"), sixteen year olds carving his name in their forearms with clasp knives. *Life* printed the following letter from Carla Jo Stewart of Amarillo, Texas:

Your article about who else but Mr. Wonderful, the pretty blue-eyed dream, Elvis Presley, is terrific. When he was here, the doors didn't open until 6 o'clock and the teen-agers were there at 4 o'clock!! I was up at the very front but got pushed away because of the more than anxious crowd. A big glass door was pushed out and I got a big gash on my leg, but who cares if it left a scar, I got it trying to see Elvis and I'm proud of it. I guess "memories are made of this"![22]

If the media mostly made Elvis the fetish of obsessive girls, it was hard to ignore the fact that boys were also Elvis fans, also went to his concerts in droves, and also enthusiastically responded to his physically seductive image. *Life*'s feature "Elvis—A Different Kind of Idol" (1956) showed boys fighting off concert hall security guards, getting their hair cut into Elvis-style d.a.'s, and miming his moves. "High school boys [in Jacksonville, Florida] have mastered Presley's ges-

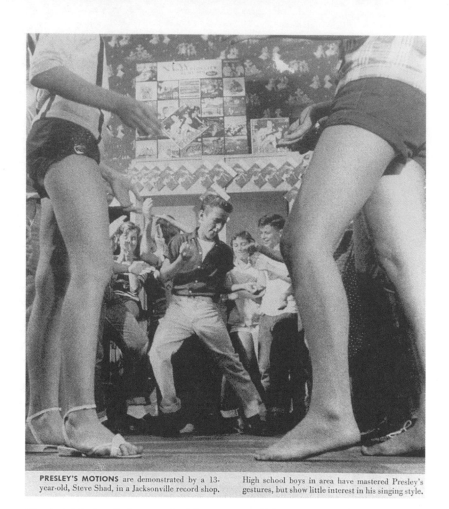

"Presley's Motions," photograph of thirteen-year-old boy imitating Elvis, as illustrated in Life, *August 21, 1956. (Photograph by Robert W. Kelley. Reprinted with permission of* Life *Magazine. Copyright Time Warner, Inc.)*

tures, but show little interest in his singing style," reported *Life*, thus admitting that males, too, were especially caught up in the kinetic energies of Elvis's body—how it moved, how it made them move.[23] Still, by framing its photo of thirteen-year-old Elvis imitator Steve Shad between the naked legs of two nubile teenage girls, *Life* backed away from truly admitting to Elvis's cross-gendered attraction.

Most 1950s fans, however, readily accepted Elvis's embodiment of gender-blurred sensuality—and adopted it for themselves. In 1957, *Life* reported that 1,000 girls in Grand Rapids, Michigan, had hacked

off their pony tails because they wanted "their hair to look like Presley's, slicked back with a lank hank over the forehead and a grippable
tuft in front of each ear." Local beautician Glenwood Dodgson pre-
dicted that within a year, 75,000 more girls would seek a Presley-style
do. The girls themselves wrote enthusiastic letters explaining how
they looked—and acted—just like Elvis. "Have big blue eyes, pretty
lips, like yours," wrote Patti Loplen of San Francisco. "I have an Elvis
scarf, Elvis pins, Elvis shoes, an Elvis sweater, Elvis hat and all of his
records. All I need now is Elvis himself. I even had my hair cut in a
boyish bob and I have Elvis sideburns," said Bobbyjean Saxon of
Seattle. And Jean Goshner of Charleston, South Carolina, related:
"All my friends tell me I look as much like Elvis as a girl possibly
could. I even wriggle like he does."[24]

"Wriggling" like Elvis was the signature performance style for
many mostly forgotten and ignored female rockabilly artists of the
1950s, including Brenda Lee, Wanda Jackson, Rose Maddox, Janis
Martin, and Barbara Pittman (a classmate of Elvis who recorded on
Sun). Martin, the first "Female Elvis," rocketed up the charts with
her 1956 single "My Boy Elvis," which let out that she, too, wanted to
ride the rockabilly "mystery train." Rejecting the tight-fitting cocktail
dresses and fluffy pink poodle-skirt ensembles that were de rigueur for
postwar female performers like Doris Day and Connie Francis, Martin did her act in jeans and white shirts; rejecting their nice-girl-next-
door concert manners, Martin rock and rolled with an explosive stage
presence and thoroughly undomesticated bravado—just like Elvis.

Postwar female impersonation of Elvis, whether in haircuts or in
performance style, was possible only because his image encouraged
this sort of gender-skewing experimentation. Girls didn't want to be
boys; they wanted—like the boys who also imitated Elvis—to be liberated from the limitations of a rigidly gender-specific culture. Teenage
girls' "enthusiasms" for Elvis, as Wini Breines remarks, represented
"tentative forays into alternative notions of femininity." But if postwar
America was barely able to reconcile Elvis's transgressive sexuality
with normative patterns of male behavior, it was completely at odds
with girls who attempted to do the same: not surprisingly, female
rockers like Martin met with only minimal success and staying power
in the 1950s.[25]

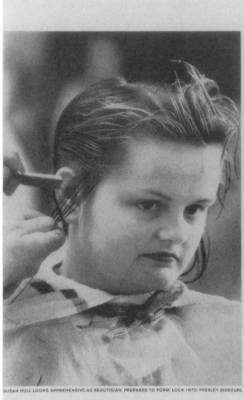

SUSAN HULL LOOKS APPREHENSIVE AS BEAUTICIAN PREPARES TO FORM LOCK INTO PRESLEY SIDECURL

AIN'T NOTHIN' BUT A HAIRDO

In Grand Rapids 1,000 girls trick up locks for love of Presley

In Grand Rapids, Mich. the Elvis Presley rage has reached the critical point where teen-age girls aren't satisfied just to adore him; they want to look like him. Or at least they want their hair to look like Presley's, slicked back with a lank hank over the forehead and a grippable tuft in front of each ear.

The new style is the creation of a male Grand Rapids beautician, Glenwood Dodgson, and in the last six weeks more than 1,000 customers, the youngest 5 and the oldest 60, have swarmed into his chain of shops to surrender their hair at $1.50 a clip. One of them, 17-year-old Susan Hull (*above*), took her foot-long pony tail home in a paper bag, burst into the house shouting, "Look Ma! No hair!" Susan's boyfriend took one stunned and unbelieving look at the locks on her forehead, and then said, "I could hang you for that."

Dodgson, who reports some of his clients want their cuts dyed black so they will look even more like Elvis, supplies a terrifying tonsorial forecast: in the next year his 77 operators expect to shear more than 75,000 girls.

SHORN ECSTASY overtakes Susan after her Elvis cut. She pretended she had guitar, sang *Hound Dog.*

"*Ain't Nothin' but a Hairdo,*" *photograph of girls with Elvis haircuts, as illustrated in* Life, *March 25, 1957. (Photographs by Grey Villet. Reprinted with permission of* Life *Magazine. Copyright Time Warner, Inc.)*

Fans and performers alike in the 1950s, female and male, were clearly turned on by Elvis's rhythmic, rebellious body. More important, they recognized that Elvis's body represented new forms of pleasure and that those forms blatantly blurred set postwar images of manliness and femininity, of male and female sexuality. And that made the guardians of gender difference nervous. Anxiety about the body and the music that makes it move has long been an abiding current in the West; from Plato to Allan Bloom, apprehensive critics have harped about exactly what 1950s Elvis fans remember—the liberating and unsettling appeal of popular music.[26] Watching Elvis's explosive, anarchic physicality, critics echoed chronic Western fears about music's emotional appeal to the body and hence its predisposition to the inferior, "feminine" side of the mind–body axis. Framing him in typically derisive female terms (a stripper, a pelvis, a sex act), Elvis was deemed different, defective, dangerous.

Elvis *was* a different kind of man—physically beautiful *and* physically powerful, a gender-bending blend of what was supposed to define and separate women and men in postwar America. His "rhythm and ooze" (a line he plays around with in the 1960 movie G.I. *Blues*) represented the sensual subversion of reason and order, manners and morals. Of course, it wasn't just Elvis's erotic style that riled 1950s critics, but the recognizably African-American sources of that style. That Elvis borrowed his "uncomfortably unmasculine" hip and lip movements from black R&B performers of the 1950s such as Chuck Berry, Arthur Crudup, and Howlin' Wolf suggests his own sociosexual identification with black male performers, and highlights homoerotic tensions between white and black men in postwar America. And that Elvis, "the poor white messenger of poor black sexuality," was then seducing America's teenagers with that erotic style deeply violated mainstream fears of miscegenation.[27]

The demonization of Elvis's body and worry about the sensory response of his fans were part of a larger moral panic about sexual control and identity in postwar America. This was, after all, an era when novels from Vladimir Nabokov's *Lolita* (1955) to Grace Metalious's *Peyton Place* (1956) were threatened by censorship, when saucy little sex comedies like Otto Preminger's *The Moon Is Blue* (1953) were tamed for moviegoers by the removal of obscenities like "virgin" and "seduction," and when Cincinnati businessman Charles Keating (later indicted for his role in the savings and loan scandals in the 1980s) started Citizens for Decent Literature and declared holy war on *Playboy*. Elvis's gyrating body was similarly a site of sexual struggle, fully exposed from head to groin to toe during his first two appearances on *The Ed Sullivan Show* in 1956, but then visually restricted—contained—"from the waist-up" on the third date, in 1957. "It was the filthiest and most harmful production that ever came to La Crosse for exhibition to teenagers," an outraged representative from the Diocese of La Crosse, Wisconsin, wrote to J. Edgar Hoover, adding: "It is known to psychologists, psychiatrists, and priests that teenaged girls from the age of eleven, and boys in their adolescence are easily aroused to sexual indulgence and perversion by certain types of motions and hysteria—the type that was exhibited at the Presley show." Elvis, the author concluded, was "a definite danger to the security of the United States."[28]

Postwar audiences, in other words, were to be entertained, not liberated. They were supposed to politely watch and maybe clap, not explode in the aisles or in their living rooms as they "discovered" the sensual pleasures of rock-and-roll rhythms and Elvis's body. But Elvis encouraged them to cross the line from voyeur to participant, from looking to becoming, from gazing at a body they desired to *being* that body.[29] Challenging the hierarchy between audience and performer, Elvis insisted that his fans play an active role in their *own* pleasure. Other postwar artists in other media were similarly experimenting with experientiality—John Cage and Jackson Pollock, for example. But Elvis was the popular culture leader of a revolutionary creative project (because that's what rock and roll really was in the mid-1950s) that depended on the participation of a young, mixed-gender, and mixed-race audience—and that made his art much more dangerous than theirs. Once Elvis was tamed and contained—after being drafted in 1958, serving two years in the army, and then reemerging as a cooler and more conservative twenty-five year old—mainstream media aspersions about his dangerous body, and anxieties about how his image orchestrated pleasure and empowerment among American audiences, died down.

Merry Christmas Baby (1989), one of Joni Mabe's glittery mixed-media collages, captures Elvis's suave 1960s image. Minus his sideburns and shaggy mane, Elvis now looked well groomed and grown-up: his dyed black hair slicked back and Bryl Creemed, his whitened teeth capped and gleaming, his adolescent pimples buffed away, his face tanned. Sharply styled in tighter, higher-cut raw-silk jackets,

Joni Mabe, Merry Christmas Baby *(1989).* Mixed media, 12 × 8 inches. *(Collection of Robin Sandler, Atlanta, Georgia)*

Banlon sports shirts, beltless, no-pocket slacks (specially tailored, since Elvis refused to wear underwear), and high-heeled boots called Continental Gaiters, Elvis absolutely personified the swingin' 1960s bachelor—slick and charming, very Palm Beach. He was *Playboy* sexy, and the B-movie musical melodramas that he made throughout the decade, from *G.I. Blues* to *Change of Habit*, almost completely revolved around his apparently irresistible swaggering stud image. *Girls! Girls! Girls!* (1962) is typical, a musical romp full of pat production numbers and curvaceous babes intent on wedding and bedding Elvis; the added attraction of Elvis's semi-erection, evident during his tango with starlet Laurel Goodwin, makes this a hot item in many video stores.

Picturing Elvis as a guitar-strumming pop idol, clean cut and whitewashed—and now playing to angels and Santas, not screaming teens—Mabe captures his post-army persona. In the 1960s, Elvis imaged himself as a "guy"—a real man, a straight white male, an unthreatening crooner like Dino and Frank. In fact, one of his first performances after being discharged from the military was joining Sinatra in a Timex-sponsored ABC-TV special called "Welcome Home Elvis" (broadcast in May 1960). Outfitted in dress blues, Elvis sang "It's Nice to Go Traveling" with Sinatra and his crew (daughter Nancy, Joey Bishop, Sammy Davis, Jr.); switching to a tuxedo, he and Frank traded riffs—Elvis singing verses from Sinatra's pop hit "Witchcraft" (1958), and Frank covering Elvis's gold-record single "Love Me Tender" (1956). Having dissed Elvis four years earlier as a "sideburned delinquent," Sinatra now claimed him as a junior member of the Rat Pack—and Elvis was thrilled.

After two years in the army, Elvis was desperate to regain his place in fandom. When Charles Kuralt asked him at a press conference held immediately after his military discharge if he still liked "screaming girls," Elvis replied, "If it wasn't for them, I'd—I'd have to re-up in the Army, sir, I tell you."[30] And he was apparently convinced that aping Frank Sinatra was the key to lasting popular culture success. (We can only imagine what Elvis might have become had he chosen a more audacious mass-media role model, like Ernie Kovacs.) Singing Sinatra's songs was just the start. Elvis modeled himself after Frank all through the 1960s (or at least until his 1968 "comeback special"), copying his casually sophisticated, Edwardian cool clothing style, dating his girlfriends (like Sinatra's fiancée Juliet Prowse), forming his own Rat Pack (the Memphis Mafia). Most important, Elvis now identified with Sinatra's (and Dean Martin's) take on masculinity and the sexual landscape.

Playing the leading man in his 1960s movies—our primary visual evidence of him from 1961 to 1968, since he performed few live concerts during this period—Elvis abandoned his role as an androgynous performance artist and twisted his former appeal to gender liberation into a stock formula for mainstream, straight male authority. In an infinite succession of tripey flicks, Elvis was always stereotypically macho, always the red-blooded American boy (fisherman, prizefighter, lifeguard, carny, rodeo rider, navy demolitions specialist), and always pursued by countless pretty girls who were utterly absorbed in him. As Mike McCoy, rock-and-roll singer *and* race-car driver in the movie *Spinout* (1966), rated one of the "fifty worst films of all time," Elvis is chased by three women, including the oversexed author of the best-seller "Ten Ways to Trap a Bachelor," who tempts him with the line, "As soon as I domesticate you and get you housebroken, you'll be the best husband a girl ever had."[31]

As stupid as these movies were (and there may be no dumber film than *Easy Come, Easy Go* [1967], in which Elvis sings "Yoga Is as Yoga Does" with Elsa Lanchester), they bluntly projected conventional ideas about gender difference and heterosexual male mastery, and they firmly situated Elvis in a landscape of male-centered sexual pleasure. Although Elvis's movies (like Valentino's movies) were presumably made for mostly female audiences, and his B-movie body was occasionally framed as an erotic morsel for their consumption, they rarely provided the same sort of liberatory and transgendered potential as his earlier concert performances. Instead, posed as the official poster boy of patriarchy, Elvis's macho movie star image reinforced standard Western binary oppositions: male–female, mind–body. He was the guy—he controlled pleasure.

That Elvis didn't appear completely convinced by how Hollywood held the line on gender difference is evident from his listless screen presence: neither bikinied babes nor movie star mastery really seem to have turned him on (except for that moment in *Girls! Girls! Girls!*). "The Presley tough guy," says James Neibaur, "was a mere caricature throughout the sixties: sexually attractive, a good singer, able to throw a few good punches and subsequently win the girl."[32] Admittedly, Elvis's 1960s flicks were truly wretched B-pictures with awful scripts and bad production values, and we'll never know if Elvis could really even act; the Colonel apparently veered him away from genuine

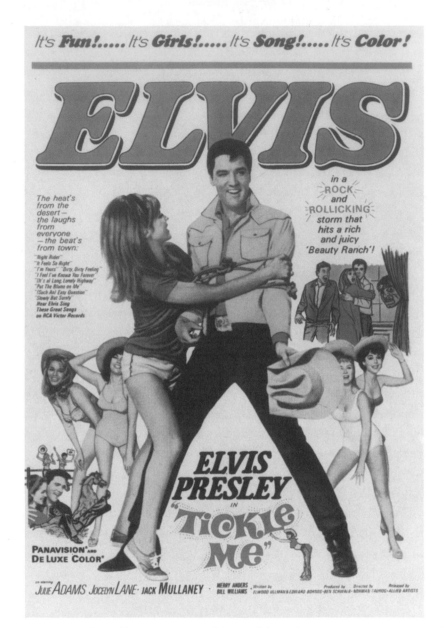

Movie poster for Tickle Me *(1965). (Collection of the author)*

screen opportunities, turning down parts in *West Side Story, Sweet Bird of Youth, Baby, the Rain Must Fall, Midnight Cowboy,* and *A Star is Born* in favor of forgettable, formulaic, low-budget, quick-profit films like *Spinout, Speedway,* and *The Trouble with Girls.* Still, it was Elvis himself who pursued Hollywood's image of chest-thumping manhood throughout most of the 1960s—playing guys like Mike McCoy, singing songs like "U.S. Male" (1967). As one fan relates, "Nobody ever put a gun to his head and *made* him make movies like *Clambake.*"

Amazingly, his records (almost all of them soundtracks for his movies) continued to sell, and the movies themselves made spectacular grosses (making Elvis and the Colonel spectacular incomes). But Elvis's physical celebration of gender-bending erotica disappeared and didn't return until he left Hollywood and got back on stage, in his caped and bejeweled jumpsuits, in the late 1960s and early 1970s. Importantly, while Elvis's movies sold tickets, the hypermasculine image that he tended to project in them has never been a favorite among fans. The image of Elvis that most fans most embrace today is either the youthful rock-and-roll artist of the mid-1950s or the Las Vegas superstar of the 1970s. Few impersonators, for example, imitate the Elvis of *Spinout* and *Tickle Me;* few fans claim the Hollywood Elvis of *Roustabout* and *Harum Scarum* as their sexual icon. All of which suggests that fans deliberately choose a more liberatory and less conventional image of Elvis when it comes to the issue of gender.

Elvis's mutation from rock-and-roll rebel to B-movie star hardly went unnoticed. Many rock fans were unnerved by Elvis's easy sway with Sinatra and unimpressed with his dispirited rendition of "Blue Suede Shoes" in *G.I. Blues.* The press made much of his metamorphosis—"The King of Rock 'n' Roll is Dead!" declared *Movie Mirror* in June 1960—and praised Elvis for his new "maturity." Tabloids and showbiz zines diligently covered Elvis throughout the 1960s, but in the later years of the decade he began to fade from mainstream media attention, except for increasingly bad movie reviews ("monotonous," "vacuous," and "insipid" were typical adjectives) and occasional gossip-column mentions of his marriage to Priscilla Beaulieu in May 1967 and the birth of their daughter, Lisa Marie, nine months later.[33] The usual take on Elvis's disappearance is that writers and reporters and a lot of fans were disgusted by his new pop persona, that they missed his rockabilly sneer, his grunt and groin moves. While this was certainly the case, Elvis's "effect" on women, or perceptions of his continued popularity among female fans, also played a role in his critical negligence.

Elvis's sexual mobility appealed to both male and female fans in the 1950s: the eroticism of his transgressive image activated both new ways of thinking about sexual pleasure and questions about socio-culturally constructed definitions of manhood and femininity. But in the 1960s, Elvis courted Hollywood's image of maleness—a one-dimensional "guy" image that reinforced gender difference. And although few said so directly, male critics (and almost all of them were male) responded to Elvis's apparent shift in style and emphasis—from them *and* girls, to just girls—with feelings of betrayal and animosity. They projected their anger, however, not on Elvis, but on his female fans.

Rolling Stone writer Langdon Winner, for example, bluntly stated: "Elvis sold out to girls," which, his former colleague Greil Marcus explained in the mid-1970s, meant that Elvis "stopped threatening and began pleading." In 1971, British jazz critic George Melly sarcastically touted Elvis as rock stud extraordinaire, describing him "as the first male white singer to propose that fucking was a desirable activity in itself and that, given sufficient sex appeal, it was possible for a man to lay girls without any of the traditional gestures or promises," a back-handed compliment that ended with: "He dressed to emphasize both his masculinity and basic narcissism, and rumour had it that into his skin-tight jeans was sewn a lead bar in order to suggest a weapon of heroic proportions."[34] Women, in other words, were basically to blame for Elvis's degeneration into nothing more than a Sinatra-esque stud: he dressed up for them; he sold out to them. It was their fault.

Critics in the 1950s—mainstream writers and journalists—railed against Elvis's erotic body because it stimulated sexual pleasure and, more dangerously, gender destabilization. A decade or so later, an admittedly different club of critics—those actually more attuned to rock and roll—continued to see Elvis as a sexualized body because, of course, he was, but more because the sexualized body he'd settled for represented a kind of ordinary, repressive masculinity that betrayed his earlier liberatory overtures. Perhaps unnerved by the sexual dynamics inherent in their own desires to see the original, gender-blurring Elvis return to rock, male critics in the 1970s suppressed their disappointment in critiques that focused on the "real" Elvis's supposed appropriation by women. Elvis's post-1950s "decline" (and that of rock in general) was primarily seen in terms of feminization: pandering to girls had domesticated, and hence diminished, the revolutionary creative project of rock and roll. Melly was particularly abrasive on this point, declaring that rock's "angry young bull" had been castrated and transformed "into a masturbation fantasy-object for adolescent girls."[35]

If such critics forgot that Elvis's appeals to pleasure and liberation were originally cast to both girls *and* boys, and were threatened by how girls and women were (and remain) important players in Elvis Culture, Elvis and his manager were more astute. The Colonel always recognized the links between women and consumerism, and hence the importance of female fans in terms of sustaining Elvis's popular culture presence. Elvis, completely locked into his identity as a sex symbol, was convinced his fandom was largely dependent on "screaming girls" and copied Sinatra's stylistics in order to keep them screaming in the 1960s. But at a time when feminism was significantly challenging sociocultural constructions of gender identity and dominance, anxieties about rock and roll's emasculation ran rampant. It's no surprise that male critics, furious about Elvis's apparent loss of interest in them and furious that women might stake claims on the mostly masculinized turf of popular music, assailed Elvis's female fans—and women in general. In early 1969, *Rolling Stone* devoted an entire issue to groupies, "The Girls of Rock," thus intimating that women in rock and roll, both performers and fans, were primarily "in it" to have sex with guys.[36]

Bob Geldof once said that, besides money and fame, guys join rock-and-roll bands to "get laid." Robbie Robertson's confession in *The Last Waltz* that the promise of "more pussy than Frank Sinatra" was the real incentive behind forming what became The Band seems to prove his point.[37] If these are sweeping generalizations, so too are those that claim that all women, and all of Elvis's female fans in particular, really want to be the submissive sex slaves of rock gods. Elvis's eroticism clearly accounts for much of his widespread appeal over the past forty years, and fans like Frankie Horrocks are pretty explicit about wanting to have sex with him. But many others, from Joni Mabe to the fictive Tyler Presley, have sexual fantasies about Elvis that center around intense emotionality and, importantly, *their* erotic freedom. In fact, as many female fans point out, sexing Elvis is often more about romance, intimacy, and friendship than about passive participation in some masculine wet dream.

Their comments bring up issues of sexual taste and speculation about preferred forms of visual erotica for men and for women. Some say that women are most attracted to the pouty sensuality of Elvis's face, the puppy dog sentimentality of his eyes, the softness of his body—that "women seem far more excited by slim, unthreatening, baby-faced types who act vulnerable and resemble them."[38] Wertheimer's and Shearer's black-and-white photographs of a young and beautiful Elvis, kissing a fan in one shot and resting his head against a chenille bedspread in the other, might seem to embody this take on what women want when it comes to sexing Elvis; widely circulated as posters and postcards over the past few years, both images have become increasingly popular. Yet to argue that women prefer these softer, gentler Elvis images suggests that there is some sort of universal or "authentic" female sexual sensibility at work in Elvis Culture (and elsewhere), which is hardly the case. Some female fans lick their lips and murmur, "Ummm, that's *my* Elvis," when looking at Wertheimer's picture; others look to other images. Some male fans find Shearer's photo of Elvis in his bedroom extremely erotic, and others don't. The diversity of Elvis's representation and the diverse sexual tastes of his fans cannot be reduced to a monolithic construction about what men and women (or men versus women) find erotic in Elvis.

In a recent series of paintings, for example, South Carolina artist Kata (born Kata Billups in 1958) images Elvis "as a sexual body who made it OK for the women of my generation to be sexual beings." Her "Elvis sightings," miniature acrylics painted in a pointedly cartoonish style, situate him in places where she has been and where she wants him to be. *I Saw Elvis at the Playboy Club*, subtitled *Elvis Was a Gentleman* (1995), shows Elvis and his Memphis Mafia drinking martinis and ogling big-breasted, bunny-tailed babes at one of Hugh

Kata Billups, I Saw Elvis at the Playboy Club (Elvis Was a Gentleman), *(1995). Acrylic on canvas, 30 × 40 inches. (Collection of Jim Matthewson, Hollywood, South Carolina)*

Hefner's swingin' 1960s sex dens, a decadent lair decorated in blood-red drapes, plush carpets patterned in the *Playboy* bunny logo, and highback lounge chairs equipped with quick-rolling feet and what Kata calls "penis-shaped arms." Elvis—the gentleman—restrains his leering, drooling entourage from the bunnies, gazing out at us with a look, says Kata, that reveals "his disgust with the lewd and vulgar behavior of other guys."

Kata studied figure painting at the Kansas City Art Institute in the late 1970s, which partially accounts for her attention to Elvis's body. But as she explains further, "I've had a lifelong love of Elvis. I think he's a beautiful man, our Adonis." She "got caught up in his image, how others see him and make up these myths and stories about him," when she first visited his Memphis mansion in 1987. Dissatisfied with the glib, one-dimensional image of Elvis (great entertainer, great humanitarian, great guy) presented by his "official" keepers at Graceland, Kata began making paintings of him that fit with her own fantasies.

Elvis Was a Real Man (1993), places him in the spacious kitchen of a suburban 1950s rancho, wearing a sleeveless undershirt that shows off his muscle-bound arms and beefcake body, getting ready to attack a stack of pots and pans. "One day I felt bogged down with housework; I had a sink full of dirty dishes and wasn't expecting any help from my husband [a Nashville songwriter, whom she divorced in 1993]. Since Elvis's image commands respect and admiration, I decided to paint him in a kitchen cleaning a sink full of dishes—in hopes of inspiring men to do more housework." Like many female fans, Kata readily admits that Elvis is sexy. She paints him in settings, however, that recast his eroticism within feminist consciousness—protesting the manhandling of Playboy Club cocktail waitresses, willingly washing the dinner dishes. Elvis the "real man" is a fully conscious sexual figure who easily transgresses the traditional constructs of "man's world/woman's place." Borrowing an already-made image that "commands respect," Kata reshapes Elvis into the man that she wants.

Without discounting Elvis's sexuality, female fans often frame it differently than many assume. Some say they "learned how to kiss" by practicing on their teenage bedroom posters of Elvis, but fandom also encouraged more anarchic kinds of female behavior. Writing about the Beatles and their female fans, Barbara Ehrenreich, Elizabeth Hess, and Gloria Jacobs remark: "To abandon control—to scream, faint, dash about in mobs—was in form if not in conscious intent, to protest the sexual repressiveness, the rigid double standard of teen female culture. It was the first and most dramatic uprising of *women's* sexual revolution."[39] While their account is somewhat overreaching— the intensity of feeling demonstrated during the peak years of Beatlemania (1964–1965) was clearly in force earlier among Elvis's female fans (and even earlier with Sinatra's bobby-soxers)—the fact is that postwar fandom empowered young girls (and boys) to override social expectations of politeness and passivity, to push toward personal emancipation by blatantly expressing their sexual desires.

For many adolescents, those desires centered more around the fantasy of Elvis, or the fantasy of his image, than of actually having sex with him—another distinction that seems to have eluded critics. Fans screamed for Elvis, but most realized he was unattainable. This was fine because while Elvis was the central figure in their fantasies, the

Kata Billups, Elvis Was a Real Man *(1993). Acrylic on canvas, 24 × 24 inches.
(Collection Susan Levy, Nashville, Tennessee)*

personal liberation that he embodied, and encouraged *them* to pursue, was what really drove their desire. Perhaps aiming to contain
those liberatory impulses, or just wanting to cash in on them, teenage
fanzines teased adolescent desire with their endless litany about how
Elvis "really believed in romance" and loved his fans the most (even
after he got married), and with their consistent visualization of Elvis as
a tender, loving pinup. Simon Frith and Angela McRobbie argue that
"dreamy fantasy" images of "teenybop idols" like Elvis—images focused on "an unformed sensuality, something sulky and unfinished in
the mouth and jaw, eyes that are intense but detached; sexiness—but
sexiness that isn't physically rooted"—encouraged girls to "interpret
their sexuality" in terms of romantic love, to sublimate their sexual
desires in deference to roles as girlfriends, wives, and mothers.[40]
But male Elvis fans say they also bought these magazines when

they were teenagers—pinning head-and-shoulder shots of Elvis on *their* bedroom walls, fantasizing about being like and being with Elvis—which complicates our picture of how boys and girls sexed Elvis in the 1950s, and how many fans see him on sexual terms today. Moreover, romancing Elvis can prompt fans to shape their fantasies around more personally satisfying relationships, into searching for lovers and partners who fit *their* fantasies. One Omaha fan remarks, "Elvis was what all women think of as the perfect man. There are the fantasies of meeting him, having him in my arms, knowing the love would never die. It's a special love I have for Elvis. One I hope to have with a viable man." Minnesota fan Joyce Noyes writes, "Elvis taught me how to feel. Everything about him excited me. Elvis influenced my taste in men, as I fell in love with two men who had similar characteristics and who also loved Elvis. My husband of 16 years has many personality traits of Elvis. When he is the most romantic, he sings Elvis to me." And as the liberatory environment of *Everything Elvis* suggests, imaging Elvis as an ideal romantic fantasy most relates to Mabe's personal quest for intimacy and sexual pleasure. Or as she puts it in her deliberately droll manner, "The King's death made it difficult for us to be together. However, in dreamland I assume the form of Ann Margaret and we carry on beyond the last frames of *Viva Las Vegas*."[41]

From a psychoanalytic perspective, fantasy embodies the desire for integration and fullness in lives circumscribed by separation, dissolution, and alienation. Fantasizing about Elvis helps many fans articulate and negotiate ("suture" in Lacanian terms) those desires in the context of real-time, real-life human relationships that occur amid the realities of sexual repression, male dominance, homophobia, and other aspects of sexual politics. To be sure, some fans sexually fantasize about Elvis without considering that "the conditions *creating* the need for such fantasies are engendered by institutional and social systems of power and control."[42] But others strive for fulfilling and equitable relationships with partners who mirror their fantasies of Elvis. Fans like Mabe and Kata clearly challenge patriarchal assumptions about male dominance and male pleasure, remaking Elvis's eroticized image into an icon that embodies *their* desires for personal satisfaction.

Sexing Elvis helps fans work out issues of desire and identity, and they don't always work them out on anticipated heterosexual terms. Sue Wise recounts how as a young teen in the early 1960s, she treated her "full-time preoccupation" with Elvis as a "solitary hobby, a private thing between 'him' and me." As a lonely adolescent just beginning to sort out the realization that she was a lesbian, Wise viewed Elvis as "a private, special friend who was always there, no matter what," a friend "to care about, to be interested in, and to defend against criticism." And, as she recalls, her feelings for Elvis were not atypical: "Flipping through the pages of *Elvis Monthlys* and remembering conversations with other fans reminds me time and again that very many female *and* male fans experienced Elvis in this way. For us Elvis the macho superhero might just as well have been another and totally different person, for he certainly wasn't *our* Elvis."[43]

As Wise points out, many fans fantasize about Elvis as an affectionate, and vulnerable, friend. South Carolina fan Jan Williamson remarks, "I love Elvis, not in a lustful, idolizer way but more as you would a lifelong, cherished friend." Judy Adams of Johnson City, Tennessee, writes, "My fantasy of Elvis is just to be able to sit down and talk with him. I believe he never truly knew just how much he was unconditionally loved by his fans." Anne Stinehart, a graduate student at the University of Virginia, comments that if she could go back in time she wouldn't travel to the medieval Germany she studies, but to Memphis in the 1950s:

> I would find Elvis before anyone knew him and I would want to befriend him, to hold his hand, to tell him he was loved. I'm ambivalent about wanting to be his lover. That would require too much vulnerability on MY part, to be with a man who needed to be with so many women. I would want to be the one Elvis could always, always depend on.

Some fans fantasize not only about being Elvis's best friend but about nurturing him. Mabe's collage *I Could Have Saved Elvis (Only If I Had Been Born Earlier)* (1983), which features a forlorn Elvis in army fatigues, captures the sentiment that Elvis needed, and still needs, the help and protection of "true" fans. "A strong woman like myself," says Mabe, "could have saved him from the pills, the drugs."

Julie Hecht's short story "I Want You I Need You I Love You," in which a thirty-something female fan fantasizes about rescuing Elvis by getting him off junk food, takes up the same theme. "I don't know why I wasted my time in college reading existentialism," says the narrator, "when there was Elvis."[44] Women are stereotypically assumed to be naturally nurturant, and mothering is a socially approved playing field for female feeling, so it is not surprising that many female fans translate their fantasies about Elvis into concerns for his protection; the female-dominant fan clubs are largely driven by such ambitions. But "taking care" of Elvis is also a way that female fans take care of themselves: Elvis is a catalyst for female collectivity, for conversation, intimacy, and friendship.

"I was sitting amongst my Elvis treasures," recalls Mary Cartaya, "and I looked at my favorite Elvis portrait, in my Elvis Room, and I asked him to show me a way I could reach out and share him with others." In 1992, she began sending hundreds of fans a chatty two- to three-page Xerox newsletter, full of personal tributes to Elvis ("the man I fell in love with") and snippets about herself (her job, her health) and other fans (marriages, babies, illnesses). She also organized an extensive network of mostly female foreign fans ("Elvis Pals"), sharing "Elvis news," orchestrating their purchase of Elvis stuff in the United States, and sponsoring their pilgrimages to Graceland. In 1995, she wrote: "I have 220 awesome pen pals from 44 beautiful countries and we all reach out and care through one great man, Elvis. How blessed am I. Elvis has never stopped bringing me happiness. Most of all he brought me each of you. You are my joy and my 'family.' Thank you Elvis for all you have given and thank you for all you have brought to my life."

A fifty-four-year-old fan who has "turned to Elvis for comfort and peace" since she was a teenager in the 1950s, Cartaya now sees him as a resource for female friendship, a stimulant to sisterhood. Elvis is still "the single most driving force" in her life, but by using him as a collective fantasy, Cartaya brings herself and other atomized female fans together into a supportive community. "Our real obsession was with ourselves," recall former teenage girl fans of the Bay City Rollers, a bubblegum group popular in the mid-1970s. "In the end, the actual men behind the posters had very little to do with it all."[45] The same might be said of Elvis's female fans, many of whom may fantasize about his image in order to attain deeper intimacy and friendship with other women.

Some argue that women organize their sexual desires differently from men, that they are more romantic, more interested in companionship and emotional commitment, more persuaded by "love" than "lust." This sort of cultural construction emerges from the different circumstances in which men and women are raised and taught about "being" sexual—following the assumptions, for example, that men are socially unrestricted and aggressive, women more contained by domesticity and submissive. Today, those circumstances and teachings are increasingly blurred. Male fans, for example, also talk about Elvis as a friend: Tommy Tomlin of Las Cruces, New Mexico, writes, "I've had a dream or two about Elvis. They've dealt with the conversations with him, sitting down talking to him, not as a fan but as a friend." And few female fans, straight or gay, when gazing at Wertheimer's 1956 photo of Elvis and a fan kissing, don't sigh and say, "God, she's got all the luck."

Importantly, it is Elvis's own gender-slippery image that permits the multiple sexual fantasies of his fans. Subverting essentialist views of male and female sexuality and of sexual identity, Elvis's image allows men to claim him as a rebel stud, women as an intimate friend—and vice versa. Or as Cartaya comments, "Elvis was a man's man and a man for all ladies, who gave each of us a part of himself." Few fans could or would freely state that by embodying both aggression and vulnerability, by being both tough and tender, Elvis was, in fact, blurring the boundaries of gender difference and sexual identity; sociocultural sanctions against admissions of gender bending, no matter that it is a lived practice for many, remain in force.

One who does is West Virginia artist Rena LaCaria, whose painting *Elvis the King* (1989) particularly evokes Elvis's sexual androgyny. A life-size portrait of a young, nude, and well-endowed Elvis casually posed on a massive throne, surrounded by flowers and wispy clouds, holding a scepter and gazing off into some dreamy distance, LaCaria's Elvis is brawny yet soft, sexually potent yet unthreatening. As she remarks, "In being an artist and thinking about Elvis I thought, why not paint him the way people actually think and see him in their

Rena LaCaria, Elvis the King *(1989). Oil on canvas, 96 × 72 inches.*
(Collection of the artist)

hearts and minds?" LaCaria's certainty that people "see" Elvis on
sexual terms has been challenged: the inclusion of her painting in a
widely traveled exhibition of Elvis art was met with considerable resistance. "We're a state institution and we've got thousands of school
kids going through here every year," said one representative of a Nashville museum that refused to show *Elvis the King.*[46] But is it LaCaria's

depiction of male nudity, or her sense of Elvis's erotic transgression of gender, that most piqued curatorial concerns?

Elvis's transgendered sexuality was perhaps no more obvious than in the late 1960s and 1970s, when he finally left behind his Hollywood guy image and reembraced the kind of androgyny that helped catapult him to popularity in the mid-1950s. Bored with making schlock B-movies and aiming to regain the adulation of a live audience—he hadn't performed in public since 1961—Elvis agreed in 1968 to a one-hour rock-and-roll variety show on NBC-TV, highlighting hits from a decade earlier ("Heartbreak Hotel," "All Shook Up") and singing to a small but enthusiastic circle of fans. Interestingly, he staged this "comeback special" by dressing, à la Jim Morrison, the Hell's Angels, and the Black Panthers, in a skintight black leather ensemble. But he didn't adhere to this macho getup for long and within a matter of months adopted the flash one-piece outfits that became stock attire during his latter concert years. Combining the comfort of the white cotton *gis* that he'd started wearing when he took up karate in the early 1960s with the outrageous fashion funkiness of Liberace (whose own sartorial performances featured feathered boas, mink capes lined in rhinestones, and red, white, and blue sequined hot pants), Elvis turned the formerly proletarian jumpsuit into the resplendent apparel of showbiz royalty.

Audiences were dazzled by Elvis's glitzy reappearance and didn't fail to notice his reinvigorated gender blurring of costume and stage mannerisms. Sammy Davis, Jr., one of many celebs who frequently turned out for Elvis's Las Vegas runs (which started at the International Hotel in the summer of 1969), exclaimed,

> You've got to see the Elvis Presley Show. He opens with that "Space Odyssey" theme—bummm, bahh, bahhh—you think it's the second coming. Then you get a spotlight just on his leg. The spot doesn't even open up. His whole first number is just shaking his leg. Then he sings "Proud Mary" and gives it that karate chop. I give it that, and people think, "Hmmm." And I'm straight.[47]

Asides about Elvis's sexual persuasions were constant throughout his career, of course: likening Elvis to a woman in the 1950s was a critical maneuver aimed at disparaging not only his masculinity but his heterosexuality. In the 1970s, rumors abounded that Elvis was gay and that the real reason his marriage failed (Priscilla left him in 1972 and they divorced a year later) wasn't his (or her) infidelity, but his preference for the all-male company of his Memphis Mafia. The ways he now dressed for performances in Vegas and in arenas all over America—his face powdered and painted, strings of pearls and gold chains draped around his neck, diamond rings covering all his fingers, his body bedecked in gaudy, custom-made costumes that he personally named "King of Spades" and "Blue Rainbow" and had detailed with Cadillac fin collars and oversize silver cummerbunds— also prompted suspicions about his sexual orientation.

Inverting, once again, mainstream assumptions about gender and sexuality, Elvis tempted audiences to rethink conventional understandings of male and female identity. He didn't focus so much on sensual liberation anymore, since the sexual revolution claimed to have accomplished what he touted during his rockabilly days. But he did return to the uncertainties of gender and, as he had in the 1950s, used his body, now cloaked in ever more flamboyant garments, as a visual hook. In some ways, he merely copied what was already on display in contemporary rock and roll: the beads and fringe Jimi Hendrix wore at Monterey Pop, the hip dandy look Roger Daltry assumed at Woodstock, the glam mode premiered by David Bowie in the early 1970s. He also continued, as he had in the 1950s, to draw on styles from black popular culture: the urban dude braggadocio of *Superfly* (1972), for example, and the moves and gestures of performers like Little Richard, James Brown, and Marvin Gaye. Elvis took these countercultural inflections and helped turn them mainstream and middle-class. He also appropriated Liberace's truly outré drag sensibility—and turned his brand of transvestism into admissible popular culture stylistics, too.

Elvis and "Lee" (as his friends called him) first compared fashion notes in late 1956, when in a PR stunt orchestrated backstage at the Las Vegas Riviera, the two millionaire performers wound up switching jackets—Elvis donning Liberace's gold lamé tuxedo top, Lee dressing down in Elvis's striped sports coat. The piano-playing Liberace (born Wladziu Valentino Liberace in 1919, in Milwaukee) was wildly popular in the 1950s; he had his own TV show, SRO concerts, tens of thousands of fans, and plenty of critics who publicly speculated about his "fruit-flavored" flamboyance. He made a lasting impression on a teen-age Elvis, who told high-school friends in the Memphis projects: "Boys, if I could ever get anybody talking about me the way they are talking about Liberace—Man! I'd have it made."[48] Liberace's blatant gender bending not only didn't disturb Elvis, in other words, but suggested an eligible stylistic pathway to the fandom and popularity he himself craved. After meeting him in 1956, Elvis began wearing a gold lamé suit designed by Liberace's designer, Nudie Cohen, posing in that outfit for the cover of the album 50,000,000 *Elvis Fans Can't Be Wrong* (1959). Reinventing himself a decade later after the 1968 "comeback special," Elvis dumped Sinatra and became reacquainted with Liberace's more liberatory, more permissive, cross-dressing persona.

That isn't to say that Elvis came out of the closet in the 1970s, but that, once again, he began to toy with the cultural constructions of gender and sexual identity. Various critics, most notably Marjorie Garber and Camille Paglia, have speculated about Elvis's androgynous image: "the face of Elvis," writes Paglia, "is a girl–boy, masculinity shimmering and blurred", "the figure of Elvis Presley," writes Garber, is that of a "male sex symbol as female impersonator."[49] Perhaps more important is to recognize how many Americans have come to understand and accept that gender is slippery, not even contained in the realm of representation, and that Elvis has been one of their primary teachers in this regard. No better evidence exists than the renewed popularity Elvis experienced when he restormed America's concert halls from 1969 to 1977. Always playing in sold-out sports arenas (whose typical capacity ranged from 40,000 to 65,000 seats), Elvis dressed in elaborate jumpsuits that teased audiences into wondering what, if anything, was essentially masculine or feminine about clothes, and the people wearing them. Refusing to marshal gender and sexual identity into socially or culturally prescribed categories, Elvis continued to shake at their foundations, and encouraged his fans to do the same.

Many gays and lesbians have long recognized, and embraced, Elvis's sexually mobile image—seizing him (and Marilyn Monroe) as the stuff of drag in clubs and parades, brooding about his homoerotic allure in underground films like Kenneth Anger's *Scorpio Rising* (1964), which features scenes of gay bikers listening to Elvis's recording of ("You're The) Devil in Disguise." For many homosexual fans, Elvis's gender play closely mirrors their own, and many describe the erotic attraction of his androgyny. "He does that gender bending thing," says one gay fan from Chicago. "He's butch *and* femme," says another, who adds that that's what most appeals: "I love the fact that here's this gorgeous guy passing for straight but wearing mascara and gold lamé." Graffiti on Graceland's fieldstone wall in 1995 included the following messages: "Elvis—I will remember you!" (signed "the world's only gay Elvis singer"), and "Elvis: You're the only man I will ever love!" (signed with the icon of lesbian fidelity—two linked "female" symbols—from "Maree" of Louisville, Kentucky).

Today, Elvis seems to have secured particularly widespread appeal among many lesbians—helped, no doubt, by k.d. lang's homage. (The "Liberace–Elvis–lang" continuum is clearly in place, with lang now dressing, too, in suits designed by Nudie Cohen.) Attempting to escape the confines of female essentialism, straight and gay women alike have claimed Elvis's image for themselves for the past forty years, beginning when teenage girls hacked off their hair in the 1950s. Since the 1980s, Laurie Anderson has occasionally punctuated her concerts with Elvis-esque costumes and asides; in 1984, Eurythmics diva Annie Lennox dressed like him during a Grammy Awards ceremony. Female performers are inevitably more self-conscious than males about gaining (and maintaining) control, about rerouting (if not altogether denying) the sexually objectifying gaze of their audiences. Lennox comments that she aped Elvis in order to transcend the "bum-and-tits thing," the chick vocalist syndrome of rock and roll. "I don't want to change sexual labels—I want to sidestep them, and to confound people," she remarks.[50]

For Lennox, who isn't gay, and for many impersonators who are, Elvis is a visual model of sexual speculation. Toni Rae's Elvis impersonation is a perfect example. With her dyed black hair cropped short and slicked back, and dressed like the 1950s Elvis in baggy mens' suits and two-toned shoes, Toni Rae easily "passes" at the "Images of Elvis" contest in Memphis, where she has been a regular performer since the early 1990s. Singing from the stock song list followed by most

Patty Carroll, photograph of Elvis impersonator Toni Rae, 1995.
(Courtesy of the artist)

impersonators (from "All Shook Up" to "You Gave Me a Mountain"), Toni Rae delights in jumping down from the stage and wrapping shiny red and gold scarves around the necks of female spectators—and sometimes kissing them smack on the mouth. Most don't seem to know she's a woman; those that do, don't seem to mind. Utilizing Elvis's transgressive image, Toni Rae negotiates her sexual difference in this public sphere, and generally finds acceptance.

In fact, one might argue that contemporary American tolerance for sexual ambiguity is especially seen today in the fast-growing phenomenon of Elvis impersonation. Some estimate that there are as many as 20,000 American "Elvii" (or Elvis Artists, as most impersonators prefer to be called). Television talk-show host Jay Leno jokes that by 2025, one out of every five people on earth "will be an Elvis impersonator." Organizations like the National Association of Amateur Elvis Impersonators in San Francisco and the Elvis Presley Impersonators International Association (EPIIA) in Chicago have seen their membership boom in the 1990s, and "Images of Elvis" in Memphis (the largest and longest running of the impersonator gigs) and the "Elvis Performers Showcase" in Las Vegas have become extremely competitive.[51] It's hard to gauge exactly how many Elvis impersonators there really are: Do they include amateurs at children's birthday parties, or are they restricted to the professionals who make a living imitating Elvis, such as Michael Hoover and Ray Guillemette? What is clear is that in a supposed nation of individualistic do-it-our-selfers, all sorts of Americans look at Elvis and say they want to be just like him. And the Elvis they most want to be—and the one most fans want them to be the most, too—is the jumpsuited icon of the 1970s.

Admittedly, the campy rhinestoned gaudiness of the jumpsuit style is, as one Dallas impersonator says, "just plain more fun" than any other Elvis image. It is also the most mediated Elvis image: via the wonders of a GlobCom satellite, Elvis's 1973 "Aloha from Hawaii" concert—in which he wore an ivory-white, gem-studded jumpsuit, a broad belt adorned with American eagles, and a superhero cape that he hurled into the crowd (and caused a riot)—was seen by an estimated 1.5 billion people worldwide. And, too, impersonators and fans favor the image of the Vegas Elvis because it best embodies the pain and suffering of the later Elvis—the Elvis with whom many American

Patty Carroll, photograph of Elvis impersonator Don Sims signing autographs at Bad Bob's Vapors, Memphis, 1993. (Courtesy of the artist)

fans say they most identify. But the fact that Elvis impersonators over-whelmingly choose his 1970s stylistics is also indicative of how gen-uinely accepted gender bending has become in Elvis Culture.

Impersonation is a kind of disguise that performers assume in order to create an alternative identity, and their success depends on the willingness of their audiences, their fans, to accept this alternative image. This isn't to imply that the culture of impersonation is entirely straightforward: "a healthy dose of ironic distance," ambivalence, and self-conscious awareness among both performers and fans of the the-atrical, and sometimes absurd, dimensions of Elvis impersonation is also part of this culture.[52] Elvis impersonators are a particular cross section of fans who pay homage to Elvis, who "take care" of him and "keep his memory alive" by dressing like him, singing his songs, mim-ing his moves. The intensity of their audience rapport depends less on exact imitation—there are, after all, Latino, Vietnamese, African-American, Jewish, female, and five-year-old Elvis impersonators—than on how they (like Elvis) generate a mood of visual sensuality. It also has a lot to do with how much of their own individuality comes through in performances that are so much about personal transforma-tion, about becoming someone else. There are many reasons why so

Elvis impersonator performing at Images of Elvis, Inc., Ninth Annual Impersonator Contest, during Elvis Week 1995, Memphis.

many Americans have this deep desire for transformation, but the fact that many of them choose to act it out by imitating Elvis suggests just how much he remains a figure of transgression.

Of course, for some fans, Elvis impersonators are simply a sexual subset of the real man; as the girlfriend of one remarked on a 1995 talk show, it's "the closest thing to real sex with Elvis." Or as forty-ish fan Karen LaVonne said at a 1993 contest in Las Vegas, after one imperson-ator draped a white silk scarf around her neck and gave her a long kiss, "We're just wishing it was Elvis and fantasizing, I suppose, that it is him. And we admire all these guys who devote their lives to honoring the one and only. It's like Elvis heaven.".The "guys" themselves are happy (imitating Elvis) to oblige their adoring fans. But as Lynn Spigel observed after attending the first annual EPIIA convention in 1990, "the sexual attraction" that most Elvis impersonators stage "is a highly exaggerated play with gender identity and libidinal pleasures."[53]

Elvis impersonators get that sense of play, of course, from Elvis himself, who set it in motion in the 1950s and returned it to popular culture consciousness in the 1970s. By choosing Elvis's Las Vegas image, impersonators revive and renegotiate Elvis's most blatantly androgynous persona for his—and their own—fans. By responding to that image of Elvis with widespread enthusiasm, fans reveal that these ongoing negotiations of male and female identity continue to have broad support. Even if most fans never dress this way themselves, their approval of others who do may suggest their basic tolerance for a gender-blurred American culture.

From the intimate ambience of *Everything Elvis* to the widespread phenomenon of Elvis impersonation, Elvis's eroticism plays an important role in his abiding presence in American popular culture. Shaped and seen as a gender-transgressive figure in the 1950s, Elvis is still imaged on such terms today. The dominance of his sexually liquid image in popular culture corresponds to the refusal of many contemporary Americans to settle with any bedrock certainty on what is meant by "male" and "female" in terms of fashion and behavior, and in the roles assumed in families, the workplace, and politics. Elvis helped to collapse the containment of gender in the 1950s, and again in the 1970s, and Elvis impersonators continue to do so today. Elvis helped to do the same with race in the 1950s, but as the next chapter explains, contemporary fans, like Americans in general, are much more divided about issues of race and don't much hold to Elvis's image as a unifying figure of racial harmony.

All-White elvis

In August 1994, just before the Seventeenth Annual Elvis International Tribute Week was scheduled to start in Memphis, Lisa Marie Presley, the only daughter of the King of Rock and Roll, announced her marriage to Michael Jackson, the King of Pop. An incredulous public and gleeful media responded to the news with a wink and a nod, skeptical about its lovebound sincerity and largely convinced that it was "a good career move" for Michael—then embroiled in charges of molesting little boys—to marry Lisa Marie, the solidly heterosexual mother of two young children. It seemed to work, too: over the course of their short marriage (Lisa Marie filed for divorce in January 1996), speculation about Michael's guilt or innocence, or his sexual orientation, largely dissolved in the wake of his newfound "family man" image.

In Elvis Culture, however, the celebrity union was widely denounced as an act of treason, an unforgivable sleight. "We want to know what's wrong with Lisa Marie's head," Judy Fielstra of Muskegon, Michigan, told one reporter, echoing the outrage of other fans who had gathered in Memphis on the anniversary of Elvis's death. "Everybody is just shocked that she would marry this creep," added Mary Fett, another Michigan fan.[1] Within days of the public announcement of the wedding, the fieldstone walls surrounding Graceland began exhibiting the following kinds of graffiti: "Elvis: Lisa Marie made a big mistake marrying that jerk. Come back and straighten her out!" and "Elvis: To bad your son-in-law is a faggit nigger" [sic]. Attendance during Elvis Week 1994 was down by half from that of the previous year, with only about 15,000 fans turning out for the Candlelight Vigil.

Some fans said they stayed away because they feared Graceland would be overrun by "Wacko Jacko"'s vast entourage and turned into "Neverland Ranch 2"—a Memphis version of Jackson's 2,700-acre Santa Barbara estate, a private park outfitted with Ferris wheels and wandering wild animals. "I'm afraid that Elvis's beloved Graceland will be forever tarnished and his home will be defaced," one fan remarked. "I'm afraid that once Michael Jackson takes over he won't allow fans to come and pay their respects at Elvis's grave site," said another. Still another declared, "As soon as we heard about that circus of a 'marriage' I told everyone, 'That's the end of Graceland. Pretty

"Michael & Elvis' Daughter: The Full Bizarre Marriage Story," cover of National Enquirer, July 26, 1994. (Reprinted with permission of National Enquirer)

soon Michael and his fans will be sleeping in Elvis's house and bed.'" Alarmist tabloid tidbits in the *National Enquirer,* the *Star,* the *Globe,* and the *Weekly World News* revealing that Michael "loved Graceland" and was planning to move right in, along with zany stories that he had hired plastic surgeons to make him "look like Elvis" and had bought the rights to "gain control over Elvis's music" in order to "save his career" and "become the new Elvis," further unnerved many fans.

Others said they were shocked by how Elvis's little girl (then twenty-six), his sole heir and the mother of his grandchildren, had obtained a quickie divorce from her husband of six years—bass guitarist Danny Keough—in order to marry a man who "liked little boys." "I know that Lisa has no respect for her father but I never imagined that she would stoop so low," said one fan. "She married that child molester just for the sake of publicity. Elvis would be disgusted to see his daughter behaving like this," said another. Pictures of Michael playing with Lisa Marie's kids (two-year-old Benjamin and five-year-old Danielle) and reports that he planned to legally adopt "Elvis's grandbabies" outraged many fans. One angrily remarked, "Would you marry a child molester if you had two small children and one of them was a little white boy, which is what Michael Jackson likes? May god protect Elvis's grandchildren."

When I first began this study of Elvis's omnipresent image, I imagined Elvis Culture as a color-blind meeting place, a multicultural mecca where white and nonwhite fans came together in mutual admiration and love for Elvis. Much of the culture of modern American popular music—swing music, for example, and to some degree jazz—has long held to an overarching ideology of togetherness and commonality, of differences abandoned in the unified search for participation and pleasure. A random encounter (very random, it turns out) during Elvis Week 1993 initially persuaded me of much the same in Elvis Culture. Eating KFC and drinking Pepsi with a retired farm couple from Iowa and a Jamaican-born fan from New York, I listened to their plans for Elvis Week 1994 and was surprised and delighted to hear the Midwesterners promise to "swing by" New York City on their next road trip to Memphis, in order to pick up the black fan and bring her along. "It's no trouble, no trouble at all. The more the merrier," I recall the elderly white couple saying, winning me over to an apparent spirit of bonhomie and brotherly goodwill among Elvis fans.

The next summer, during Elvis Week 1994, when I heard some fans damn Michael Jackson as a "faggot nigger" and denounce Lisa Marie as a "nigger loving tramp," I realized my naiveté—and began reconfiguring Elvis Culture as a more disturbing arena in which fan understandings of family, loyalty, respect, and identity are often tangled with abiding habits of American racism. When I asked fans, for example, why they cared so much about Elvis's daughter, especially since I thought it was Elvis they were drawn to, not his only child, they were quick to tell me that Lisa Marie is "essential" to "taking care" of Elvis. "She's his child, his only child. She's his flesh and blood. What she does in her life, what she does to her kids, it all is a part of Elvis," one fan explained. "When she married that freak, it was like slapping Elvis on the face. It made Elvis, and us Elvis fans, seem even more like a big joke."

For many fans, what Lisa Marie "does" is a barometer of her loyalty, or lack thereof, to her dead father. The fact that she is Graceland's official "keeper" (she inherited the estate on her twenty-fifth birthday, in 1993) strikes terror among fans who have long claimed the hallowed house shrine and pilgrimage site as their own. Fan fears for Graceland's future particularly correspond to perceptions that Elvis and his home are inadequately cared for by Lisa Marie. Her refusal to play the part of the dutiful daughter and greet each and every one of Graceland's 750,000 annual visitors with a tray of mint juleps, a southern belle smile, and a stock repertoire of "I remember when Daddy Elvis . . ." stories angers fans who feel that her life should be given over to Elvis's memory—and their own interests. Tabloid stories about Lisa Marie's allegiance to Scientology have worried some into thinking she might tithe Graceland to "those weird cult people" and further exclude fans from his home. "She has never loved Elvis and his beautiful house like we have," is a common fan complaint.

Fan fears for Elvis's grandchildren (children he never knew, of course, since he died when Lisa Marie was only nine years old) are similarly prompted by their expectations of her and her children's fidelity to Elvis. *National Enquirer* stories in the early 1990s, reporting that Lisa Marie had "banned" all of Elvis's music, his image, and any mention of his name around her young children in order to "give them a chance at a normal upbringing," incensed fans like Cathy Ferguson of Florida, who remarked that it was Lisa Marie's "duty" to tell her kids about their "wonderful grandfather." British fan Katie Vanstone was especially indignant: "How could anyone even dream of bringing up a child without the sound of Elvis, let alone when that child is his own flesh and blood?"

But it was the contagion of Michael Jackson, and the threat of a union that might sully the Royal Presley bloodline (especially after the couple announced their plans to "start a family"), that really escalated fan fears about their role, their presence, in Elvis Culture. The marriage of Elvis's only daughter to a black man brought out deeply felt anxieties among many white fans about Elvis's power and authority—and their own—in an increasingly nonwhite America. It hardly seems surprising that when news of the marriage hit the press, and especially during Elvis Week 1994, proprietors of various gift shops up and down Elvis Presley Boulevard noticed a run on the always popular Elvis Flag—a banner featuring Elvis's smiling face right smack in the middle of the former battle flag of the Confederacy.

Much of Elvis's popularity in the mid-1950s and the media attention he then received can be ascribed to his cross-race stylistics—to the ways that he mixed and blended black and white music and black and white modes of performance into the emergent hybrid of rock and roll. Clearly, it is quite possible to love and imitate black music and black culture and still hold, and even act on, racist beliefs. But Elvis's actual racial beliefs and attitudes are not the main issue in Elvis Culture, or in this book, although their historical context is crucial to an understanding of the particulars of his popularity. Rather, it is the "all-white" Elvis of Elvis Culture, the Elvis who has been made into and is seen by many fans as an icon of whiteness, that demands critical examination. This does not pretend to suggest that all Elvis fans hold to this all-white image of Elvis, either, but to complicate an understanding of what it means for those who do. The fact is, many contemporary fans are unaware of, or more blatantly ignore Elvis's undeniable appropriation of African-American rhythms and sounds, his personal acknowledgment of lessons learned from black musicians, and the significant role he played in negotiating the nascent terrain of civil rights in post–World War II America. Instead, they claim Elvis as a singer who emerged out of what they choose to remember as an essentially white culture, and as a star who appealed mostly to white audiences. Imaging Elvis on a flag flaunted by today's right-wing separatists and Aryan Nation adherents, and denouncing his daughter as a race traitor, many contemporary fans fix him within what they claim as a specifically white racial identity.

Race itself, like sexuality and gender, is hardly fixed but an arbitrary and abstract set of assumptions that are constructed, and decon-

Elvis Flag, featuring Elvis's face on the Stars and Bars.
(Photograph by Nick Havholm)

structed, within visual, cultural, social, political, scientific, and legal systems of meaning [2] We tend to use terms like "black" and "white" with great abandon but are, in fact, hard-pressed to actually define, let alone represent, what we mean. Images of whiteness and blackness, in other words, are conjured out of irrational biases and stereotypes: golfers and Wall Street moguls standing in for "whiteness"; basketball players and gangsta rappers signifying "blackness." Each racial "category" is thoroughly unstable—there are, of course, black golfers and white rappers, black CEOs and white basketball players—which betrays our basic inability to construct American images and identities that are distinctly white or black. Yet while racial difference isn't "natural" and racialized images and understandings of what they truly represent are unfixed and capricious, many of Elvis's fans hold onto a certainty about his "whiteness" and, perhaps more important, his centrality in "white" culture.

The look of American identity has dramatically changed over the past few decades. Norman Rockwell's *Saturday Evening Post* images of straight, white, middle-class guys may have helped shape a national narrative about the "average" American in the 1950s, but we have no corresponding set of images in today's polyglot America. Contemporary American culture is thoroughly racialized, with black athletes (Michael Jordan, Dennis Rodman), black musicians (Babyface, Whitney Houston), black actors (Morgan Freeman, Denzel Washington), and black celebrities (Oprah Winfrey, Bill Cosby) held up as the icons, the heroes and heroines, of youth and adults, black and white. And America's racial mix doesn't simply consist of only "black" and "white": Selena, Jackie Chan, Antonio Banderas, and Margaret Cho also coexist in this country's pantheon of multicultural celebrity. But anxieties about Elvis's place, and their own, in America's obviously pluralistic popular culture have prompted some Elvis fans to image him in terms of racial difference, as a white figure distinct from— meaning different from and superior to—nonwhites. Their blanket condemnation of his daughter's second marriage and their invectives against Michael Jackson speak to the racialized, and racist, narrative that also underlies Elvis's popularity in contemporary America.

Elvis himself didn't tout whiteness, nor was he the racist that some critics seem to think he was. Consciously courting black music, black musicians, and mixed audiences in the mid-1950s, Elvis participated in the creation of a powerful form of popular culture—rock-and-roll— aimed at crossing and even dissolving a racially divided postwar America. His early rockabilly style stemmed from any number of sources, from country ballads and hillbilly twangs to southern gospel, revivalist church hymns, even slick pop ditties. But it was his liberal borrowing from what the recording industry then called "race music"—rhythm and blues, black gospel, and soul—that really set him apart and, importantly, set into motion his popularity.

Elvis's identification with black culture was intentional and deep. While still in high school, he hung out at Henry's Record Shop in Memphis, where black musicians congregated and proprietor Robert Henry booked acts like Fats Waller and Earl "Fatha" Hines for local shows. As a teen, Elvis bought 89-cent singles by black artists, such as "Bear Cat" by Rufus Thomas and "Rocket 88" by Jackie Brenston. He listened to regional R&B radio programs like *Tan Town Jamboree* on WDIA and *Red, Hot and Blue* on WHBQ. He frequented the Club Handy, the Gray Mule, and other Beale Street blues clubs where B. B. King, Charlie Burse, Arthur "Big Boy" Crudup, and Chester "Howlin' Wolf" Burnett often performed, occasionally playing alongside black

Ernest Withers, photograph of Elvis with B. B. King, backstage at the WDIA Goodwill Revue, December 7, 1956. (Photograph © Ernest Withers. Courtesy Michael Ochs Archives)

contestants during Amateur Night at the fabled Palace Theater. He greased his hair with Royal Crown Pomade and shopped at Guy and Bernard Lansky's Men's Fashion Store on Beale Street, emulating black "process" hairstyles and buying the same cool duds as blues artists Jimmie McCracklin and Little Junior Parker.[3] By the time Elvis jumped on stage for his first solo Memphis performances and began recording his first hits at the studio of Sun Records in 1954, his looks and his sounds were undeniably drawn from black musicians and black music.

This is clearly evident in his music: singles like "That's All Right (Mama)" (1954), written and recorded by Arthur Crudup in 1946, and "Mystery Train" (1955), recorded two years earlier on the Sun Records label by Little Junior Parker, obviously demonstrate Elvis's debt to rhythm and blues. Megahits like "Hound Dog" (1956), written by two white songwriters from Los Angeles (Jerry Leiber and Mike Stoller) and recorded in 1953 by blues chanteuse Willie Mae "Big Mama" Thornton (and reaching number three on *Billboard*'s R&B chart that year), further embodied Elvis's deliberate attention to the multi-metered cross rhythms, syncopations, and "rhythmic creolization," of popular post–World War II African-American music.[4]

But it was Elvis's image, and his onstage body movements, that really transgressed postwar notions about the supposed differences between "whiteness" and "blackness." Seizing the moves, the poses, the clothes, and the general attitude of various R&B artists, Elvis showed his physical alliance with what people in the 1950s assumed was an authentically "black" style. For whatever reasons—he liked the beat, he liked the look, he was subversively drawn to a repressed subculture, he was drawn to difference—Elvis adopted a performance style that said "black" in the 1950s. He claimed that style for himself— singing "black," dressing "black," acting "black"—but he mixed it into a self-conscious blend of Pentecostal, pop, Tin Pan Alley, honky tonk, and country styles and sounds. On the one hand, Elvis's version of rock and roll played against narrow American ideas about racial and musical purity, openly inviting audiences to join him in crossing post-war color and culture lines. On the other, while Elvis's white fans in the 1950s clearly reveled in his manipulation of black sounds and styles, they incorporated that blackness into their own reimaging of white identity. There's no doubt that Elvis's "whiteness," backed by photographic "proof" of his Caucasian ethnicity, helped establish his success: if some white disc jockeys refused at first to play Elvis's music because it "sounded black," once they saw he was "really a white guy," they helped take him to the top of the charts.

Elvis at least, from the start of his career, publicly acknowledged his borrowings from black culture. During some of his earliest regional radio and print interviews, he relayed his debts to various blues musicians. "I got it from them," he told a reporter from the *Charlotte Observer* in 1956. "Down in Tupelo, Mississippi, I used to hear old Arthur Crudup bang his box the way I do now, and I said if I ever got to the place I could feel all old Arthur felt, I'd be a music man like nobody ever saw." Backstage later that year at Ellis Auditorium, at the Goodwill Revue, a benefit concert sponsored by radio station WDIA for Memphis's black children, Elvis was overheard saying "Thanks, man, for the early lessons you gave me," to B. B. King. A year later, when a *Portland Journal* staff writer suggested that Elvis had "discovered" rock, Elvis was quick to correct him: "Rock 'n' roll was around a long time before me—it was really rhythm 'n' blues. I just got on the bandwagon with it."[5]

Getting on the R&B "bandwagon," Elvis was postwar America's most obvious "white Negro," a teen version of the hipsters who Norman Mailer portrayed as being infatuated with the sights, sounds, and styles of urban black culture. If Mailer's essay focused primarily on the racialized romance of white intellectuals (like himself) with black jazzmen, Elvis's own identification with African-American culture wasn't terribly different; indeed, Eric Lott argues that "the legacy of blackface" lies behind Elvis's "not-quite and yet not-white absorption of black style." What was different, however, was that the interest Elvis expressed was reciprocated; in the mid-1950s, more than a few black Americans were drawn to Elvis, too. Sun Records office manager Marion Keisker expressed amazement at the cross-race attraction of Elvis's first single: the bluesy rocker "That's All Right" backed with his version of Bill Monroe's country standard "Blue Moon of Kentucky." "The odd thing about it," she told Memphis reporters in 1954, "is that both sides seem to be equally popular on popular, folk and race record programs. This boy has something that seems to appeal to everybody."[6]

Odd, maybe, but shrewd business practice. However obnoxious Sun owner Sam Phillips was when he made rock and roll's most infamous (and misstated) quote—"If I could find a white man who had the Negro sound and the Negro feel, I could make a billion dollars"—he was realistic about long-standing patterns of institutional racism (still in force) that prevented black musicians from achieving success in the mainstream record industry. The modern music business deliberately segregated record distribution, directing R&B to black stores and black audiences, country to whites. *Billboard,* the industry bible, developed separate charts to track the success of mainstream "pop" (white) and "race" (black) music; it also tracked "hillbilly" music, or records directed specifically to southern whites. In the late 1940s, "race" was changed to "R&B," "hillbilly" became "country and western," and mainstream music was fixed on pop's "Hot 100" chart.[7] By aiming Elvis's music at different audiences, by backing his blues-influenced singles with his country-flavored ballads, Sun played as many sides of the profit margin as possible.

In fact, the rise of rock and roll in the mid-1950s was partially the result of its abilities, and those of its audiences, to weave in and out of racially and culturally distinguished music industry charts. There was no "rock-and-roll" chart (there still isn't) and when Elvis emerged, his music went to the top of all three of *Billboard*'s separate, segregated charts: country, R&B, and pop. Elvis's success showed the money to be made by diversifying distribution: record sales in general soared from $195 million in 1954 to $438 million in 1958, and recording opportunities, while hardly equitable, opened up for increasing numbers of black and white musicians. While Elvis alone was hardly responsible for all of this, his sure success helped. As Little Richard put it years later:

> Let me tell you this—when I came out they wasn't playing no black artists on no Top 40 stations. I was the first to get played. . . . [B]ut it took people like Elvis and Pat Boone, Gene Vincent to open the door for this kind of music, and I thank God for Elvis Presley. I thank God for Elvis Presley. I thank the Lord for sending Elvis to open the door so I could walk down the road, you understand?[8]

More than a few of Elvis's concerts in the mid-1950s were aimed at multiracial audiences, and the black fans who bought his singles clamored for his attention at shows. Nathaniel Dowde Williams, a black d.j. at WDIA in Memphis and a nationally syndicated columnist for the black press, described the reaction of some 9,000 teens in

December 1956 at the Goodwill Revue, the benefit concert that Elvis watched from the wings as luminaries like B. B. King and Ray Charles performed. At the end of the show, someone asked Elvis to come on stage and wiggle his hips, and the crowd went crazy. Williams reported that the "black, brown and beige teen-age girls in the audience blended their alto and soprano voices in one wild crescendo of sound that rent the rafters . . . and took off like scalded cats in the direction of Elvis."[9]

Rufus Thomas was there that night, too, and said the scene was a "near riot" as black teens rushed to get Elvis's autograph, and to "get a look at the boy who sounded like one of theirs." In addition to cutting R&B singles like "Bear Cat" for the Chess and Sun labels, Thomas was a d.j. at WDIA. With its 50,000-watt transmitter and black broadcasters, including Thomas, Williams, and B. B. King, WDIA was one of the strongest providers and promoters of postwar black music in the South. Thomas recalls playing Elvis records early on, but being told by the station's program director to "stop" because "he didn't feel like black folk liked Elvis." The night of the Goodwill Revue, however, Thomas says he "took Elvis by the hand and led him onto the stage. He was holding my hand, leaning back, and wiggled that leg two or three times. People stormed the stage! They even stormed backstage, trying to get to Elvis. The next day I started playing Elvis on the radio again."[10]

Black fans surely helped secure Elvis's popularity in the mid-1950s, although Williams, for one, found their response more than a little ironic, and wondered why black teens "would take on so over a Memphis white boy when they hardly let out a squeak over B. B. King." Postwar black teens were drawn to Elvis for the same reasons as other teens—he embodied a kind of dynamism and sexuality that they found appealing, he made it clear that *their* pleasure was central to his own, and his performances spoke to their dreams and their needs. More pointedly, at a time when Jim Crow laws were just beginning to make their slow retreat in the South and racially divided concert halls and lunch counters were tentatively moving toward integration, Elvis's respectful emulation and acknowledgment of black style was perhaps seen by many African-Americans as vindication for centuries of cultural marginalization. Black fans didn't embrace Elvis because he "sounded like one of theirs," but because, as Greil Marcus writes, he had "the nerve to cross the borders" of race. Elvis's blatant assertion of race mixing, his basic refusal to be contained within the limited parameters of "whiteness" and white culture in mid-1950s America, was key to his popularity among many black—and white—fans. As Williams mused after witnessing Elvis's interracial popularity at the WDIA revue, "Beale Streeters are wondering if these teen-age girls' demonstration over Presley doesn't reflect a basic integration in attitude and aspiration."[11]

In a profoundly segregated country, however, Elvis's slippage between racial categories, his apparent ease with various forms of musical, cultural, and especially social integration, made him deeply disturbing to many. In the mid-1950s, the rabidly segregationist White Citizen's Council warned that Elvis, and rock and roll in general, embodied the racial ruination of America's white teens.[12] The double whammy of Elvis's transgressive sexuality *and* subversive racial mixing made him a potent mainstream threat that parents and politicians alike did their best to undermine, to little avail.

Elvis's edginess, his rebellious enthusiasm for testing the boundaries of both race and sex, made him the central icon for a body of mixed-race, mixed-gender fans equally commited to rejecting postwar America's repressive racial and sexual codes. His crossover image made for crossover audiences. In 1956 and 1957, "Don't Be Cruel," "Jailhouse Rock," and "Teddy Bear" climbed to the top of all three of *Billboard*'s major charts. A decade later, in 1968, Elvis's "comeback special," whose eclectic repertoire zigzagged among sweaty, sexy rock and roll, R&B, gospel, and frenetic Broadway-esque pop tunes, and whose finale featured Elvis, styled sharp in a white suit and singing "If I Can Dream" (a tune inspired by the Reverend Martin Luther King, Jr.'s "I Have a Dream" speech), drew some of that year's highest TV ratings—and generated a rush on Elvis's music in record stores all over the country. Intentionally muddying the musical waters of rock and roll, Elvis seemed to say that race didn't matter, and—at least in the 1950s and until he died—his fans seemed to agree.

That isn't to say charges of racism didn't occur during Elvis's career, or that they don't continue today. The "shoe shine" legend— whereby Elvis supposedly once said "the only thing a nigger is good for is to shine my shoes"—has widely circulated since the mid-1950s.[13] If widely believed, the rumor has never been confirmed: no witness has ever emerged to detail when or where Elvis reportedly said this, or that he said it; it has always been a matter of "I heard" or "they told me." Verifiable standards of evidence are not exactly obligatory, of course, when it comes to rumors. More to the point is that hearsay about Elvis's bigotry stems more from legitimate black anger about how Elvis profited from black culture and how Elvis—not Little Richard or Chuck Berry—has been crowned the King of Rock and Roll. Cyclical rumors of Elvis's supposed racism, rampant in America in the 1950s and again today, correspond to historical moments when racial prejudice and discrimination are also rampant.

Nor are they relegated only to America: in the late 1950s, Elvis was widely quoted in several Mexican newspapers for saying he'd rather "kiss two Negro girls than one Mexican girl." A fierce anti-Elvis campaign ensued, including a public protest in Mexico City's Chapultepec Park, where a bonfire was made from huge piles of Elvis records and photographs. In 1960, the Mexican government banned Elvis's movies after riots broke out at the Mexico City premiere of *G.I. Blues*. It is doubtful Elvis really made such a comment; U.S. reports from Mexico suggested that it received such "tremendous publicity" that it appeared to be "contrived." In all likelihood the entire affair, which started with a mistranslation of a radio interview that Elvis gave while promoting his movie *King Creole* (1958), was orchestrated by Mexico's national press and various trade unions, furious at the inroads being made in the country by American popular culture. (In 1958, for example, almost half of the new movies shown in Mexico, which had its own well-financed cinema, were American productions.) Elvis's supposed insult of Mexican womanhood thus became the rallying cry behind struggles over Mexican identity. His handlers (the Colonel and PR expert Hank Saperstein) put the spin on Mexican cultural nationalism by appealing to Elvis's provocateur status, selling him with ads proclaming: "Death to ELVIS PRESLEY! Burn his records, his pompadour, his photographs, his guitar, burn anything you want, but give yourself a treat with the true king of happiness and of rock and roll."[14]

It seems to have worked: José Agustín reminisces that listening to Elvis hits like "Hound Dog" and "Heartbreak Hotel" on Radio Mil, the Mexican station that blasted popular music all over Latin America, shaped his own career as Mexico's foremost rock critic. He wasn't alone: Agustín notes that by the late 1950s, many other middle-class Mexican teenagers were also listening to rock and roll, and eagerly snapping up RCA-Victor's foreign issues of Elvis's albums. In order to generate sales among non-U.S. fans, RCA often altered its releases— changing the flip side of "Hound Dog" from "Don't Be Cruel" to "Guadalajara" for Mexican teens, for example.[15] Catering to international audiences, record companies played to pervasive cultural and racial stereotypes, especially in packaging. Mexican album covers, for example, were modified to make Elvis "look" Latino—his hair slicked back, eyebrows darkened, lips painted red, mascara applied thicker, clothes colored brighter and flashier. Japanese releases were customized to make Elvis "look" Asian—elongating his eyes, darkening his hair to jet black, whitening his teeth, flattening the bridge of his nose, morphing his jawline to eliminate the semblance of "Western" cheekbones.

Manipulating Elvis's image in terms of racial and ethnic difference helped secure his foreign popularity. Rendered dark and swarthy, a rock-and-roll mariachi, for Mexican audiences, and imaged lean and energetic, a guitar-playing samurai, for Japanese fans, racial stereotypes helped sell Elvis. Today, Elvis continues to be imaged by foreign fans as "one of them"; he has astounding popularity, for example, in Brazil, and the Gang Elvis Brasil fan club in São Paulo regularly draws 600 or more fans to its monthly meetings. "He's just like one of us," said one Brazilian fan attending the Elvis Week 1997 festivities. Elvis impersonator Robert Lopez, better known as El Vez, "The Mexican Elvis," has much the same take on Elvis. Growing up in East Los Angeles (he was born in Chula Vista, California), Lopez says he always thought Elvis came from south of the border. "I had uncles with continental slacks and slight pompadours in that Elvis style," he remarks. "I thought Elvis looked like my uncles, he looked Latin."

If the black velvet paintings and plaster-of-paris busts that stream out of Ciudad Juarez tend to feature the Latino Elvis, the Elvis stuff conjured in various Chinese and Indonesian factories seems to sug-

DE LA BANDA DE SONIDO DE LA PELICULA

PARAMOUNT PRESENTA A

BAILABLE

RCA VICTOR
AVE-220

NUEVA /ALTA FIDELIDAD ORTOFONICA

elvis
presley

en

MELODIA
SINIESTRA

(KING CREOLE)

VOLUMEN
II

Record album cover for Melodia Siniestra (King Creole) (1959).
(Collection Geoffrey Thrumston)

gest an Asian Elvis. *The King Comes to Colorado* (1994), a painting by Gao Min, formerly a social realist artist in Communist China (and now an assistant to pop artist Peter Max), depicts a grinning Elvis decked out in his famous gold lamé suit, propped against a backdrop of snow-capped mountains. While a visiting artist at the University of Colorado's fine arts department, Gao Min offered to paint a picture of Elvis for me. Working from the cover of the album *50,000,000 Elvis Fans Can't Be Wrong*, he projected and traced Elvis's image onto the canvas. But photo-realism evaporated when he added the Rocky Mountains and painted Elvis's face in yellowish hues with almond eyes.

Accordingly, in contemporary America, many white fans tend to see Elvis as a "white" guy. There are differences, of course, in the ways

Gao Min, The King Comes to Colorado (1994). Acrylic on canvas, 30 × 20 inches. (Collection of the author)

that Elvis is imaged by foreign and nonwhite fans as a crossover specimen of exported American consumerism, and the ways that white fans
claim him as theirs, the most profound of which stems from white
nationalist anxiety. If many white fans in the 1950s embraced Elvis's
appropriation of black culture—and mixed it into their own constructions of whiteness—today's fans tend to deny that that appropriation ever took place. Instead, they image an all-white Elvis who corresponds to their nostalgia for an American culture that never really
existed, but that they fear is fading from national consciousness. Much
like the supporters of anti-immigration measures such as Proposition
187, the "Save Our State" (S.O.S.) initiative aimed at cleansing California of its undesirables (meaning nonwhites), most Elvis fans deny
they are racist.[16] They say they are simply "taking care" of Elvis and
preserving his memory. But the historical memory of Elvis that they
insist on preserving, and that which they deny, betrays their racial
animus, and the race-based claims they make on Elvis.

This is evident in plenty of Elvis images, including displays made
for the motel window-art contests held in Memphis during Elvis
Week. In 1993 and 1994, two prize-winning pictures were assembled
by members of the Elvis Country Fan Club, the Dallas club primarily
responsible for the Candlelight Vigil each year. Episodic time lines of
Elvis's rise to fame, his concerts, his movies, and his family, the collages consist of gilt-trimmed Elvis photos, hand-painted vignettes of
Graceland and the Tupelo shack where he was born, thick applica-
tions of glitter and foil, and lots of tiny, handwritten script. *The Boy
Who Would Be King*, the window piece from 1993, is divided into sec-
tions titled "The Begining [*sic*] 1953–1958" and "The Legend 1958–
1977." *Elvis The King Lives On*, the 1994 picture, features "Memories
of Elvis" and "The Presley Legacy," and includes insets of Lisa Marie
and her former husband, Danny, and teensy photos of Elvis's "new-
born grandbabies" surrounded by puffs of pink and blue flower decals.

Given the fan furor over Lisa Marie's second marriage, it's not
surprising that Michael Jackson didn't figure in the 1994 picture.
More conspicuous still was the complete absence in either piece of
visual or textual references to the black artists and black music that
enabled Elvis's success. The road drawn from Elvis's Tupelo beginnings to his Memphis "mansion on a hill" (and the words from that

*Days Inn Motel window decoration by members of the Elvis Country Fan Club,
Elvis Week 1993, Memphis.*

Hank Williams hit are highlighted in gold glitter) showed no detours
to the blues clubs and black record stores where Elvis honed his rock-
and-roll sensibilities. Instead, Elvis's "country" roots are emphasized,
complete with photos of his numerous appearances at the *Louisiana
Hayride* and lists of his country-style ballads.

Much as Mexican admirers tend to image Elvis in Latino terms, it might seem obvious that Elvis Country fans would celebrate his country roots. But they go further, claiming that Elvis's music stems *only* from the country sounds of the Carter Family, Jimmie Rodgers, Bob Wills, and Hank Williams—not from the R&B of Rufus Thomas and Arthur Crudup. That it was both, and more, and that country music itself is a complicated cross-race cultural mix, is dismissed out of hand. These fans, along with others, seem to deny Elvis's self-conscious racial synthesis in favor of an ahistorical racial myopia that privileges whiteness. They may not recognize, of course, that the "all-white" image of Elvis that they have shaped depends on the existence of other equally chimerical racial categories: that whiteness depends on its opposites in order to sustain its supposed superiority. They also ignore the "blackness" of country music: black musicians like DeFord Bailey, who played harmonica in the original Grand Ole Opry house band from 1926 to 1941, and Charley Pride, who won the 1971 Performer of the Year Award from the Country Music Association; black musical traditions of call and response and three-bar, twelve-line blues that have become part of the country style; black fans who turned out, and still do, at the Grand Ole Opry.[17] Country music, like American popular culture in general, cannot be simplified to a single category within the false construct of "race." Yet for certain fans, Elvis—and country music—is white.

Perhaps no better contemporary image of Elvis's fan-created "whiteness" is that which fixes him on the Confederate flag. The Confederacy's original inflammatory battle flag dates to 1861, designed by General P. G. T. Beauregard to be seen at long distances and be visibly distinct from the flags carried by Union soldiers. Commonly called the Stars and Bars and today heralded throughout Dixie as the Southern Cross, the flag consists of a red field emblazoned with a blue cross, upon which are dotted thirteen white stars—the states the Confederacy claimed as its own.[18] Elvis Culture's version of the Southern Cross features Elvis in a cowboy hat (a still from his movie *Stay Away Joe* [1968]), center stage among the flag's other white stars. Marketed by Fast Line, an Italian outfit that also sells "poster flags" of Marilyn Monroe and Mack Trucks, the Elvis Flag sells for $19.95 and is a staple among the Elvis stuff collected by many fans. During Elvis Week, it appears in infinite variations—hung in Memphis motel windows, draped on the sides of parked vans, unfurled at fan club get-togethers. It is the official logo of the Elvis in the Heart of Dixie Fan Club, based in Somerville, Alabama. Each August, club members fashion a Meditation Gardens grave-site offering of red, white, and blue carnations shaped into the Stars and Bars, with a picture of Elvis planted in the middle.

Lots of fans love "American Trilogy," too: the Mickie Newberry number that Elvis often sang to close his 1970s shows is an arrangement combining the black spiritual "All My Trials" with the Confederate theme song "Dixie" and the Union standard "The Battle Hymn of the Republic." If Elvis tried to suture a racially divided Vietnam-era America by mixing a slave song with Civil War standards, he failed; racism tends to beat out paeans to unity in America. Whether or not Elvis himself sang "Dixie" as an expression of personal pride in southern history (which is what some fans say) is irrelevant: it gained its popularity—like the Stars and Bars—as the rallying cry of racist separatism. Today, the Confederate flag appears on bumper stickers and license plates all over the South, often accompanied by the slogan "Heritage Not Hate."[19] It's doubtful, however, that many African-Americans feel that the Stars and Bars appropriately embodies *their* heritage and history, especially since it's currently the emblem of choice among more than a few American hate groups—from the Ku Klux Klan to the National Association for the Advancement of White People. The fans who attach Elvis's image to this symbol say they're motivated mainly by Elvis's southern roots, his "heritage." But by pinioning Elvis's head to this flag of secession, they imply their own— and Elvis's—secession from a multiracial and multicultural America.

Ironically, the same argument applies to the ways fans link Elvis to the Stars and Stripes, and to the ways they generally picture his patriotism. In a satirical 1959 song about "how to become an All American Boy," Bobby Bare poked fun at Elvis's evolution from a long-haired, Cadillac-driving rock and roller ("impressing the girls" and *American Bandstand* with his "hot licks") to one of Uncle Sam's boys, a rifle replacing his guitar. Fans in the 1950s were generally horrified when Elvis was drafted, begging the "damn Southern goons" of the Memphis Draft Board to reconsider, weeping when he was inducted into

Floral arrangement donated by the Elvis in the Heart of Dixie Fan Club, placed at the fence next to Meditation Gardens, Graceland, during Elvis Week 1995.

the army on what they called "Black Monday," March 24, 1958.[20] But many contemporary fans relish Elvis's image as an army private who "did his duty" and "served his country" as a infantryman from 1958 to 1960, and Elvis Week usually abounds with pictures glorifying Elvis as an all-American soldier. One 1996 motel window, captioned *Red White and G.I. Blues*, featured a huge painting of Elvis in his army greens, along with a collection of various patches of the Third Armored Division and a real army uniform similar to the one he would have worn in service. Another window, titled *To the Greatest G.I. of Them All*, was filled with photographs of Elvis driving tanks and saluting officers, Elvis dolls and teddy bears dressed in military camouflage, and tiny American flags. Still another, an Elvis Culture appropriation of the opening scene of *Patton*, propped a picture of a khaki-clad Elvis (a still from *G.I. Blues*) against the backdrop of Old Glory.

As America's premiere icon, the Stars and Stripes ostensibly speaks to shared notions of national—not just white—unity, purpose, and patriotism. And the U.S. military is hardly an all-white domain: having steadily pursued integration policies since the early 1950s, the American military continues to be the country's leading multiracial employer. Yet both the American flag and the American military manifest exclusionary pretensions: recurrent debates over flag desecration speak to political efforts to monopolize the flag for "appropriate" (meaning nondissenting) use, and only recently have nonwhite soldiers such as the Tuskegee Airmen and the Japanese Fighting 442nd, the mostly highly decorated infantry division of the U.S. Army during World War II, been officially included in America's pantheon of patriotic nationalism. Notions of white (and particularly white male) centrism continue to dominate popular understandings of the American flag and the military, and by repeatedly imaging Elvis as an upstanding soldier and, more directly, by repeatedly attaching his image to that of Old Glory, fans further imply that they claim him on exclusionary terms, as a distinctly "white" American. Simply by stressing his "Americanness" fans bolster his whiteness; as Toni Morrison remarks, "American means white" and people who aren't white "struggle to make the term applicable to themselves with ethnicity and hyphen after hyphen after hyphen."[21]

Many fans further extend Elvis's whiteness to his (and their own)

Days Inn Motel window decoration featuring image of Elvis as G.I., Elvis Week 1995, Memphis.

idealized working-class image. As an economic term, "working class" connotes wage labor, but it also embodies (especially among those who are working class) sociocultural values like sincerity, loyalty, self-improvement, industriousness, and perseverance—values that many fans feel Elvis was born with and always maintained. "People in the working class—all types of work—truckdrivers, cops, seem to like him a lot," remarks New Jersey fan Tom Thatcher, a forty-four-year-old police officer.

> He had that American dream come true. You know, a back woods country boy started off driving a delivery truck for an electric company. . . . The man's a legend. Reached the top of his chosen career which was show business. He started out at carnivals, high school plays singing. And he knew that this was what he was meant to do. And he continued polishing and polishing and perfecting until he got as we see him in the big Las Vegas shows and *Aloha from Hawaii*. He reached his maximum.[22]

Most fans enthusiastically recite Elvis's material triumphs: his money, his houses, his gold and platinum records, his airplanes. But their admiration for his apparent achievement of the American dream is always underscored by how it didn't really change him, how he "stayed loyal" to his working-class roots and fans. They further qualify Elvis's megasuccess by emphasizing how hard he worked—"polishing and perfecting" his musical skills as he climbed his way up the ladder of show biz stardom. Fan readings of Elvis's working-class image are doubly tied to his fealty to them and to their estimation of his steady dedication to craft. As Shirley Gomez, a fifty-seven-year-old fan from West Sumner, Maine, remarks: "Elvis fans relate to him because he was one of them. Born poor, he achieved tremendous success because he was *sincere* with a *real* talent."

Labor historian David Roediger argues that the terms "work" and "working class" are deeply imbricated with whiteness, that the formation of American working-class identity in the nineteenth century was anchored to assertions of racial superiority by whites. Fearing their growing dependence within a capitalist system of wage labor, white workers sharply distinguished themselves from the slaves and former slaves with whom they shared economic oppression. Artificial, alienating, and yet powerfully convincing categories were established whereby white laborers self-consciously defined themselves as hard working, independent, skilled, honest, and industrious, in direct counterpoint to nonwhite (black, Asian) workers, whom they viewed as lazy, needy, unskilled, undisciplined, untrustworthy, and "preindustrial." The racist underpinnings of an American working class emergent in the industrial age remain prevalent today; in everyday language, as Roediger observes, "the very term *worker* often presumes whiteness (and maleness)."[23] This is not to imply, of course, that racism is only or even particularly a working-class disease, but to recognize the complicated intersections between race and class identity. Thus when many white working-class fans highlight Elvis's progress as a rock-and-roll pilgrim, and when they romanticize his (and their own) working-class leanings, they speak to their shaping of his essentially white racial identity.

In the worlds of popular culture and sports, race-based assumptions linking work with whiteness might appear to break down: James Brown is "the hardest working man in show business"; Michael Jordan is the "workhorse" of the Chicago Bulls. But lionizing the labor of black musicians and black athletes doesn't ease or erase longstanding patterns of racism that denigrate blacks as lesser than whites, that link blackness with laziness and inferiority, whiteness with work and supremacy. Moreover, it often simply reinforces biases about the supposedly "natural" affinities between African-Americans and athleticism—on the dance floor, on the court.

This naturalized and unquestioned pairing of work and whiteness may help explain the fury with which many fans generally respond to accounts of Elvis's drug abuse—the reports that he consumed hundreds of pills a week and the autopsy evidence that showed a body stuffed with Dialaudid, Placidyl, Valium, quaaludes, Percodan, Demerol, Seconal, Nembutal, phenobarbital, morphine, codeine, cortisone, and lots of other uppers, downers, and painkillers. Despite plenty of evidence to the contrary, many fans recite the mantra "Elvis was no drug addict," unable to reconcile his workingman image with one of stoned self-abuse. Others qualify their denial by stressing that Elvis used only "prescription drugs," not "street drugs," and those only "because he was always in so much pain" from a variety of physical ailments and from working so hard to satisfy them. These fans find links between Elvis and drugs repulsive not only because addiction is associated with dependence and weakness, but also because drugs have been stereotypically associated with nonwhites—jazz musicians in the 1950s, crack addicts in the 1990s. Attributing drug abuse exclusively to nonwhites is ludicrous, of course, but it is another way in which many fans strive to distinguish Elvis's fundamental whiteness.

This may also allow yet another explanation for the popularity among today's fans of Elvis's Las Vegas image—the image of an older Elvis working a crowd of thousands, sweating it out on stage at the International Hotel or in a huge sports arena wearing a lily-white jumpsuit. Among all of Elvis's various guises, it is this image that best embodies the values of work and whiteness held dear by many fans. The white jumpsuit has a lot to do with it: it's basically the same one-piece uniform originally worn by World War II parachutists and then by American blue-collar workers, albeit gussied up into royal grandeur. And it's white—the color of purity, of power, "of positive myths that celebrate imagined virtues and conceal real failings" in the popular imagination.[24] That the blatantly androgynous image of Elvis in a

Elvis in all-white jumpsuit.
(Photo collection of William J. DeNight, Streamwood, Illinois)

jumpsuit speaks to gender transgression suggests just how much limiting assumptions about sex and gender difference seem to have collapsed in contemporary culture; that this image of Elvis also serves to reinforce the racist beliefs of many fans suggests just how much notions of racial difference persist. If few other Elvis images have this hold among today's fans it's because they don't appropriately convey the man they want Elvis to be: a white guy who made it big the "right" way through talent, ambition, and sheer hard work. Elvis's 1950s rockabilly rebel image is too outlaw, too flip, and his 1968 "comeback special" costume comes too close to the leather look courted by the Hells Angels in the 1960s, and the S/M trade today.

In fact, contemporary American outlaw or bad-boy images seem mostly relegated to nonwhites: to gangsta rappers and barrio homeys. If fans, and impersonators, have largely abandoned Elvis's incarnations as a teen delinquent or a leather-clad outlaw it's because today's white stars mostly seem to signify law and order. Popular culture images of rebellion and dissent, images Elvis certainly embodied in the mid-1950s and tentatively reclaimed in his "comeback" to rock in 1968, have mostly become the property of nonwhites. Real life belies these wildly stereotypical configurations of race difference: Oklahoma City bomber Timothy McVeigh is a white guy; Supreme Court Justice Clarence Thomas is not. Yet a larger popular narrative persists, one that divides Americans into obviously capricious racial categories. The explosion in the streets of South Central Los Angeles on April 29, 1992, after a suburban Simi Valley jury acquitted the police officers who had beaten Rodney King, is but one example of this yawning contemporary racial divide. The fact that whites generally called the events that transpired in L.A. that spring a "riot" (on a nationally televised address on May 1, President George Bush termed it "the brutality of mob, pure and simple"), and that many black Americans saw them as an "uprising" and a "rebellion," suggests just how wide this gap really is.[25]

Elvis's generally reviled status in much of contemporary black culture hinges on this racial chasm. The image of an all-white Elvis that has been produced by many fans has also become "*the* grand metaphor for the racial (and racist) politics of US popular music" for many black Americans. Two interrelated arguments, one economic and the other aesthetic, specifically target Elvis's appropriation, and hence mainstream white America's appropriation, of black culture. The "Elvis bilked black America" argument centers on his financial success and his popular culture stardom—and the lack thereof for the black musicians he "ripped off." Alice Walker's short story "Nineteen Fifty-Five" (1981), for example, tells the tale of blues singer Gracie Mae Still, who sells one of her songs to a pop-star wannabe named Traynor, a "womanish looking" boy "with real dark white skin and a red pouting mouth." Her song makes him a star ("the Emperor of Rock and Roll"), and while she doesn't exactly languish in poverty, it's Traynor who becomes rich and famous. Substitute Gracie Mae Still for Willie Mae Thornton and Traynor for Elvis, and Walker's story loosely stands as a parable about how a black woman's recording of "Hound Dog" never made it very far, while Elvis's rendition became a mainstream hit in 1956 (never mind that "Hound Dog" was originally written by two white guys).[26]

Walker's quick read attributes Elvis's mid-1950s success to the economic inequities of a racially segregated music industry. And she's right: if Elvis had been black, he probably wouldn't have become a mainstream music success. The fact that he sounded "black" kept him off certain radio playlists at the start of his career; the fact that he looked "white" certainly helped make him mainstream material. Of course, Elvis's own talents and ambitions, his personal popular music commitment to racial and cultural integration, and his popularity among white *and* black teens also contributed to his rock-and-roll fame. But this history tends to be devalued in favor of an economic one, which recognizes that in the postwar American music business, fame followed race: greater economic rewards went to white pop performers, not to the black artists whose work they often covered and copied. It still does: ask anyone to name the most important figures in an emergent mid-1950s rock and roll and see how many include Chuck Berry, James Brown, Ray Charles, Sam Cooke, Bo Diddley, Fats Domino, Little Richard, Ike Turner, and Jackie Wilson in the mix.

Justifiable bitterness about the profits that white culture made off the backs of black labor, and the persistent invisibility of black artists in popular understandings of rock and roll, segue into widespread disgust with what happened to the black music that white musicians appropriated. Walker hints at this when she reveals that Traynor/Elvis never quite understands what the blues song he bought, and hence the black culture he borrowed it from, is all about. "I done sung that song seem like a million times," Traynor tells Gracie May Still. "I've sung it and sung it, and I'm making forty thousand dollars a day offa it, and you know what, I don't have a faintest notion what that song means." Critic Nelson George is more directly disgruntled with how Elvis not only stole the blues, he turned them bland. "Elvis was just a package, a performer with limited musical ambition and no real dedication to the black style that made him seem so dangerous," George writes in *The Death of Rhythm and Blues* (1988), charging Elvis, and white crossover aesthetics in general, with the betrayal and dilution of black cultural control.[27]

Having recently heard an unbelievably schlocky rendition of Marvin Gaye's "What's Goin' On" sung by a bevy of topless showgirls in a glitzy Las Vegas revue (a newly sanitized, family-values Folies Bergères doing popular American music—Gershwin to Village People, "Old Man River" to "YMCA"—in inimitable, jaw-crashing fashion), I'm more than a little sympathetic with George's argument. The first rock records churned out by the major national labels, once they awakened to the mainstream appeal—and hence profitability—of black culture, were white versions of songs written and performed by black artists: Pat Boone singing Little Richard's "Tutti Frutti," Elvis singing Big Joe Turner's "Shake, Rattle, and Roll." And there's no doubt that most of these covers smoothed over and flattened the edge and zeal, the liberatory pleasure, of the originals. Even Elvis remarked, "My music wasn't the same after Sun."[28] But saying that Elvis profited from black music and black musicians didn't is one thing; saying that the blues are black and rock and roll is white is quite another. The messy history of crossover—from Elvis to Living Colour, an all-black band that fused hard rock, jazz, dance, funk, rap, and soul during its ten-year career (they broke up in 1995)—disrupts superficial assumptions of racial ownership and racial stereotyping in music as much as anywhere else in American popular culture. As Living Colour vocalist Corey Glover remarked, "We're black. We play rock and roll. Now maybe everybody will give that a rest."[29]

Probably not: the appropriation of black music and its subsequent watering down for mass consumption is too common in the histories of jazz, rock, and hip hop for Elvis's image as a rip-off artist to ease anytime soon in black culture; his stature as a "Klansman in blue suede shoes" persists. As *Ebony*, the slick monthly aimed at middle-class African-Americans, noted in an article titled "How Blacks Invented Rock and Roll:" "It continues to be the biggest lie in the music industry—that Whites created rock 'n' roll. . . . Look no further than Presley's 'Hound Dog' to see how White artists exploited the creations of Black musicians.·. . . Graceland was built off the backs of Black artists." Or as the rap group Public Enemy put it in "Fight the Power," on their best-selling *Fear of a Black Planet* (1989):

Elvis was a hero to most
But he never meant shit to me you see
Straight up racist
That sucker was
Simple and plain
Motherfuck him *and* John Wayne.[30]

In a racially divided America, Elvis's image (along with John Wayne's) clearly signifies "whiteness," but whether that means hard-working patriot or racist profiteer depends on who's looking.

Who's looking at Elvis also has a lot to do with who views him as the King of Rock and Roll. If Elvis's regal status is taken for granted by many fans, it is scorned by many others as the biggest racist lie of all. As Living Colour guitarist Vernon Reid protested in 1990, "It's not enough for the powers that be to love Elvis, for him to be *their* king of rock and roll. [But] Elvis has to be the king of rock and roll for everybody. And that is something I cannot swallow." That isn't to say that Reid, and other black musicians, want to deny Elvis's cultural importance, but that crowning him king renders everyone else in the rock-and-roll pantheon, especially black musicians, as lesser figures. As Gil Rodman argues, "Elvis's coronation implicitly helps to reinforce the resegregation of the musical world into neat and (supposedly) mutually exclusive racial categories" where whites dominate. Or as funk bassist Me'Shell NdegéOcello shouted in 1994: "If Elvis is King, then who the fuck is James Brown—God?"[31]

All of which makes it difficult for many African-Americans to openly admit that they like Elvis, or that they once were or still are Elvis fans. Or to descend upon Memphis with other fans during Elvis Week. Although Graceland is situated in the midst of a predominantly black neighborhood (ironically called Whitehaven), few blacks take the house tour or shop in the gift stores, or belong to many of the Elvis fan clubs. Going to Graceland, or to Memphis, didn't even rate on a list of vacation hot spots that *Ebony* assembled in 1997 for its readers, beaten out by Walt Disney World, Las Vegas, New Orleans, and the Zora Neale Hurston Festival in Eatonville, Florida.[32] Neither Memphis, despite its "birth of the blues" reputation, nor Graceland, despite being the caretaker for the King of Rock and Roll, projects an image of a "color comfortable" public space the kind of space carefully constructed in Disney's tourist zones. That isn't to say that many black workers don't staff the shops and the restaurants that surround Graceland, or supervise the house tours, especially in the summer when many fans visit Elvis's mansion and burial spot. But most believe that Graceland, and Elvis Culture in general, is a "white thing." Some white fans shrug this off as "a political stand in the black community which precludes admitting to admiration for a white man who became popular performing 'black' music."[33] Others more astutely recognize that the black absence in Elvis Culture is due more to the concerted manner in which the culture itself has been organized as a distinctive, deified even, site of whiteness.

There are black Elvis fans, of course. Georgia King, longtime president of the Elvis Presley International Fan Club Worldwide, a Memphis outfit aimed at Elvis "outreach" around the globe, avows that Elvis "is the instrument" of God and adds: "When Jesus was here, he had disciples. Different name, same meaning." And in 1984, African-American fans Nancy Rooks, Elvis's maid for some seventeen years, and Mae Gutter, an Oklahoma City secretary, described themselves as "true-blue Elvis Fans" in their fifty-one-page tract *The Maid, the Man, and the Fans*. Writing that they "have always loved and admired this great man," both repeatedly asserted that Elvis "was not prejudiced; he was all kind heart."[34]

Their conviction that Elvis "loved each and every one of us" is shared by some white fans who also idealize Elvis Culture as a grand mecca of multiculturalism. New Jersey fan John Sheyka, who saw Elvis at Madison Square Garden in 1972, reminisces that the crowd at that concert consisted "of all color, nationalities, sexes, and age groups." Elvis, says Sheyka, "had the ability to appeal to ALL GROUPS. He was the true AMBASSADOR of the world on goodwill." Another fan makes similar comments: "Elvis crashed through barriers, bringing the people of the world together via his gifts. That's one hell of a man. World leaders with all their big words and big treaties CANNOT do what this good ol' boy can do, even in death!" And Sue Wiegert, longtime president of the Blue Hawaiians for Elvis Fan Club, writes that "the love Elvis shared with all of us came straight from his heart without manipulation or prejudice or guile," and adds: "Maybe *we* can be the generation that actually loves as Elvis loved, and reaches out to our brothers and sisters as if they really *are* family."

Maybe, but admiring Elvis's goodwill and brotherly love doesn't automatically translate into living it in Elvis Culture; the color-blind milieu that fans like Sheyka fondly remember from Elvis's 1970s concerts seems to have largely evaporated in today's America. Most fans seem to practice a kind of vicarious brotherhood, coming together in the spirit of fellowship at fan club get-togethers and during Elvis Week. Some like to quote lines from Paul Simon's song "Graceland" (1986), with its "poorboys and pilgrims with families" who've got "reason to believe" they'll all "be received in Graceland." But few seem to closely consider why blacks might feel unwelcome in a racialized fan culture whose favored images include Elvis the southern separatist, Elvis the working-class hero, Elvis the all-American soldier, Elvis the country rocker, and Elvis the Las Vegas showman—all images that reinforce the claims of whiteness that many fans extend to Elvis.

Brouhaha over Elvis's image on a 29-cent postage stamp further reveals the racial chasm in Elvis Culture. Shortly after Elvis's death, the United States Postal Service was besieged by fan demands that Elvis join the flag and the eagle as lickable icons. Pat Geiger of Vermont headed their lobbying efforts, writing daily letters to Postmaster General Anthony Frank and organizing petitions from fan clubs. In 1992, well after Elvis had met the Postal Service's "ten-years dead" rule, Frank orchestrated the first-ever nationwide vote for an American stamp, and the Postal Service printed 5 million ballots posing a

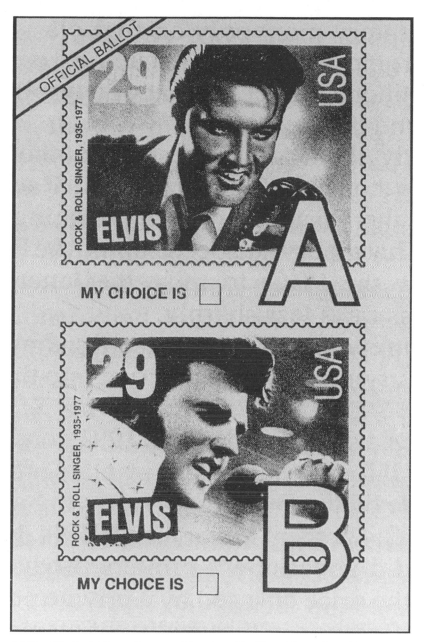

"Official Ballot," Elvis poll postcard distributed by United States Postal Service in 1992, featuring choices for the Elvis stamp competition.

choice between the younger Elvis (painted by Mark Stutzman) and the older one (painted by John Berkey). Certain politicians decried the stamp campaign: "What are we saying to our young people?" growled Representative Marge Roukema, a New Jersey Republican. "We're trying to teach them to say no to drugs, then look who we're lionizing on a stamp." And certain philatelists sneered, "Elvis is to stamps what Barbara Cartland is to serious literature."[35] Fans, however, concentrated on hotly debating which Elvis image was more appropriate—the 1950s teen rebel crooning "Teddy Bear" or the 1970s "Aloha from Hawaii" showman decked out in a high-collared and bejeweled white jumpsuit. And while thrilled by Elvis's impending honorific status, they worried about democracy in action. As the president of the Elvis Love Forever Fan Club sniffed, "A lot of non-fans and people who don't know very much about Elvis will vote [and] I'm not sure you will get the nicest picture."

Dismayed when the public, by a 3 to 1 margin (over 1 million votes were cast), picked the 1950s Elvis over the Las Vegas image most fans prefer, fans were even more upset by his inclusion in the "Legends of American Music" series, along with Ritchie Valens, Dinah Washington, Buddy Holly, Hank Williams, Patsy Cline, Otis Redding, and Clyde McPhatter. "I don't like the idea of Elvis being part of a group because he is too unique," complained Geiger. If fans were distressed because the Postal Service seemingly sought to contextualize Elvis within the country, R&B, and pop musical mix from which he actually emerged—thus making him one of many popular culture legends, instead of *the* legend—others wondered about the prevailing whiteness of the entire stamp campaign. "What about T-Bone Walker . . . or Joe Turner, whose 'Shake, Rattle, and Roll,' covered by Bill Haley and many, many others is considered by some critics the first rock-and-roll record? Or Roy Brown, whose 'Good Rockin' Tonight' was covered by Elvis?" asked one reporter, questioning why "all the black rock-and-rollers who are part of this tradition of American music" were mostly overlooked when the federal government went looking for "official" images.[36]

Elvis Culture's organization of a dominant and "unique" whiteness was most blatantly revealed in the summer of 1994, when the union of

Lisa Marie Presley and Michael Jackson brought to the surface the virulent racism of many Elvis fans. Some implied they were simply disgusted with how "that fake marriage" was "just a stunt to try and rebuild a faltering Michael Jackson image." As a fifty-six-year-old female fan from Michigan stated, "This business with Michael Jackson was a joke dreamed up by their agents." And a seventy-eight-year-old fan from Florida remarked, "I think it was a business arrangement made so that Michael would appear to be a normal, respectable person and enhance his image. I remember the interview between them and Barbara Walters [actually Diane Sawyer] which seemed to confirm my observation." Many fans were certain that Elvis himself would have "hated" the union: as a seventeen-year-old male fan from Colorado commented, "Elvis would have had a canary about Lisa's marriage and put a halt to it." Or as another fan, a woman from Omaha, put it, "I think for both Lisa and Michael it was an ego trip. They used each other. And I think Elvis would be, as they say, turning over in his grave."

Other fans were more up-front about what, exactly, might be making Elvis "turn" in his grave. "I feel Lisa Marie disgraced her heritage and that Elvis would have been deeply disappointed at the lack of loyalty," a "forty-something, divorced, white, female, single parent" fan from Tennessee asserted. "I felt his daughter did a terrible, selfish injustice to her father's memory by marrying Michael Jackson," said a forty-seven-year-old female fan from Colorado. A man from Tennessee (a white fifty-one-year-old "ex-Elvis fan" who asserts that the "roots of rock 'n' roll" come from "the 'Natives' of the world who used this type of music to call up demons in their Voodoo Worship. Which is Devil Worship. So rock 'n' roll is Devil Worship. God used Elvis Presley and his rock 'n' roll to ruin America and turn it from God"), decisively stated: "As for Lisa Marie, it was a sin for her to marry a Black. God tells us nationalities are not to mix. It is a sin." His comments were echoed by a longtime female fan from South Carolina (now fifty-four, she started an Elvis fan club in 1956), who stressed that Elvis "would NOT have given his Blessings" to the marriage, and "would have more than likely RAISED HELL with her and tried to lead her elsewhere. Southern roots go DEEP and 99% of us Black and

White folks DO NOT believe in mixed marriages—God made m. & f. of ALL colors and 'birds of a feather flock together' not crows & doves, ravens & cardinals, orioles & sparrows."

One of the more poisonous sites of Elvis Culture racism was the Elvis Presley Burning Love Fan Club, based in Streamwood, Illinois (a Chicago suburb), and founded by Bill DeNight in 1983. Elvis's "love and his caring for others are the reasons I love Elvis and why I started the club," DeNight explained in the early 1990s, yet many of the ways he imaged Elvis rebuked and betrayed the integrated consciousness that Elvis originally embodied. DeNight presided over a very large and very visible fan club, holding monthly meetings, sending members (around 1,200 by 1995) Elvis photos and information about Elvis collectibles, sponsoring fan festivals during Elvis Week, raising funds through raffles and auctions. An exceptionally active and well-organized fan club president, DeNight was also extremely generous, frequently sharing personal photographs that he had taken at Elvis concerts with club members, as well as donating his own Elvis stuff to charity. The club and DeNight's personal charity efforts (Burning Love contributed more than $130,000 to various Memphis hospitals) were recognized for their "Outstanding Contributions in Elvis's Name" by *Elvis International Forum Magazine* in 1993. Like most fan club presidents, DeNight also produced a quarterly newsletter, a twenty-plus-page tract packed with Elvis stories excerpted from the press as well as features like "What Elvis Means to Me." In 1992, the newsletter even included a lengthy article on Sun Records' support of black music and musicians, with comments on how Sam Phillips's father "didn't raise him to be racist."

But starting in 1993, more and more of Burning Love's newsletter was given over to DeNight's fury with how Graceland's managers were turning Elvis's home into "Greedland." Anger about the high cost of Elvis stuff in the Graceland gift shops and about the estate's attempts to license the Elvis fan clubs prompted most of DeNight's attacks, but they were furthered by his contempt for Lisa Marie and Priscilla Presley, neither of whom was, in his view, "taking care" of Elvis or Graceland with the same sort of love and attention of the "true fans." In the summer of 1994, when Michael Jackson entered the picture, DeNight's rage turned racist. After going to that year's Elvis Week festivities, he wrote: "Young black Michael Jackson fans were EVERY-WHERE. They were yelling dirty words at the ELVIS fans and holding out the 1 white glove, from their car windows. They even were up at ELVIS's grave. They were there causing trouble, with the WONDERFUL GRACELAND SECURITY letting them do as they darn well please. Must be orders from Lisa." Fears for Elvis Culture's future, now seemingly contaminated by nonwhite outsiders, prompted DeNight to declare that Graceland had "become a very bad place to visit" and to recite a litany of its dangers: "During the 10 days of Tribute Week, a young girl got shot, 2 blocks from Graceland, there was an armed robbery at the Wilson World Motel, several Elvis fans were mugged and robbed, and there was an attempted child snatching, right in the Graceland shopping plaza."

Fan club members responded to this race baiting with "hundreds of letters," all of them, said DeNight, "stating the same view that I had had during Tribute Week." In the Fall 1994 issue of the Burning Love newsletter, for example, one fan wrote that the scene was "much, much worse" than DeNight described: "Besides the HARD CRIME being everywhere, the JERKY JACKSON NIGGER FANS got away with anything . . . throwing things at each other in the driveway, and running in and out on the grass." Another fan relayed "the anger that is built up inside of me" and wrote the following:

> I know the crime in Memphis is rising, in a survey it was listed in the Top 10 of the worst cities of crime. Those Damn blacks taking over Graceland, the holdup at Wilson World, that TRAMP Lisa marrying that FAGGOT, CHILD MOLESTER Michael. How she can have her children around that black piece of s— is beyond me. I am so sick over this I told my wife that maybe we should not go to Memphis anymore, if I want to get shot or mugged, we can take a ride on the subway to Harlem.

Other outbursts included "Elvis would be completely ashamed of Lisa Marie. She has turned out to be AN EVEN BIGGER TRAMP than her mother, Priscilla," and

> Our God does not make mistakes but he had to be mighty tired the day he created these two jerks! They are both a disgrace to the

human race. They are both totally confused: Lisa doesn't know if her dad is dead or alive and M.J. doesn't know if he's black or white. So how can they even know if they are in love? One thing for sure though, M.J. knows how to make love to little white boys.

One fan wrote, "Go kiss a nigger, Lisa!"

Among many fans in Elvis Culture, understandings of Royal Presley Family dynamics tend to break down into the following assumptions: Elvis the patriarch was betrayed by Priscilla, the unfaithful, greedy bitch. Only Lisa Marie, the King's daughter, was viewed with any sort of regard, and fans delighted in stories of her princess childhood (her father buying her extravagant gifts like mink coats and ponies, or spending $30,000 to charter a jet from Memphis to Utah so that she could see snow), her marriage to Keough, an aspiring country musician, and her continuation of the Presley bloodline with the birth of "Elvis's grandbabies."[37] But when Lisa Marie married Michael Jackson, her royal princess status in Elvis Culture immediately dissipated: she had sullied the clear path of royal inheritance and succession by marrying a rival king—the King of Pop—and had endangered Elvis Culture's "whites-only" hierarchy by marrying a black man. Her brief partnership with Jackson may have worked to moderate his deviant image in media culture, but it only reinforced fan phobias in Elvis Culture that Elvis and Graceland were under siege by false claimants to the throne.

The Lisa Marie–Michael union became a convenient dumping ground for widespread fan fears for Elvis's future, and their own. The racial dimensions of that paranoia were actually well in place before Michael Jackson's appearance in Elvis Culture, however. In the late 1980s, for example, Elvis Inc. began offering side trips for Elvis Week attendees to various Memphis music haunts such as Beale Street and Sun Records. "Fans told us they wanted to see Beale Street," remarked Stacey Sheppard, Elvis Inc.'s marketing coordinator, "but people are afraid to go downtown and tour Beale Street themselves. They think they'll get mugged."[38] Fearful of venturing out into any of Memphis's black and hence "bad" neighborhoods, most American fans tend to stick close to Graceland. (European fans tend to be far more adventurous.) In 1997, one fan posted this inquiry on the alt.elvis.king newsgroup: "I heard that in the town of Memphis around Graceland it is really run down, like my friend described it 'really awful kinda like the ghetto.' Is this true?" Another fan responded: "Your friend was right. I am pretty good friends with one of the security guards at Graceland and he always told us not to stray too far from Graceland in either direction at night. And from the looks of the areas, I just take his word for it."

Most Elvis Week attendees stay cloistered within a three-block area of Elvis's mansion—touring the house, making the pilgrimage to Elvis's grave site, hitting the souvenir stands, eating at fast-food restaurants, staying at nearby motels. Elvis Inc. doesn't do much to discourage this, either—a captive audience, after all, is a paying audience. Nor has Graceland, Memphis's top-grossing tourist spot, shown much interest in improving community relations with its predominantly black Whitehaven neighbors: deserted car lots, boarded-up buildings, and pawn shops border Graceland on both sides of Elvis Presley Boulevard. In the past few years, a few trees, historical markers, and better sidewalks have been added to the landscape, but Graceland mostly remains an island of whiteness, a white mansion and a dead white rock star, attended by legions of white fans.

In September 1994, the tabloid *Globe* played to this racial divide in a feature headlined "Oprah's Amazing Link to Elvis." Tracing "a direct bloodline" between Elvis's nineteenth-century ancestors and the slaves they owned and fathered, including the forebears of talk-show host Oprah Winfrey, "accredited genealogist Ron Stucker" declared: "Oprah and Elvis are distant cousins!"[39] Given its timing, *Globe*'s piece may have been an attempt to ease the antimiscegenation fallout of the marriage of Lisa Marie and Michael. The one-shot effort didn't appear to work, however; the "amazing link" was never covered again (and none of the other tabloids picked up on the story), and Elvis fans almost uniformly dismissed the story as an "out-and-out lie." Despite its constancy in American history, race mixing remains taboo, and the *Globe* soon returned to what it and the rest of the popular press do most in their constant Elvis coverage: bouncing back and forth between stories of his drugged-out decadence and tales of his devotion to family, friends, and fans.

They treat Michael Jackson in the same way: veering from exposés

September 20, 1994 $1.25/$1.29 Canada

TOP HISTORIAN UNCOVERS PAST EVEN OPRAH DIDN'T KNOW

OPRAH'S AMAZING LINK TO ELVIS

Her family slaved for his — they may even be related!

In his own chilling words — not for the squeamish!

INSIDE THE SICK MIND OF THE GAINESVILLE KILLER

"*Oprah's Amazing Link to Elvis,*" *cover of* Globe, *September 20, 1994. (Reprinted with permission of Globe Communications Corporation)*

of his plastic surgery ("first photos ever of Michael's face falling apart") and his "hush money" payouts to those accusing him of child molestation ($40 million, according to the *National Enquirer*), to celebratory photos in spring 1997 of a beaming Michael, second wife, Debbie Rowe, and newborn son, Prince Michael Jackson Junior. The fact is, Michael Jackson *is* Elvis's heir—the King of Pop to the King of Rock. He's more like Elvis than many Elvis fans want to admit: the same sense of stylistic difference, the same androgynous sexuality, the same fantasy-life existence, and, despite the scandals, the same sort of mega-success and mass appeal. And his fans image him in much the same way that Elvis's fans image Elvis: as the Michael Jackson Internet Fan Club proclaims, "Michael Jackson is a great artist and humanitarian" who "exudes hope, acceptance, joy, and love. He has touched and improved the quality of life for so many fans."[40]

Yet for all his similarity to the King of Rock, the King of Pop is generally despised in Elvis Culture. At first take, that's not surprising;

Michael Jackson is a regal rival, a threat to the rock/pop throne that Elvis fans claim for Elvis. To be sure, some fans are offended by the crotch-grabbing antics of "His Royal Weirdness," and plenty more are disturbed by intimations that "The Gloved One" prefers the company of young male children to most adults. But their loathing of Jackson more clearly stems from the dominant racial hierarchy that lies at the core of contemporary Elvis Culture: many Elvis fans are outraged by Michael Jackson's refusal to stay within the parameters of "blackness."

Ironically, of course, it was Elvis's own racial slippage that largely accounted for his postwar success. But he was a white man appropriating black culture; he started from the supposedly dominant racial position of whiteness. In a contemporary America where race difference is understood in terms of race hierarchy, where whiteness dominates and blackness is seen as its inferior opposite, Michael Jackson's efforts to dismantle the boundaries of race—whether physically by narrowing his nose and whitening his skin, musically by creating a kind of pop music that knows no racial parameters, or socioculturally by amassing a truly multiracial and increasingly international audience of fans—are far more revolutionary. As the King of Pop, he threatens not only Elvis's regal status, but his white power base. If that terrifies many of Elvis's white fans, many black Americans see Michael's "moves" as a pleasurable kind of comeuppance. As black comic Paul Mooney exclaimed on his album *Master Piece* (1995): "Go Michael, Go! Yes, Yes, Yes, Elvis Presley's daughter. Wonderful! Elvis Presley stole so much from niggers, it's about time that he gave us something back. It's about time."[41]

Deeply disturbed by Michael Jackson's attempts to erode the supposedly natural categories of a superior whiteness and an inferior blackness, or simply by his refusal to "be black" (a refusal that obsesses many more Americans, white and black, than just those who live in Elvis Culture), many Elvis fans scapegoat Jackson as the scary, savage, dark-skinned other. While hardly an in-your-face rap artist like the late Tupac Shakur, many fans see Jackson as a stereotypical "uppity nigger" threatening the prevailing dominance of their "white" culture and its dominant icon, Elvis Presley. It's the same sort of racial anxiety that underlies contemporary debates about blacks in sports and blacks in business, where casually tossed phrases like "physical superiority" and "taking over" really stand in for the less explicitly voiced fears that many whites have about nonwhite competition and domination. This is all relatively recent in Elvis Culture, too: while many white fans eagerly incorporated Elvis's manipulation of black sounds and styles into their own reconstruction of white identity in the 1950s, and many championed the color-blind "family of man" zeitgeist that Elvis embodied in the 1970s, many of their counterparts today have re-formed his image, and hence his historical meaning and memory, into one of a reified whiteness.

Interestingly, race-based biases in Elvis Culture are pretty much configured only along black and white lines; many fans may vehemently deny that Elvis and Oprah share the same bloodline, but they generally accept and even boast about his "Indian roots" (Elvis's maternal great-great-grandmother was Cherokee). They're ambivalent or just plain confused by Elvis's popularity among Asians and Latinos, tending to see the busloads of Japanese and Brazilian fans who flock to Memphis during Elvis Week as "proof" of Elvis's global popularity. They even tend to tolerate certain nonwhite Elvis impersonators who occupy Elvis Culture, like Mori Yasumasa, Japan's leading Elvii and the 1992 winner of the "Images of Elvis" contest in Memphis. But if all of this is bearable, it's because Elvis as the object of foreign fan consumption, and even Elvis as an American Indian, doesn't seem to radically challenge his fans' own understandings of what they assume is his universally acclaimed all-white status.

Many fans are less pleased, for example, with El Vez, largely because they think his hysterically campy act, replete with Chicano Power parodies of Elvis songs like "You Ain't Nothin' but a Chihuahua," "En El Barrio," and "Viva La Raza," and backed by the bouffant-coiffed, maracas-shaking, high-heel-wearing El Vettes (Priscillita, Lisa María, Que Linda Thompson, and Gladysita) *and* the salsa rhythms of the Memphis Mariachi Band, borders on blasphemy, even regicide. El Vez (a former Los Angeles art gallery owner who also fronts a punk band called the Zeroes) says he's simply trying to return Elvis to his origins, "showing some of the possibilities for mixing, matching, and translating different cultures." "You don't have to be white to do what Elvis did. I do it because Elvis was a revolutionary in 1956, a bad

Elvis impersonator El Vez, 1991. (Photograph © Paul Beauchemin)

boy, tearing things up," he remarks. "El Vez is the idea of the melting pot, and everyone's welcome. It's Elvis as the American Dream."[42]

African-American Elvis impersonators like Robert Washington and Clearance Giddens share the same dream. The fact that both claim Elvis as their guy, too, does a lot to subvert the whites-only ethos that many fans have fabricated in Elvis Culture. Washington, a factory worker from South Portland, Maine, has placed first in numerous "Elvis Competitions" all over the country and has his own gathering of devotees (Tender Memories of "The King" Fan Club), who follow him from contest to contest. Giddens, formerly a house painter from Virginia, has met with similar success and now makes a living by playing the impersonator circuit up and down the east coast, backed by the White Trash Band and his own loyal following of fans, the Black Heads. "Elvis to me," says Giddens, "is exciting, dazzling, motivating, energy and control." He adds, "Elvis was a Martin Luther King, Jr., in the music field. He did not see music as divided by color."[43]

With utmost sincerity, El Vez and Giddens highlight the historical Elvis that more than a few contemporary fans seem to want to ignore and deny, the egalitarian Elvis who stormed postwar popular culture with an image that evoked a multiracial America, an integrated America. Indeed, Elvis impersonation in general provides a tangle of contradictions within Elvis Culture. Eric Lott, who rather overreaches by arguing that the "great majority" of Elvis impersonators are "working-class white men," nevertheless points out the "double mimicry" of Elvis impersonation: when impersonators imitate Elvis, they imitate the many black artists that Elvis himself imitated.[44] While convoluted, this pattern of impersonation seriously scandalizes the racial hierarchy that many fans have constructed in Elvis Culture: even dressed in the ivory-white jumpsuit that has become an emblem of whiteness for many of these fans, the Elvis impersonator cannot escape Elvis's "blackness," his own self-conscious transgressions of race. Perhaps this is why some fans thoroughly detest Elvis impersonation: it comes too close to the racially complex image of Elvis they've come close to burying.

In 1956, while Elvis was topping the charts and gaining national attention on prime-time TV, the Reverend Martin Luther King, Jr.,

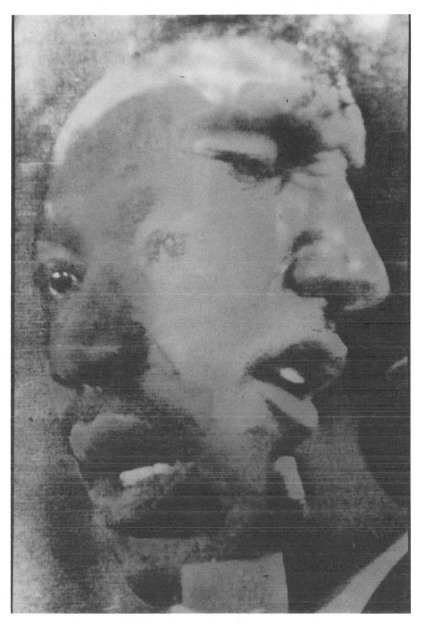

Fred Stein, The Kings (1997). Handcolored photograph, 18 × 13 inches. (Collection of the artist)

was leading the Montgomery, Alabama, bus boycott and drawing national attention to civil rights. Forty years later, the fans who mourn for Elvis forget that another King died in Memphis, murdered at the site of what is now the National Civil Rights Museum. A recent photo-collage by Milwaukee artist Fred Stein awkwardly blends the faces of America's two Kings into an "I Have A Dream" sort of scenario—Elvis with his eyes closed, painfully emoting an interior integration of body and soul; King confidently looking outward, a national leader captivating the hundreds of thousands of Americans gathered at the 1963 March on Washington with a spellbinding speech and a spirit of optimism about the country's future, and its commitment to racial justice and human rights. "I got the idea that Martin Luther King and Elvis had the same purpose, the same dream," says Stein, a longtime Elvis fan. "They had different styles and perspectives but they shared the same image of a better America." They did, but they don't anymore, Stein seems to suggest: in his print, as in the larger culture, Elvis's face overshadows King's, taking up most of the visual frame.

In a late-twentieth-century America dominated by a loss of faith in liberal humanism and racial equality, by an emphasis on personal wealth and individual entitlement, by a yawning gap between haves and have-nots, and by even bigger yawns of "Who cares?" from many quarters, Martin Luther King, Jr., is no longer an icon: his vision of an integrated American dream no longer commands credibility. Integration itself, for that matter, seems to have largely evaporated in the popular and political imagination; the word "integration" seems to appear only infrequently in either academic or mass-media discourse. The Elvis who shared King's dream of American racial harmony is no icon, either. Today's Elvis, for many of today's fans, personifies the triumph of whiteness, of race-based privilege and hierarchy. Locked into an ideology of oppressive racial essentialism, many of the fans who occupy today's Elvis Culture favor an image of Elvis that symbolizes a divided and oppositional race consciousness. In the segregated and stifling world that their Elvis Culture has become, there's no room for the liberatory barrier-breaking ethos of the original, interracial Elvis.

In 1995, the Burning Love Fan Club was "disenrolled" by Elvis Inc., and removed from the rosters of other "official" clubs associated with Graceland and Elvis's estate. At the same time, the club disbanded. But whether Elvis Inc. simply wanted to outlaw attacks on the Royal Presley Family—and gain further control over what it deems to be Elvis's "appropriate" image—or truly condemn Elvis Culture racism, is open to question.

Who Owns elvis?

Velvet Elvises have long been a staple in Elvis Culture. Tens of thousands of the fuzzy black, handpainted or airbrushed pictures of a sad and swarthy Elvis have been churned out since the 1950s, mass-produced in small factories in Tijuana and Ciudad Juarez along with similarly painted pictures of poker-playing dogs and full-bodied Vargas babes. Shipped by the truckload to furniture warehouses and souvenir stores all over America, velvet Elvises are cheap—around $14.95 a canvas. They're even cheaper at "starving artists sales," or at those makeshift stands hastily assembled around Ford pickups and Econoline vans parked at abandoned gas stations: two black velvet paintings for $25, three for $35, whatever you can bargain, whatever you can pay.

"It's the art we love to hate," the "blue-light specials" of the art world, says Jennifer Heath, author of a book on black velvet paintings that looks at the attraction of a so-called "bad taste" aesthetic in these postmodern times. "Elvis was probably the first celebrity to be featured on velvet," she adds, and he remains the premiere velvet icon.[1] Before him, velvet artists tended to focus on Spanish themes like matadors and flamenco dancers. The popularity of the velvet Elvises ushered in all sorts of other celebrity portraits—John Wayne, Bob Marley, John Lennon—but Elvis still leads the pack. Today, in fact, "black velvet" and "Elvis" are practically synonymous, so much so that phrases like "velvet Elvis" and the paintings themselves embody not only the image of Elvis but the aura of an entire contemporary popular culture sensibility, of visceral tackiness, of the pleasurable profane.

That's what Canadian pop singer Alannah Myles discovered when her bluesy song "Black Velvet," sort of a contemporary female version of the Rolling Stones' "Brown Sugar," met with broad popular acclaim in the early 1990s. The tune, with the catchy riff, "Black velvet with that slow southern style / A new religion that'll bring ya to your knees," never directly names Elvis but hints around at what his image, or the memory of his image, has come to mean. "Black Velvet" is about "America's love for a legend," says Myles, "for a new religion that brings you to your knees—rock 'n' roll—and Elvis is the guy that exemplifies that in American history."[2]

A lonely legend: a teardrop of sweat streaking his cheek, Elvis always looks lonely in these black velvet paintings, like the sad-faced pictures of Emmett Kelly clowns or the big-eyed kids and puppies that

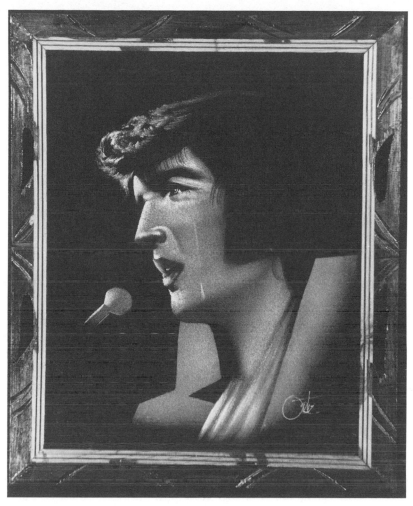

Black velvet painting of Elvis, 1996. (Collection of the author)

Margaret and Walter Keene painted. Leaning into the floating microphone with his brow knotted and his forlorn eyes looking upward, or
out toward the fans in the far, far rows of the Astrodome-scale sports
arenas he played in the 1970s, trapped between the interlocking
planes of his sideburns and his jumpsuit, Elvis seems to fade into the
void, a desolate figure on a dark stage. It's an image of Elvis that a lot of
fans cherish; the image of Elvis in pain, Elvis suffering, Elvis crying
out to be taken care of. They treasure these black velvet paintings—
and never more so since 1995, when they were outlawed by Elvis Presley Enterprises, Incorporated. As one company spokesman scorned,

"We feel Elvis on velvet just doesn't meet the criteria of the *quality* of the Elvis merchandise we want on the market."[3]

Elvis Inc.'s apparent concern about issues of taste stems from its inability to control the *quantity* of Elvis stuff pouring out of multiple markets along the Mexican–American border and elsewhere. And EPE, headquartered in Memphis (with additional offices in Los Angeles), does has fixed claims on Elvis's image: Colonel Parker was legally displaced from managing Elvis's estate in the early 1980s, when state and federal courts in Tennessee upheld EPE's ownership of Elvis's name, voice, likeness, and image. Elvis Inc. is now the sole proprietor of Elvis's "official" image and promotes him via its "official" Elvis merchandise, its "Official Elvis Home Page," and its tours of Graceland, all of which conspicuously avoid much attention to Elvis's fandom, his sexuality, his important relationships with black popular culture, or how and why he died.

Having "offical" claims to Elvis's image, the company has pursued a number of legal blockades aimed at containing and curtailing that image. Elvis Inc. was horrified, for example, over widespread media attention in the early 1990s to the sales of serial killer John Wayne Gacy's brightly colored prison paintings, including several acrylic canvases of Elvis now owned by some fans in Sydney. Artists have received letters from EPE demanding that they "immediately stop the promotion and sale" of paintings and prints featuring Elvis's image. Fan clubs have received "cease and desist" memos for selling unregistered Elvis arts and crafts at fan fests and charity auctions. The Velvet Elvis, a Houston bar, was sued for violating EPE's claims to exclusive ownership of Elvis's name. And for years, Elvis Inc. has tried to figure out how to license and control Elvis's impersonation, even demanding that the most successful Elvis Artists and big-scale acts like the Las Vegas revue "Legends in Concert" stop imitating Elvis without its permission. In late 1996, Elvis Inc. signed with Optical Security Group, Inc., to make holographic ID tags for all "official" Elvis merchandise.[4]

Conflicts over image ownership have recently exploded as control of imagery has more and more become tied to corporate power and profit. Under the Reagan, Bush, and Clinton administrations, neo-conservative legal appointees employed the rhetoric of economic

John Wayne Gacy, paintings of Elvis, dates unknown
(Private Collection, Sydney, Australia)

"protection" in order to strengthen corporate monopolization of intellectual property—ideas and, by extension, the various forms of material culture they become.[5] Driven in part by the emergence of new technologies and by perceptions of the need to "protect" burgeoning U.S. computer software and database exports from piracy in global markets, copyright laws have been redrafted to safeguard and essentially limit the ownership and use of intellectual property. Ideas, in other words, are regarded as "property" protected by copyright and trademark. Despite their base intangibility, ideas—and, hence, images—are increasingly understood as owned and fixed things, as exploitable and immutable goods.

However real the need to protect U.S. markets, these restrictive legal mandates have had an inarguably potent effect on fortifying corporate claims to ideas, and how they're expressed. Legal activist Peter Jaszi warns that protecting corporate markets threatens the marketplace of ideas, that as the public domain of knowledge—ideas and images—becomes the private property of a few, America's "informational commons" disappears from the public sphere.[6] Indeed, longstanding principles of "fair use" and "freedom of expression" recently seem to have been relegated to the dustbin, replaced by an intellectual property imperialism by which exclusive corporate ownership of American stuff—from CD-ROMs to Elvis merchandise—is championed as the weapon of economic protectionism.

The fight to license and make money from intellectual property, especially from a steadily multiplying culture of images, increasingly drives corporate investment and litigation—from Microsoft's $6 million purchase of the Bettmann Archive, a collection of some 16 million photographs, to the innumerable lawsuits aimed at "protecting" Disney's exclusive ownership of Mickey Mouse, Mattel's exclusive ownership of Barbie, and Elvis Inc.'s exclusive ownership of anything Elvis. These sorts of battles over image ownership parallel those over other forms of intellectual property, too—over who owns what in popular music, for example, when new technologies like digital storage and sound sampling throw into chaos traditional modernist (and capitalist) understandings of authorship and creativity. Such issues are at the heart of the future of image culture, and they're at the heart of Elvis Culture's future, too.

Elvis, of course, didn't "own" the songs he sang, all of which were written by other people. And he didn't "own" the various images, from rockabilly rebel to Las Vegas showman, that he lifted from bits and pieces of other images and shaped into his personae. He understood the fabricated nature of his identity, too, and shrugged it off in one widely quoted remark: "The image is one thing and the human being is another. . . . [I]t's very hard to live up to an image."[7] Yet despite his history of musical and visual hybridity, Elvis is today claimed by his estate as a legally held, legally enforceable, and essentially monolithic entity. The history of twentieth-century modern art has tended to focus on the "crisis" of representation, showing us again and again that images are, in fact, tenuous constructions whose meaning is inconsistent and undependable, ever open to changing modes of interpretation. But the contemporary crisis in visual culture is one of ownership—of claiming the inconstant image as a solid thing, as a commodity, as something to guard and possess.

We never look at images, of course, without thoughts of ownership. The very act of looking, writes James Elkins, "immediately activates desire, possession, violence, displeasure, pain, force, ambition, power, obligation, gratitude, longing."[8] Given that looking is active and subjective, a complex and constantly fluctuating dialogue that goes on between us and what we see in random yet deeply nuanced places and spaces, how can we isolate any image into any fixed reading? Given that images multiply in meaning as we look at them, how can they be claimed and possessed for any fixed purpose? Who, then, really "owns" Elvis: his estate, his fans, or anyone? Who owns popular culture? What happens when a popular American icon, itself a construction long dependent on intermittent and generally unharnessed levels of interpretation, becomes the exclusive property of a few?

If Elvis himself never had any real control over his image (although he did, of course, help to shape it), he never had any real problems with how he was imitated and appropriated, either. His own calculated creation of a multiformed image, of an identity derived from diverse sources, was central to the ways he thought about himself and acted around others. He was apparently amused, for example, by many of the impersonators who worked Elvis Culture early on, some of whom even opened for some of his 1950s shows. In 1976, he invited Douglas Roy, a Canadian singer who'd been doing an all-Elvis act since the mid-1960s, to join him on stage at the Sahara Tahoe Casino in Stateline, Nevada, and grinned and clapped along with the rest of the crowd as Roy belted out "Hound Dog."[9] And Elvis was always, of course, enthusiastic about his fans, ever willing to sign an autograph or kiss a pretty girl, clearly aware of how their attentions had helped make him a star and how much he depended on their continuing to look at him—and hence their abiding ownership of him—in order to stay a celebrity.

Yet if Elvis never insisted on his own originality or authorship and allowed his fans great freedoms in terms of accessibility and appropriation, his estate now claims sole copyright on his name, his body, and his representation. (EPE even tried to gain ownership of the term "The King," but that was legally rebuffed.) If Elvis saw himself in terms of the circuitous relationships of fandom, his estate isolates and valorizes him as a product requiring their legal protection.[10] Such eagerness to control the widespread application of Elvis's image speaks volumes about the abiding popular appeal, and profitability, of that image. But it also threatens the perpetuation and sustenance of an image made meaningful for the past forty years primarily through the desires, rituals, and behaviors of a popular audience, especially Elvis's fans.

This yoking of Elvis's image isn't anything new, of course: Colonel Parker and Henry G. Saperstein were as image-conscious about Elvis in the 1950s as EPE is today. But if the Colonel avidly pursued copyright infringement cases when manufacturers tried to sell unsanctioned Elvis stuff, Elvis Inc. has more ambitiously, and quite successfully, pursued the wholesale harnessing of Elvis Culture. With annual revenues currently exceeding a conservatively estimated $100 million, EPE is a major corporate player completely dependent on Elvis's image. Divided into three arms—Graceland, retail merchandising, and music publishing—Elvis Inc. employs an executive staff, marketing consultants, financial advisers, and teams of lawyers whose primary responsibility is to grow and protect its primary property: a dead rock star and popular icon named Elvis Presley. "The goal is to expand the profitability and the financial depth of the company," remarks CEO Jack Soden, formerly a money manager with a Kansas City investment firm. "We're working to bring Elvis into the twenty-first century," echoes Priscilla Beaulieu Presley, the president of EPE and the real wizard behind Elvis Inc.'s image-conscious industry.[11]

Lisa Marie Presley inherited her father's estate when he died in 1977, but being a nine-year-old minor, management passed to a trust managed by Elvis's father. When Vernon Presley died two years later, Priscilla Presley became co-executor of Lisa Marie's inheritance. Priscilla found Elvis's empire in shambles, with the costs of maintaining Graceland exceeding $500,000 annually, with millions owed to the IRS, and with very little income. (In 1973, for instance, Parker allowed RCA to purchase Elvis's entire master catalog, a deal that cut Elvis, and then his heirs, out of future royalties for any music he had recorded prior to that date.) In 1982, just as the estate was practically bankrupt, Priscilla turned to its only real asset: Elvis's image. Taking the long view of the gaining number of fans making the pilgrimage to Elvis's grave site (Vernon Presley had opened it free to the public shortly after his son was reinterred in the mansion's Meditation Gardens), who then bought tons of Elvis stuff at the privately owned mom-and-pop souvenir stands directly across the street from Graceland, and seeing that Elvis's records were still selling like hotcakes

(RCA sold more than 200 million of them in the four months following his death), the Presley estate began to seriously rethink Elvis's postmortem money-making potential.[12]

Their first move, in June 1982, was to open Graceland—for a $5 fee, of course. Beforehand, Priscilla Presley and Jack Soden spent a year studying other private home tours—including Mount Vernon, Monticello, Biltmore, and Hearst Castle—analyzing their crowd flow, tour guides, and gift shops. They also took a look at how Disney and the National Park Service were managing cultural tourism. William Randolph Hearst's San Simeon estate in California was adopted as Graceland's main crowd-control model, such that today groups of twenty are shuttled at staggered intervals from the Graceland Plaza ticket office to Graceland's front door, and then bused back to Graceland Plaza—and its attendant souvenir stores—at the end of their tour. Unlike Hearst Castle, which is miles from the highway, shuttle buses at Graceland aren't really necessary to travel the 200 yards or so from Graceland's ticket office to Elvis's front door, but they do keep visitors confined and controlled, and ultimately funneled back into the terrain of Elvis stuff. The same is true at Disney's theme parks, where most rides end with a smooth transition into a gift shop.

If Disney's model of "consumer tourism" was adopted at Graceland, so too were Disneyland's and Disney World's upbeat and unshakable employees.[13] They became the role models for Graceland's guides, trained to stay with a script that emphasized Elvis's rags-to-riches success story, and nothing more. (Guides have since been replaced by prerecorded tapes, audio headsets, and "self-paced" tours, but the script remains the same.) The tour itself was originally restricted to Graceland's main floor and its basement, its backyard, Trophy Room, racquetball court, and Meditation Gardens; recently, the house kitchen and a downstairs bedroom (where Elvis's grandmother slept) were unveiled. The dark and tempting secrets of the second floor—Elvis's Bedroom! Elvis's Bathroom!—were (and still are) strictly screened from public view.

The entire operation required an extensive security system and EPE replaced Elvis's uncle Vester, Graceland's longtime guard and constant Melody Gates personality, with a professional police force. Priscilla Presley decided that it also required a thorough makeover, and she quickly replaced the blood-red shag carpets, teardrop lighting, leopard-skin pillows, and fake-fur throw rugs ("a Mae West type of look," she sniffed) that Elvis and girlfriend Linda Thompson had handpicked for Graceland in the early 1970s, with the regal blue and white decor that pervades the house today. "We wanted an all-American look," remarks Jack Soden, "the high road. We didn't want to give people what they expected—music blaring, tour guides in poodle skirts. We wanted a dignified, super-conservative presentation." Priscilla also insisted that Graceland acquire an estate manager like Soden, who shared her take on "good" taste and, importantly, wasn't a fan. "I liked that," she remarked in 1993. "It indicated to me that all the B.S. would be out of the way. A lot of times, when you have major fans, they can't see the whole vision, or the goal. They'll say, 'We have to do this or that for Elvis.' They get in the *way*."[14]

Not surprisingly, a lot of Elvis fans were incensed and insulted by the changes Elvis Inc. put into play at Graceland. Some, like Paul and Elvis Aaron MacLeod, were used to dropping by Graceland at any old time, chatting up Vester Presley and taking their own "self-paced" tours of the house and the grounds. Others were angered by Priscilla's "high road" redecoration of Graceland, rightfully recognizing it as a collision of taste between Elvis and Priscilla, and between Priscilla and his fans. But many fans were especially outraged by how Priscilla (and Priscilla, disparaged as the unfaithful ex-wife of the King of Rock and Roll, always takes the fall in Elvis Culture) had reimagined Elvis's image and Elvis's estate on corporate terms, as a big business that didn't seem to need, or even particularly want, his fans. "Priscilla said that *SHE* made Graceland what it is today," fan club president Bill DeNight blasted in one Burning Love Fan Club newsletter. "WHAT ABOUT US, THE FANS? Graceland would *HAVE NEVER* been a success without us!"

If such fans are unnerved by a corporate Graceland's exclusion of them, they're even more disgruntled by the "official" image of Elvis promoted by EPE, which frames Elvis as an uncomplicated American success story. Refusing to license merchandise featuring an overweight Elvis, to sanction any product that calls attention to either his rebellious cross-race and cross-gender beginnings or his decline, or even to condone Elvis stuff—like velvet paintings—that it deems inappropriately lower-class or kitschy, Elvis Inc. tends to focus on a generic Elvis: a sanitized, drug-free, fat-free, all-white Elvis. The estate was "not happy," for example, with the "stoned Elvis calling President Jimmy Carter" stories that surfaced in the summer of 1997, and apparently refused to entertain requests for further details from Carter biographer Douglas Brinkley.[15] Ironically, while Elvis Inc.'s central interests clearly lie with the profits to be made from Elvis's image, the company insists on a limited understanding of that image, which also stands to limit its own commercial capitalization and, more important, Elvis's future popularity and profitability.

Tours at Graceland, and all of EPE's recorded and published information about Elvis, completely avoid any impertinent discussion of his sexual rendevous, his drug escapades, or his bloated demise inside a bathroom on Graceland's second floor, and reinforce the company's "official" image of Elvis. The prerecorded tape, for example, that visitors now listen to while walking through Graceland opens with strains of "Dixie" and with B-movie star (and former Elvis stand-in) Lance LeGault rhapsodizing, "It all started with the dream of a poor young boy in Tupelo, Mississippi. He dreamed of a better life of music and wealth and a fine home for himself and his family." The tapes tend to keep tourists from asking too many questions, and that's exactly why they're used; as Todd Morgan, EPE's director of communications, notes, the tapes keep folks from putting "their own spin on things."[16] It's not surprising, of course, that Elvis's estate avoids all the "negative" stuff about their main product (although, whether EPE wants to admit it or not, it's that stuff, too, that draws millions to Elvis's image). What's more disheartening is the company's basic historical amnesia about Elvis's transgressive identity, its obvious disinterest in his fandom, and its insistence that there is only one "spin" on Elvis.

Contrast EPE's "official" take on Elvis's image with that at GracelandToo, which not only retains the bordello ambience that Graceland embodied at the time of Elvis's death but strives to visually complicate Elvis's entire history. Paul and Elvis MacLeod's Holly Springs house is jam-packed with Elvis stuff ranging from the tacky to the tasteful, a presentation style that immediately alerts GracelandToo's tourists to the real facts of Elvis's nonhierarchical presence and meaning in American culture. And the MacLeods don't shy away from

Elvis's messy personal history; they don't overemphasize all the girls and all the drugs, but they don't deny them either. Visitors tend to appreciate the MacLeods' imaging of Elvis; comments in Graceland-Too's guest books suggest that people yearn for more complex understandings of Elvis that encompass their own diverse and ambiguous readings of him. "Your museum shows that Elvis was a real talent who led many lives," one fan wrote in 1996, while another remarked, "You know more about Elvis than those tour guides at Graceland."

GracelandToo, of course, is a monument not only to Elvis, but to a family of fans who have devoted their lives to "taking care" of Elvis's memory. Graceland, on the other hand, while certainly a monument to Elvis, seems to pay special tribute to the smooth efficiency and growing net worth of his estate. And its superficial and ahistorical representation style seems to have great appeal for other outfits anxious to get on the cultural-tourism bandwagon and cash in on image. Dexter King, for example, son of the Reverend Martin Luther King, Jr., and CEO of the King Center, the Atlanta complex dedicated to promoting King's philosophy of nonviolent social change, has repeatedly consulted with Jack Soden about strategies to "sell" his father. In 1994, the King estate signed with an intellectual property management company to ensure that King's name and image were officially licensed and controlled; in 1996, the estate sued CBS for allegedly misappropriating King's "I Have a Dream" speech on its program "20th Century with Mike Wallace." Memphis's financially troubled and poorly attended National Civil Rights Museum, built on the site of the Lorraine Motel, where King was murdered in 1968, has recently turned to Graceland for advice, too. Soden, who's on the museum board, commented in the local press: "There are some people who will never be comfortable with this as a tourist attraction, but like all things, it's for naught if it can't sustain itself financially. Every effort should be made to try to help a business operation find its way to economic self-reliance."[17]

Graceland is the leading model for this neoconservative vision of American culture's economic "self-reliance," drawing well over 750,000 paying visitors a year. (The house tour alone today costs $10 per adult; the "Platinum Tour," which includes admission to the mansion and the Elvis Presley Automobile Museum, and quick peeks at

Elvis's personal jets, costs $18.50.) More than 8 million people have visited Elvis's mansion since 1982, 90 percent of them out-of-town tourists who spend an estimated $200 million in Memphis each year, especially during the summer months. "It's unfortunate that Elvis Presley died, but it is very fortunate that he died in August—before Labor Day, when the kids were back in school—it's when people take their summer vacations," observes David Less, president of Gibson Entertainment. And as Jack Soden remarks, "There is no reason to think people won't be coming here in 2050, 2060, or 2089. Look at Stephen Foster; his home is one of the top two to three biggest attractions in Kentucky, and Stephen Foster hasn't had a hit song in a long, long time."[18]

Graceland is only one of EPE's arms. The company's other revenue streams come from royalties on the $50 million worth of Elvis CDs, tapes, and records sold each year (EPE and RCA "renegotiated" the royalties in the 1980s, and RCA still derives some 50 percent of its own annual revenue just from Elvis's music) and from royalties collected whenever any of Elvis's thirty-three movies or TV specials are sold or shown (EPE is part owner of those movies and entirely owns video rights to the 1968 "comeback special" and the 1973 "Aloha from Hawaii" shows). But EPE's biggest gold mine of all comes from the annual sales of hundreds of millions of dollars' worth of Elvis stuff.

EPE receives some forty phone calls a day about Elvis product proposals, and rejects some 95 percent of them. "We could sell anything with Elvis," says Danny Hiltenbrand, director of merchandising. "Just because we can doesn't mean we want to." Rejected items include Elvis sweatsuits ("we stay away from stereotypical aspects," says Hiltenbrand), Elvis toilet paper ("total poor taste"), and Elvis wallpaper ("tacky"). There's still lots of money being made from 35-cent postcards (over 1 million are sold each year), T-shirts ($16.95), and collector's plates ($34.95), but Elvis Edition Wurlitzer Jukeboxes ($12,000), Harley Davidson motorcycles, replicas of his favorite Gibson guitars, and Limited Edition Elvis Screenprints (set of four, $4,300, by "Andy Warhol protégé Steve Kauffman") are some of the tonier Elvis items the company has recently licensed. "As long as we tended to license small operators and distributors selling inexpensive items," says Soden, "that's the way we would be regarded. The mar-

Elvis stuff for sale, Graceland Crossing shopping mall, 1997.

ketplace would regard us as the licensor of trinkets and beads, of truck stop paraphernalia."[19]

Selling Elvis today, in other words, is about good taste and Elvis Inc. is adamant that its increasingly upscale image of Elvis is the Elvis the world sees. Given its stated financial objectives, the exclusivity of EPE's "marketplace" position is somewhat surprising, but it clearly demonstrates how the company has aligned itself with a limited image of Elvis that it believes, incorrectly I think, is the most profitable image of Elvis. Gone is any Elvis stuff that might draw a laugh or might seem tacky—vials of Elvis sweat, plastic-wrapped locks of his hair, paperweights filled with Real Graceland Dirt, fuzzy acrylic bedroom slippers with Elvis's tennis-ball-size head perched on the toes, velvet paintings—despite the fact that it is this sort of Elvis stuff that many fans (and many others) love and cherish. And gone too are the mom-and-pop stores that once sold this stuff, much of it unlicensed by Elvis's estate, across the street from Graceland. In the 1980s, Elvis Inc. acquired the entire strip mall, renamed it Graceland Plaza, replaced it with its own stores (today called Good Rockin' Tonight, Elvis Threads, and Gallery Elvis), and restocked it with its own Elvis stuff. Down the street at a privately owned mini-mall called Graceland Crossing, Elvis stuff is still sold in several shops (The

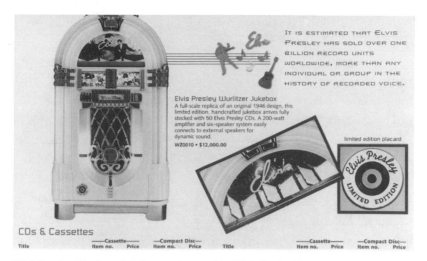

It is estimated that Elvis Presley has sold over one billion record units worldwide, more than any individual or group in the history of recorded voice.

Elvis Presley Wurlitzer Jukebox
A full-scale replica of an original 1946 design, this limited edition, handcrafted jukebox arrives fully stocked with 50 Elvis Presley CDs. A 200-watt amplifier and six-speaker system easily connects to external speakers for dynamic sound.
WZ0010 • $12,000.00

limited edition placard

CDs & Cassettes

Title	Cassette Item no.	Price	Compact Disc Item no.	Price	Title	Cassette Item no.	Price	Compact Disc Item no.	Price

Elvis Presley Wurlitzer Jukebox, as featured in Elvis Presley Enterprises, Incorporated, 1997 catalog. (Reprinted with permission of Elvis Presley Enterprises, Incorporated)

Wooden Nickel, Souvenirs of Elvis) that are not managed by EPE. But at Graceland Plaza—as inside Graceland—EPE presents Elvis's "official" image.

As this book argues, there are many different, messy, and complicated images of Elvis: saint, sexual fantasy, icon of whiteness. Elvis's representation is contradictory and provisional and has never been understood or agreed upon with any unanimity of interpretation. But within the world of EPE, there is only an "official" image of a clean and generous Elvis who seems to have burst forth from his Tupelo/Memphis womb a fully developed, heroic, and autonomous Rock and Roll King. His real history—his transgressive cross-race, cross-gender history—ignored and denied, his dirtier and more decadent parts swept away, his putrefaction corrected, the "official" Elvis presented at Graceland is like some exotic stuffed animal on display in a natural history museum. Taxidermy, after all, is about gutting and mounting the lifeless in ostensibly lifelike, and hence real (or "official") poses and settings.[20] As preserved at Graceland, Elvis is still the teddy bear of his 1957 hit single, but gone is all the verve and dynamism—and scat—of that cuddly and dangerous rockabilly rebel. EPE's "official" Elvis is hygienically sterile, a specimen of upwardly mobile middle-class normalcy and achievement. He's conservative and controlled, seamless and uncomplicated, fixed—even paralyzed—as not much more than a symbol of monopoly capital.

It's an image that obviously conflicts with those actually shaped and embraced by his fans, many of whom bitterly complain that Elvis Inc.'s take on Elvis is too simple, too sanitized, and too commercial. EPE's proclamation, moreover, that it is the "official" authority in Elvis Culture—the proprietor of the "Official Elvis Home Page," for example, and the purveyor of "official" Elvis merchandise—further arouses fan indignation because it not only excludes their claims to Elvis, but forces them to choose to be either "official" adherents or unofficial heretics. This struggle for authority in Elvis Culture is not unlike that examined by Art Simon in his study of the representation of John F. Kennedy's assassination—with the Warren Commission claiming to be the "official body of knowledge" about the president's murder and with artists and filmmakers, including Bruce Conner, Ed Kienholz, Alan Pakula, and Oliver Stone, as well as a large body of the American public, engaged in quite a different construction and understanding of JFK's death.[21] Elvis's representation and meaning are similarly the site of fierce contestation and debate, with "official" and heretical representatives claiming his image as their own on their own terms, and disclaiming others.

Elvis Inc.'s "official" claims to that image extend from litigation it pursued and laws specially written after Elvis's death. Legal rights to profit from the commercial use of one's likeness were actually established earlier, in 1953, in a New York case involving rival chewing-gum/baseball-card manufacturers battling over the rights to pictures of ball players. In his opinion, Judge Jerome Frank coined the term "right of publicity," establishing the property rights inherent in a person's identity and denoting publicity as a form of property—specifically, intellectual property. Those rights were deemed capable of being assigned and licensed and were deemed infringed by the "unpermitted use of a person's identity in a commercial setting." In the 1970s and 1980s, right of publicity claims burgeoned as the estates of dead celebrities like Bela Lugosi, Groucho Marx, Agatha Christie, and Elvis sued for the legal inheritability of postmortem publicity/property rights—and generally won their cases.[22] Overturning the commonly held notion that "the dead have no rights," courts ruled that the right of publicity survived the death of the rich and famous and passed to their heirs.

Elvis Inc. first gained that right by successfully challenging Colonel Tom Parker's commercial hold over Elvis. Even after the death of his single client, Parker's management contract (which Vernon Presley renewed on the day of his son's funeral) continued to give him an astounding 50 percent of the income from Elvis's estate. After a labyrinthine number of injunctions and hearings (a "mountain of lawsuits," a veritable *Bleak House* of "convoluted litigation," writes legal scholar J. Thomas McCarthy), EPE was eventually able, in 1983, to depose Parker (especially after courts took a close look at his shady commercial-licensing deals, his failure to retain Elvis's record royalties, and his status as an illegal alien who stowed away to America aboard a Dutch freighter in 1929 and never pursued U.S. citizenship).[23] It didn't come cheap; Parker reportedly received a $2 million payoff, and in 1990 EPE paid him much more for his private collection of Elvis memorabilia—some 70,000 pounds of scrapbooks, photos, Elvis fan club archives, unseen video footage, clothes (including Elvis's gold lamé suit), and other stuff currently cached in a Memphis warehouse.

Once the Colonel was out of the picture, EPE seriously stepped up its "official" claims to Elvis, helped along by the governor of Tennessee signing into law the Personal Rights Protection Act of 1984, which provided a statutory right of publicity, and by a 1991 decision in federal appellate court granting EPE "exclusive rights to commercially exploit the name, likeness and image of Elvis Presley." Initially, in 1980, the Tennessee Sixth Circuit Court decided that in the absence of state court direction, the legal rights to Elvis's name and image had died with him. But EPE heavily lobbied the Tennessee General Assembly to remove legal ambiguities in state inheritance laws, and then convinced various courts to overturn the 1980 decision. Tennessee's legal decisions regarding Elvis's ownership have helped to establish important precedent: in 1985, California enacted Civil Code 990, the so-called Celebrity Rights Act, which grants statutory postmortem rights of publicity lasting for fifty years and prohibiting the unsanctioned use of the "name, voice, signature, photograph, or likeness on or in products, merchandise or goods" of any person. Since then, twelve additional states have adopted similar right of publicity legislation. Media coverage of the potential profitability of the late Frank Sinatra's image (and forthcoming legal battles) referred repeatedly to Elvis, one reporter noting that Elvis's estate had "made an estimated one billion dollars" from Elvis's name and image since his death.[24]

In their decisions and opinions, the legal community seem to have given little or no consideration to the ways in which celebrity is, in fact, often dependent on unharnessed publicity. Protecting the rich and famous from commercial exploitation by granting them the exclusive right of their own publicity may, as intended, protect their rights to privacy. But it also restricts others—the public—from their own interpretations and expressions, indeed constructions, of celebrity "property." If, as some argue, including First Amendment considerations within the framework of right of publicity only serves to muddy or confuse those rights, so be it. Images, like ideas, are complex and open to multiple interpretations; they are not simply or only fixed property. Failure to recognize this is concomitant with a larger failure to recognize the contemporary erosion of both individual and public rights to free expression, particularly in the past two decades of legally mandated "protectionism" for intellectual property. It is one thing to argue that Elvis Inc. has the right to control the commercial use of Elvis's identity, but what of the company's insistence that artists, authors, script writers, Web servers, impersonators, and fan clubs are also subject to its legal hold on his image?

How, after all, can we legally determine standards of taste, and who's to determine those standards in Elvis Culture? For some people, everything about Elvis is tacky; for others, velvet Elvises are the epitome of good art and good taste. And Elvis Inc.'s insistence that its real interest in Elvis is to improve and guard his image is ludicrous, as even a cursory look at the stuff the company licenses and the litigation it pursues suggests. Are $9.95 Elvis Socks and $49.95 Elvis Bowling Shirts really tasteful? Are they more tasteful than the Elvis sweatsuits that Elvis Inc. refuses to market?

EPE's real interests are obviously financial: how else to explain its demands that the Lady Luck Casino in Tunica, Mississippi, remove an image of Elvis from a large wall mural or pay a licensing fee of $1 million a year? (The casino opted to paint out Elvis and replaced him with Frank Sinatra.) Or that software engineer and Web server Andrea Berman withdraw her "Cyber Graceland Tour" from her personal "Elvis Home Page," on the grounds that it "improperly infringes on EPE's proprietary rights" to its own tours of Graceland, physical and virtual? Or the company's twelve years of litigation against British businessman Sid Shaw, proprietor of an east London gift shop that owns the trademark "ELVISLY YOURS" and sells lots of Elvis stuff? Or EPE's insistence that artist Joni Mabe "cease and desist" making and selling small $1 buttons displaying "Elvis' Hair" (of which Mabe says she "sold like 30") or immediately compensate Elvis Inc. $5,000 "for the damages caused by your company's [!?] violation" of EPE's "rights" to Elvis's image?

"We take no joy in going after these people," says Mark Lee, an attorney with Manatt Phelps & Phillips, an entertainment law firm in Los Angeles. "But we're obligated to defend the rights of EPE."[25] In August 1994, Elvis Inc. hired Carol Butler, former manager of licensing for Anheuser-Busch, to direct its worldwide merchandising and licensing. During Elvis Week 1994, Butler's staff delivered "cease and desist" memos to the multiple fan club conventions and booths that had been set up in local hotels and restaurants around Graceland, warning fans that they were operating illegally if they were selling unauthorized Elvis memorabilia or crafts, and that they could be in violation of copyright if they refused to sign licensing agreements with EPE. Longtime Elvis artist Betty Harper, who has drawn more than 10,000 portraits of Elvis since the 1960s and who usually, during Elvis Week, sets up a stand of her sketches in the lobby of the fan-dominated Wilson World Hotel, about a block from Graceland, was one of those targeted by EPE. Harper basically ignored the company's memo and refused to sign any licensing agreement. "They're trying to scare people," she remarked. "It's the authority of Graceland over the image of Elvis."

That authority has been sweeping. Since the late 1970s, EPE has pursued hundreds of "infringements" and "violations" of its right of publicity to Elvis's name and image. Policing Elvis's image is handled by an eight-person international licensing office in Memphis and several outside law firms. Not surprisingly, most of EPE's complaints

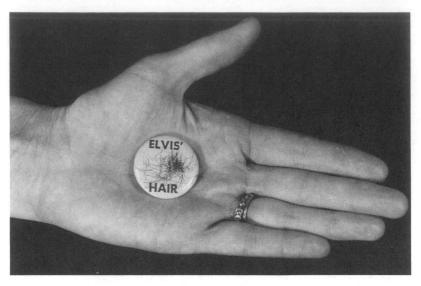

Joni Mabe, "Elvis Hair" button (1993). Limited edition. (Collection of the author)

have ended in the company's favor: the threat of litigation and the sheer financial burden of constructing a defense against a Fortune 500 corporation like Elvis Inc. tends to persuade most people who receive one of the scary "cease and desist" memos to settle, fast. Americans tend to be notoriously underinformed about their legal rights and the law in general, especially when it comes to areas of copyright, intellectual property, fair use, and free speech. Corporations take advantage of that ignorance and use their well-oiled authority to provoke real and imagined legal threats, especially when big bucks are at stake. As the Internet, for example, has become more and more the domain of capital and commerce, more and more companies have sought to enforce their ownership of copyrighted material—hence EPE's threat of a suit against Berman's "Elvis Home Page." Original visions of a "free Net" of accessible information and, perhaps more important, multiple opportunities for free-flowing exchanges in a high-tech version of America's "informational commons." seem to have fallen by the wayside.

A certain refusal, however, to allow Elvis Inc. complete control over Elvis's image framed the important decision in the lawsuit *EPE Inc. v. Capece and Velvet Limited* (1996). In 1991, Barry Capece, a former entertainment lawyer turned nightclub entrepreneur, opened the Velvet Elvis, a campy Houston bar featuring blues and lounge music and decorated, à la 1970s retro aesthetics with red vinyl furniture, lava lamps, cheap ceramic statues, beaded curtains, disco balls, *Playboy* centerfolds on the walls of the men's bathroom, and about forty black velvet paintings. In addition to its life-size "Aloha from Hawaii" velvet of Elvis highlighted above the bar's small bandstand, Capece's nightclub displayed velvets of Bruce Lee, John Wayne, Chuck Berry, Malcolm X, John Lennon, Stevie Wonder, the Mona Lisa (with her breasts exposed), lots of nude women, and the ubiquitous "Dogs Playing Pool."

"We're not an Elvis bar and we're not commercializing Elvis Presley's image," said Capece. "We're named after a tacky velvet painting—and damn proud of it." EPE wasn't so proud and sued Capece for trademark infringement, asking for legal fees and bar profits and demanding that the Velvet Elvis's registration of its own name (received in 1993) be revoked by the U.S. Patent and Trademark Office. Capece pled exemption, arguing that his tongue-in-cheek saloon was a "cheesy, tacky, off-the-wall parody" of American kitsch and bad taste, and didn't expressly capitalize on Elvis's name.[26]

The fact that Elvis Inc. had its own plans for an Elvis nightclub—its upscale eatery Elvis Presley's Memphis, a 12,000-square-foot full-service 330-seat restaurant with bars, banquet rooms, gift shops, and multiple stages for live bands opened on Beale Street in Memphis in June 1997—certainly colored the company's interest in the Velvet Elvis. This, however, didn't come out in the suit against Capece. Instead, during the two-day trial, EPE tried to prove that the Velvet Elvis caused confusion in the minds of consumers who mistook the bar for an Elvis gift shop or some other site of EPE-sanctioned Elvis commercialism. EPE also argued that Capece's bar served to tarnish Elvis's name and reputation and offered four witnesses to prove its point, three of them members of the Elvis Presley Fan Club of Austin. One said he had specifically gone to the Velvet Elvis to buy Elvis stuff, and was sorely disappointed. Another testified that she was offended by the image of "Elvis in a bar," especially in a bar that also featured pictures of "nude women."[27] Utilizing these fans in its defense, EPE aimed to show that everyone in Elvis Culture was on the same wavelength when it came to issues of taste, that everyone shared the

Interior of the Velvet Elvis, Houston, 1997.
(Courtesy of Barry Capece. Photograph by Jaime Siff)

company's concerns that Elvis's image be "appropriately" rendered and placed, and that everyone agreed that Elvis required EPE's legal protection.

The judge didn't buy any of it. In her hilarious opinion (thank God some folks in the legal community see the humor in some of this), U.S. District Court judge Vanessa Gilmore ruled that the Velvet Elvis was not in violation of EPE's trademark rights and granted none of the estate's requests: "Stated simply, the court must determine if the Defendants stepped on the Plaintiff's blue suede shoes. . . . Defendants plea, 'Don't be cruel, we have a registered service mark' [and] maintain that Plaintiff is merely a victim of suspicious minds." For federal court, this counts as comedy, but Gilmore's thirty-eight-page decision was also filled with blunt legal directives dismissing EPE's sweeping claims to Elvis. Importantly, the judge challenged EPE's claim that it is the only, or "official," tastemaker in Elvis Culture. Remarking that "the phrase 'velvet Elvis' has a meaning in American pop culture that is greater than the name, image or likeness of Elvis Presley," Gilmore shrewdly observed that Elvis means more than the physicality of his image: he embodies an entire culture and restricting ownership of that culture to a single corporation is tantamount to monopolization. Or as Capece's attorney commented after the trial (which cost Capece well over $100,000), "Look, [Elvis] may have been a famous singer of the era, but that doesn't mean the whole era's off limits."[28]

Elvis Inc. may hold the legal right of publicity to Elvis's image, in other words, but an image is a conceptual construction much broader than any single product or piece of art. And, as such, an image cannot be legally contained or controlled. The significance of the Houston decision was to challenge the idea that anyone or anything can own the "idea" of Elvis, because the boundaries of that idea are too huge and too multifaceted. Sadly, on appeal these noble sentiments were not borne out; the Fifth Circuit Court of Appeals reversed the lower district court, holding that there was a substantial likelihood of confusion among the public regarding the Velvet Elvis and EPE's claims to Elvis.[29]

Andrea Berman and Sid Shaw have also challenged EPE's totalizing claims to Elvis's image and have met with more success. Berman put her "Cyber Graceland Tour" back on her personal Web site after receiving thousands of e-mails from other Elvis fans outraged by EPE's totalizing claims to Elvis, and after lawyers informed her that the doctrine of "fair use" still applies online. "My first reaction was fear," she remarks. "EPE is a huge, powerful organization, and their intimidation tactic worked perfectly with me. I later regretted giving in to them so quickly. Little did I know there were hundreds, if not thousands, of people ready to support me, including many lawyers and legal specialists."[30] Her case has, in fact, since become a rallying point for those concerned about legal issues involving the Internet.

Shaw successfully defended his trademark "ELVISLY YOURS" against EPE in a London court, winning the right to continue to market his Elvis stuff without EPE's permission. "Just as Elvis Presley did not own his name so as to be able to prevent all and any uses of it by third parties, so [EPE] can have no greater rights," declared High Court justice Hugh Laddie in 1997, adding, "Even if Elvis Presley were still alive, he would not be entitled to stop a fan from naming his son, his dog or goldfish, his car or his house 'Elvis' or 'Elvis Presley,' simply by reason of the fact that it was the name given to him at birth by his parents." Shaw was ecstatic after the decade-long legal battle and is now considering how to pursue his case in the United States, where EPE has won a court order prohibiting sales of Shaw's Elvis stuff to American consumers. "You cannot monopolize industries in America. Why can you monopolize the Elvis industry?" asks Shaw. "You can't own Shakespeare. You can't own Che Guevara. How can you own Elvis Presley?"[31]

Joni Mabe asks the same question. She plans to stop traveling her *Traveling Panoramic Encyclopedia of Everything Elvis* and open it up as an Elvis museum in an old boardinghouse she's inherited in Cornelia, Georgia. But she's worried about how Elvis Inc. will react. "You think twice about dedicating your life to Elvis after what I've been through with this big enemy called 'Graceland Incorporated,'" she remarks. Mabe, who really has dedicated the last twenty years of her life to Elvis, has reason to worry. In 1990, the Memphis Brooks Museum of Art commissioned her for a single-person show based on her Elvis artwork, but the show was abruptly canceled. Mabe feels that Jack Soden exerted pressure on the museum board, protesting that her work was "too outrageous" to be seen in the hometown of Memphis's number-one son. But Mabe also refused to sign a licensing contract with EPE that would have given the company total rights to the profits of any Elvis artworks she might have sold from the show. "I try to figure out where that line is drawn between Elvis art and merchandise," Mabe remarks. "What I consider art, they don't. If I do a series of prints, I consider it art. When I open my Elvis museum, I'll consider that art. But they don't, they see it all as Elvis merchandise."

Conflicts over Elvis's ownership have burgeoned recently as artists and fans have tried to figure out how to freely express themselves without arousing Elvis Inc.'s interest and demands. When Core New Art Space, a Denver art gallery, organized a show of Elvis artwork in 1997, the title of the exhibition and its promotional materials never even mentioned Elvis's name. Show organizer Linda Pickrell-Takata explains that Core originally intended to call the show "Elvis International" and was advised by Colorado Lawyers for the Arts to ask EPE for permission to use Elvis's name. When EPE refused, the gallery decided to turn the issue of Elvis's ownership into the show's central motif. Core's exhibition brochure featured the head shot of a sneering, black-haired figure with a black band reading "CENSORED"

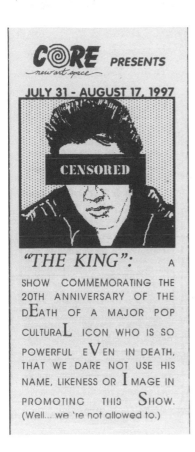

Publicity for 1997 exhibition of
Elvis art, Core New Art Space, Denver.
(Courtesy Core New Art Space)

over his eyes. The exhibit itself was titled "THE KING" and was described as "a show commemorating the 20th anniversary of the dEath
of a major pop culturaL icon who is so powerful eVen in death, that
we dare not use his name, likeness or Image in promoting this Show."
Everyone knew who it was, of course, and what the show was all
about—further evidence that Elvis means much more than his name
and his image. More than 200 paintings, sculptures, shrines, and
collages from a diverse international pool of artists were eventually
featured in Core's juried show. As Pickrell-Takata observed, "Our
exhibit showed how Elvis's name and image are universally recognized. It's hard to understand how EPE can own all of that."

EPE's general unwillingness to "share" Elvis is evident from other
conflicts it's had with organizations and museums. In 1980, for example, the company (or, more correctly, Factors, Etc., Incorporated,
EPE's exclusive licensee at the time) took issue with the Memphis

Development Foundation, a nonprofit neighborhood-improvement group that aimed to help downtown tourism by erecting a large bronze statue of Elvis in a Beale Street park. Those who donated $25 or more to the project were to receive eight-inch pewter replicas of the sculpture. EPE, however, completely discounting the statue's civic and charitable context, claimed the "exclusive right to reap commercial value" from Elvis's name and image, and forced the foundation to halt its funding process.[32] The statue was eventually dedicated (in 1996, it was moved to a Tennessee Welcome Center on the fringe of downtown), but EPE's actions set the tone for a dead Elvis's participation in the public sphere. Without Elvis Inc.'s permission, Elvis doesn't participate. Although Elvis, in 1986, was one of the first inductees into the Rock and Roll Hall of Fame in Cleveland, Elvis Inc. reluctantly donated only a pitifully small pile of memorabilia, apparently fearing more stuff might draw tourists away from Graceland. Likewise, EPE rejected requests to lend any of its reported 300 Elvis jumpsuits for an exhibition at the National Museum of American History of the Smithsonian Institution.

Admittedly, Elvis Inc. has engaged in some small charitable ventures. The Elvis Presley Memorial Foundation, a small 501(c)(3), was created in the early 1990s to provide an annual scholarship for an undergraduate student attending the University of Memphis; the foundation also gives around $20,000 to $30,000 annually to various Memphis youth programs. And in August 1997, EPE unveiled a new Elvis statue on Beale Street (by Memphis artist Andrea Holmes Ungar), announcing that "in the future," miniatures of the sculpture would be sold, with a portion of the proceeds going to the Memphis Development Foundation. However, even Jack Soden admits that EPE has not "put a great deal of focus" into philanthropy, explaining that the company's most important "job is to conserve and protect [its] assets."[33] More than a few fans resent the fact that Elvis Inc.'s efforts at civic welfare have not come anywhere close to the charitable giving of the fan clubs themselves, particularly for Memphis-based hospitals.

Many fans have also been offended by EPE's recent efforts regarding fan club licensing, making each club pay an annual membership fee to Elvis Inc. and forcing the clubs to ask the company's permission to use Elvis's name and image. This is not, in fact, unusual (organiza-

Elvis statue and fans, Tennessee Welcome Center, Elvis Week 1996, Memphis.
Bronze statue by Eric Parks.

tions from the Girl Scouts to the National Rifle Association demand annual fees of their local chapters), and lately, more than a few clubs have willingly come under EPE's big corporate umbrella. The Elvis Chicago Style Fan Club membership form, for example, now asserts that it is a "not-for-profit organization licensed by the Estate of Elvis Presley," and the Elvis Memphis Style club promotes itself today as a Tennessee nonprofit that has a "permission agreement signed with EPE, Inc." Perhaps beholden to Elvis Inc. for their status as "official" Elvis fan clubs and appreciative that during Elvis Week they are feted at a special EPE-sponsored luncheon and that year round the company deluges them with "News from Graceland" and information about new Elvis stuff, these clubs seem to have taken the path of least resistance in terms of Elvis Inc.'s overall interests in Elvis Culture.

Other clubs, however, have refused to submit to EPE's efforts to control that culture, seeing it as a threat to their own independent and different imaging of Elvis. "The Last Elvis Fan" (1994), a parable written by Keith Mitchell of the Oklahoma Fans for Elvis Fan Club, is the story of John Presley Stephens, the last living defender of Elvis Culture in the mid-twenty-first century. Explaining how "it all went wrong" after Elvis died and his blood relatives "formed a corporation to make sure there was only quality Elvis stuff on the market," Stephens, now an old man, relates how the "Elvis Police" drove the fan clubs out of business in the 1990s by forcing them to pay licensing fees to the corporation, or suing them if they used Elvis's name or image without permission: "Most clubs couldn't afford it. They just folded up and quit doing their charity work." All he has left (the Elvis Police having confiscated his Elvis collection for "a new exhibit at Graceland") is a battered tape of *Elvis's Golden Hits*, which Stephens plays to the delight of his grandkids. Mitchell ends his parable with the lines: "They had almost exterminated the Elvis fans. He had been the last one. But now Elvis would survive for another generation, in spite of what they had tried to do in the name of greed."

Thin as it might be, "The Last Elvis Fan" captures the valid fears among many fans about EPE's monopolization of Elvis. Fan anxieties about their voice and authority in an increasingly corporate Elvis Culture have taken various forms, from parables to protests. In 1993, Bill DeNight, president of the Burning Love Fan Club, became so outraged at "Graceland's plans to have total control of Elvis and to suck every dime of our money" that he mounted a boycott of Elvis Inc. and encouraged the club's 1,200 members not to buy their Elvis stuff at the Graceland Plaza stores, and not to participate in EPE-sponsored events like the Fan Club Presidents' Lunch. Riding into Memphis during Elvis Week in a purple van painted with slogans like "Graceland Spells Elvis M-O-N-E-Y," DeNight took his stand. Over the next several years, his club newsletters increasingly focused on Elvis Inc.'s "power hungry ways" and how Priscilla Presley, Jack Soden, and Lisa Marie had "taken over" Elvis Culture. "We, the fans," wrote DeNight, "made Graceland what it is today, thru our love, support, caring and our *money*! Not Priscilla, not Soden. Elvis would be completely ashamed of these people running (ruining) Graceland, and some day in the near future, the media will be referring to it as 'Greedland.'"

After Elvis Week 1994, during which EPE distributed "cease and desist orders" at the fan conventions and the marriage of Lisa Marie Presley and Michael Jackson obsessed many fans, DeNight's anger erupted. Conflating his racist rage about Lisa Marie and Michael with his fury about "Greedland," he demanded: "We *must* get these care-less people *completely removed* from their plush jobs before it's too late!! I have been trying to tell all of you people now for over 2 years that these care-less, money hungry, power crazy, slimeballs that run (ruin) Greedland (Dis-Graceland) WANT IT ALL and they won't stop until they have it all!" In January 1995, DeNight assembled a "hit-list" of those he advised Burning Love Fan Club members to "avoid like the plague," including "money hungry Priscilla," "Lisa the nigger loving tramp," "Patsy 'Airhead' Anderson," "Tutti Frutti Todd Morgan," and "Jerky Jack Soden."[34] It was his last stand. Shortly thereafter, DeNight informed club members that due to ill health (he had been complaining of "very bad headaches" for several years), he and Burning Love were taking a hiatus. At the same time, the club was disenrolled as one of EPE's "official" Elvis fan clubs.

As virulent as DeNight's diatribes were, they foregrounded Elvis Inc.'s apparent interest in gaining "total control" over Elvis Culture for financial reasons. Licensing the fan clubs would generate a fairly substantial revenue stream for EPE; as DeNight observed, "Imagine if every Elvis fan in the world had to pay 'Greedland' $10 a year!" It would also reinforce EPE's legal ownership of Elvis and further promote its "official" image of him as the only image. Interestingly, however, the more rapacious Elvis Inc. has become, the farther some fans have retreated into an Elvis Culture all their own. Joni Mabe's decision, for example, to create her own Elvis museum demonstrates her unwillingness to give up on "her" image of Elvis, or to give in to EPE's demands. "I look at my relationship with Elvis as a long term marriage," says Mabe. "I'm not that crazed, obsessed person I was twenty years ago, but I'm definitely in it for the long term. And Elvis tends to work his way into whatever I'm interested in."

That sense of personal commitment and long-term constancy informs Roanoke Elvis fan Kim Epperly's artwork, too. Epperly is best known as the maker and keeper of *Miniature Graceland*, a collection of dollhouse-size replicas of Elvis's Memphis mansion and Tupelo birthplace, the Roanoke Civic Center (where he performed four times), and several other three- to four-foot-tall buildings staffed with Barbie, Ken, and Skipper dolls dressed like Priscilla, Elvis, Lisa Marie, his band members, and his fans. Epperly, her husband Don, and their eight children started building their Virginia version of Elvis Culture in 1986, shortly after Don, a self-employed pesticide exterminator and handyman, was diagnosed with multiple sclerosis. That year, they built a mini-model of Graceland, complete with Melody Gates, tiny swimming pool, and Meditation Gardens, on the sloping side yard of their one-story bungalow on Riverland Road. Over the next decade, they added the other buildings, replicas of Elvis's airplanes, cars, and motorcycles, dwarf trees and boxwoods, and a working fountain. "I feel like during my lifetime," says Kim, "that Elvis has given me so much pleasure—music, concerts, seeing him at airports—that this is the least I could do for him, keeping his memory alive. I do it, too, for all those Elvis fans who can't get to Graceland."

Seen by an estimated 10,000 people each year, some of whom visit after making a pilgrimage to nearby Mill Mountain to gaze on "the world's largest man-made star," *Miniature Graceland* is the material manifestation of Kim Epperly's personal love and admiration for Elvis. Ten years after his death, she commissioned a special poem about *Miniature Graceland* from her friend Mary Cantrell, parts of which read:

Kim Epperly with Miniature Graceland, *1995, Roanoke, Virginia.*
(Courtesy of Kim Epperly)

"The Wonder of You" shall never diminish
We shall stay loyal until the finish
To the world you added such a special "touch"
To the needy, to the lowly, you gave so much
Miniature Graceland flows with your music
Open to the public, we shall never abuse it

You shall always live on in my heart and my mind
Miniature Graceland, Elvis Presley's memorial shrine
Memories like you are far and few
Elvis, we built it for the love of you.

Miniature Graceland is about making an accessible Elvis, about shrinking him and his estate down to a controllable scale and reclaiming him from a personal perspective as a dear friend, a lost companion, an intimate memory. It is also about reaffirming Elvis as an important member of the family, about nurturing him under the umbrella of a fan culture where Elvis is more than just stuff. "When he died it was like my world ended," Kim Epperly recalls. "He was like a friend, a relative. He's a big part of my life and I miss him." By rebuilding Elvis's estate in her side yard, Epperly blends Elvis's world into her own and combines his family into hers. She's the caretaker for both, too, providing Elvis with the same sort of everyday attention and sustenance that she provides her own family.

Epperly's Elvis shrine exemplifies the powerfully expressive and creative means by which fans include Elvis in their daily lives and nurture him as one of their own, on their own terms. At night, tiny colored spotlights pan over *Miniature Graceland*'s fifty-five-foot spread and Elvis's songs play softly in the background. Cars pull up curbside and park, their passengers often sitting for hours while looking over the scene, listening to the music, sharing in one fan's loving devotion to Elvis. Although there is a small sign encouraging donations for *Miniature Graceland*'s maintenance and upkeep, there's no admission fee. "I would never charge admission," says Epperly, surprised at the suggestion. "This is free, it's for everyone." And that's the point: despite Elvis Inc.'s understanding of Elvis as a lucrative commodity, fans insist that Elvis is free, that he's for everyone.

Elvis has always, of course, been both: a physical, accessible, marketable image and something more ethereal—a feeling, a soulmate. But many contemporary fans recognize that Elvis Inc. has shifted the balance of Elvis's identity to a more completely commercialized representation that essentially excludes his deeper and more emotive meaning in their everyday lives. They also realize that EPE's new upscale Elvis, an image propped by a lot of pricey stuff they simply

Velvet Elvis in Elvis shrine made by Margaret Martinez, Embudo, New Mexico, photographed in 1996.

can't afford (like $12,000 jukeboxes) and that excludes a lot of the cheaper and more accessible stuff they have long collected and cherished (like $14.95 velvet Elvises), champions the estate's "official" image of Elvis over the multifaceted images they have long constructed. It is clear to many fans that their tastes—however diverse they really are—are broadly perceived by Elvis Inc. as lower-class and hence out of sync with the estate's corporate image of Elvis. Jack Soden's arrogant remark that EPE is deliberately avoiding an Elvis Culture aesthetic of "truck stop paraphernalia" deliberately targets many fans, and makes it clear that they aren't the audience of Elvis's intended future.

This sort of "us versus them" mind-set, whereby fans see Elvis Inc. as an all-consuming big-business monster that denies them autonomy in Elvis Culture, and Elvis Inc. tends to view Elvis fandom as primarily a lower-class phenonemon, is fairly pervasive. In June 1997, for example, script writers for the NBC soap opera *Days of Our Lives* decided to run a typically far-fetched story line about an obsessed Elvis fan named Susan, a drawling, buck-toothed southern gal who has an illegitimate baby and names him Elvis, and fantasizes that another character, John Black, actually *is* Elvis. Susan eventually cons John into a marriage proposal, and one whole week of *Days* was given over to an elaborate Elvis Theme Wedding, complete with the female characters dressed up in what *Days* staff assumed to be cheesy white-trash costumes (lots of tight-fitting spandex, cheap jewelery, heavy makeup, and really, *really* big hair), with Susan looking like Priscilla, circa 1967 (complete with black bouffant) and John impersonating Elvis.

That the script writers were hell-bent on presenting Elvis fans as lower-class unsophisticates is one thing. What is equally interesting is that EPE apparently "approved" that presentation well in advance of its production. *Days* producers were advised by in-house legal staff to send a script outline to EPE seeking permission to use Elvis's name and image, and a few Elvis impersonators, in the show. "Whenever we used an impersonator, they were concerned over how we would portray Elvis," recalled *Days* coordinating producer Janet Spellman-Rider. "They really didn't say anything," she added, about the script, or about the soap opera's derogatory class assumptions about Elvis fans. "It didn't seem to bother them."[35]

Days of Our Lives was a big topic of conversation among many American fans during Elvis Week 1997. While some said they saw the humor in it all and breathlessly watched from day to day just waiting for "that wacko Susan" to pull her next stunt, others were upset that "the media" continued to insist that Elvis fandom was, basically, ridiculous: deviant, lower-class, the subject of bad jokes and bad hair. Dismay that Elvis Inc. seems to side with that view, and even promote it, has prompted some fans to reconsider the nature of their fandom and, in particular, their relationship with his estate. Although many fans continue to obsessively collect every possible bit of Elvis stuff they can get their hands on, others are trying to reconcile their material desires (and EPE's steady supply of merchandise to whet those desires) with their profoundly intangible, even spiritual, understandings of the man they adore.

The fact is, of course, that for the past forty years, Elvis has held an extraordinary position as an emblem of transgression and transformation in American popular culture precisely *because* of his material culture visibility. His multivalent image as a secular saint, a sexual fantasy, an all-white guy, and even a corporate logo is rooted in the culture of his materiality. Few fans have decided to completely opt out of the materialist dimensions of Elvis Culture, but some have begun to question their culture's dependence on Elvis stuff, "It's a real shame," says Martha Clark of Maryland's the Wonder of You Elvis Fan Club, "how the fans keep handing over hard earned money for trashy pieces of plastic, paper, glass and various other souvenirs. It is just a sad way to remember someone like Elvis, who stood for so much more." Florida fan Mary Cartaya agrees, remarking, "God bless the fan who does not feel that owning a piece of the ten thousands of items produced monthly is being a true fan. God bless the fan who may own only one photo but remembers Elvis in his thoughts, prayers, and most of all by reaching out to someone in need as did and still does Elvis."

The rising costs of collecting Elvis has prompted some of these antistuff sentiments, many fans saying they are "disgusted" with the "outrageous" prices demanded in the Elvis collectibles market. "Look, I'm the biggest fan around," remarked a fifty-something female from Eugene, during Elvis Week 1996. "But even I can't see spending so much money on some of this Elvis stuff. I buy small, or not at all." Some fans are more disgusted with the cost of Elvis stuff sold in EPE's own stores; in the early 1990s, Bill DeNight was particularly outraged because the Graceland gift shops were "overcharging" fans for Elvis Trading Cards that could be purchased for half the price down the street. Still others are disgusted with what they describe as an Elvis Inc. "mafia" for grossly commercializing Elvis Culture and turning Graceland "into a carnival atmosphere." A fan from Johnson City, Tennessee, writes that she feels "betrayed" by Elvis's estate "because it has not been evident that they have tried to promote his [Elvis's] image as an entertainer, but have only promoted things that would keep their coffers filled." As Clark puts it, "I'm not against the fans gathering for memorials. But the Graceland Atmosphere does nothing to honor a man of dignity and class."

Despite these shared grievances, fans have not collectively addressed their frustrations, nor, with the exception of fans such as DeNight, have they directly targeted Elvis Inc. with any grassroots activism. The real complexity surrounding the consistent commercialism of Elvis's image partially accounts for this. The fact is that the Elvis Culture industry is as internally differentiated as Elvis's fandom, with various merchants and entrepreneurs ranging from the "unofficial" makers of Elvis stuff in the 1950s to Sid Shaw and Barry Capece in the 1990s also questioning EPE's apparently exclusive, or monopolistic, ownership of Elvis's commercialized image. Their eagerness to also profit from Elvis makes the simple dichotomy of "fans versus Elvis Inc." untenable, especially since more than a few of the business-people who inhabit Elvis Culture are also Elvis fans.

Arguments over Elvis's "correct" image also seem to preclude much Elvis Culture consensus on the issues of fan disenfranchisement and Elvis's commercial exploitation. Fans like Joni Mabe and Kim Epperly have, however, chosen to recenter the material culture of Elvis Culture in their own homes, building museums and miniature versions of Graceland that allow *them* to control Elvis's image, and their own images as Elvis fans. Likewise, fans like Mary Cartaya and Martha Clark encourage their colleagues to recenter Elvis's meaning around fund-raising and charitable giving. Both ways of imaging Elvis reinforce his importance on personal, emotive, and even social and communitarian levels; both undermine Elvis Inc.'s understanding, or a strictly commercialized understanding, of Elvis as simply and only a marketable product.

The clash between Elvis Inc.'s "official" claims to Elvis and those shaped by his fans is more than simply a struggle over his image; it is a collision of values. It is a collision not unlike that raging, for example, over Native American art, which is understood by many American Indians as the very embodiment of traditional ritualistic and spiritual existence, and viewed by many non-Indian collectors, including most museums, more superficially, as tribal trophies and objets d'art. But if these apparently oppositional understandings compete, they are also mutually enabling. In Elvis Culture, the fact that fans so completely depend on Elvis's materiality—his image in a velvet painting, a photograph, or a sculpture; his "trace" collected in a case or displayed in a home shrine—means that they often covet the "official" marketable stuff that his estate promotes. Even their personal and hybridic images of Elvis do not operate completely apart from the "official" commercial image claimed by his estate.

More important, this "official" image and its concomitant set of values is steadily gaining ascendency in the public sphere. EPE is growing at an unbounded rate, its voracious thirst for greater profits leading it to many new revenue streams. Elvis Presley's Memphis, for example, which cost $6 million to open, is but the first in an international chain of nightclub-restaurants that EPE plans to build. "It's going to be a jumping point," says Jack Soden. "Raw, gritty, authentic, like Elvis." Following the expansionist cue of the Hard Rock Cafe and Planet Hollywood, EPE plans to sell pulled pork shoulder specials, meatloaf plates, and fried peanut butter and banana sandwiches (Elvis's favorite) to the image hungry all over the globe. They'll get high-tech multimedia, too, with R&B, gospel, and rock-and-roll combos playing in front of ("accompanying") huge-screened images of Elvis live in concert. At least eight Elvis clubs (or "Elvis embassies," as Soden calls them) are scheduled to open in cities like New York, Los Angeles, Honolulu, Paris, Berlin, Tokyo, Hong Kong, Kuala Lumpur, London, and/or Sydney by 2001, each of them accompanied by a requisite retail merchandise shop.[36] In June 1997, after only two weeks of operation, Elvis Presley's Memphis was reporting around 4,000 to 5,000 transactions a day, and was almost completely sold out of what gift-shop managers had predicted would be a three-month supply of Elvis stuff. After two months, it still took up to three hours to get a table for lunch.

"We are creating a place," says Priscilla Presley, "where Elvis, who was a consummate host and entertainer, would have enjoyed entertaining his friends between road tours and filming movies. Guests will experience Elvis' hospitality firsthand in an incredibly fun environment." Never mind that EPE's overdone restaurant was built on the site of Lansky's, the clothing store where Elvis and lots of other Memphis musicians bought their threads in the 1950s, or that the club presages a grossly ahistorical "revitalization" of lower-downtown Memphis that largely ignores its black cultural roots. Not unexpectedly, remaking Beale Street into Elvis Street has prompted some angry local response. "The building of the oversized, gaudy Elvis Presley's Memphis club and the proposed building of a Hard Rock Cafe on the hallowed ground of Pee Wee's Saloon where W. C. Handy wrote some of his famous songs are a travesty and a tragedy," complained one Memphis resident in a letter to the *Commercial Appeal*. "The culture and character of Beale Street have been damaged if not destroyed. Its place on the National Register of Historic Places should be denied."[37]

On the one hand, historic preservation isn't exactly central to EPE's all-Elvis expansionism. On the other, when asked if EPE has any interest in connecting with the majority of black consumers who see Elvis Culture as a "white thing," Soden replied, "I think that there's a black community that lumps Elvis in with Pat Boone and everybody else. Most of [Elvis's] favorite singers were black. He didn't try to fool anybody into believing that he invented this stuff." He added, "It's a great, great story, and telling it is going to be part of the fun. And we'd love to reach a black audience somehow by doing that."[38] Maybe, but inviting black consumers into a nightclub where an overarching icon of Elvis looms suggestively behind live blues acts, or blatantly cleansing both Beale Street and Elvis of their rhythm-and-blues heritage, or generally ignoring how black culture helped shape and direct Elvis Culture in the first place probably won't draw much enthusiasm from black audiences.

In addition to more nightclubs, an Elvis-themed Las Vegas casino (and casinos abroad, perhaps in Australia and Asia), an Elvis Ice Show, and an Elvis on Broadway musical are also said to be on EPE's development calendar. Elvis Town U.S.A., a six-acre Elvis amusement park near Tokyo Disneyland, was all set to go until the bottom fell out of the Japanese economy in the mid-1990s; it is now on hold. Back in Memphis, EPE aims to open an Elvis museum, Elvis and the Rock Era, at Graceland Plaza where the 800 to 1,000 people who wait in line each hour to take the shuttle bus to the mansion could take a look at the estate's vast collection of Elvis stuff, including some of the recently acquired items from Colonel Parker's collection. Plans to house all those tourists include the development of a Graceland hotel similar in theme and scale to the grandiose Opryland Hotel in Nashville, which features more than 1,800 rooms and numerous meeting and exhibition spaces.

All these ventures require a lot of capital, of course, which means that EPE's charitable giving probably won't increase dramatically in the near future. More to the point, all these ventures are come-ons; the real money is in the merchandise—the Elvis stuff, the CDs and records. As any movie theater owner knows, the real money is in the popcorn and candy. To this end, EPE announced in 1997 that it had signed with International Creative Management, a Hollywood talent agency, to "do more with the Elvis Presley name and image."[39] Together, EPE and ICM say they plan to pursue new venues for Elvis's image in mass merchandising, TV commercials, general advertising, network programming (including a cable channel that would show only Elvis's movies), popular music, and live theater. On the one hand, this sort of corporate expansion will make Elvis even more omnipresent, more iconic. On the other, is the Elvis of the future only an icon, as Jack Soden says, of "profitability and financial depth?" Is Elvis, finally, just an ice show?

Ironically, Elvis Inc. claims to understand the multiformity of its main product. As Soden remarked in 1997, "The more business we do overseas and around the world, and the more opportunities we get to see what drives the Elvis Presley phenomenon, the more we come back to the fact that Elvis is this extremely multifaceted icon, a symbol for the whole post-war American era." In "every instance," he added, EPE's future will be driven by "tapping into that iconography." But Soden also says that he sees Elvis mainly as a nostalgic icon for happier days. "There's this mythologized image of life in the '50s and '60s, when Elvis came on the scene and changed things so dramatically," he comments. "Life was fun and fresh, the choices were simpler, and if you were a teenager, life was easier."[40]

There's no doubt that for a lot of people, Elvis *is* an icon of this revisionist image of an "easier" postwar America; many fans and many others overlook such historical and cultural moments as the Cold War, civil rights, and Elvis's own transgressive personae in favor of some sort of homogenized *Leave It to Beaver*, family values, 1950s fiction. And EPE is working overtime to ensure that the "official" image of Elvis that will be seen everywhere in the twenty-first century will be exactly, and only, that "fun and fresh" and "simpler" Elvis. Yet given Elvis's success, for example, in topping all three major music charts (R&B, country, and pop) in the 1950s, it is worth asking why Elvis Inc. is so anxious to adhere to this "official" image. Corporate assumptions that the sanitized image of Elvis is the most profitable one are unfounded, given the historical record and the fact that celebrity in general depends on the free flow of meaning. The most troubling aspect of EPE's superficial understanding of Elvis's meaning lies in its sweeping authority: even while limited, EPE's corporate image of Elvis has had the effect of neutralizing, if not entirely eliminating, many others. Elvis Inc.'s exclusive ownership of Elvis effectively shuts down public debate about his image. And despite EPE's confidence otherwise, it threatens to erase Elvis's image from the public sphere.

Struggles over Elvis's image have been in play, of course, since the mid-1950s, when teenage fans claimed him as a transgressive icon of liberatory pleasure, and critics stigmatized him as a no-talent Cold War enemy. Importantly, these struggles have been absolutely central to Elvis's popular endurance: his image has remained significant in American culture for the past forty years *because* of its unrestricted ambiguity and instability, its diversity and illegibility—and because Americans have never stopped arguing about what Elvis means and what he represents. Today's struggles over Elvis's image, however, seem to be less conversational and less tolerant, both because some fans have constructed narrowly essentialist views of Elvis's "correct" image and because Elvis Inc. has had great success in shaping the "official" image of Elvis rapidly taking hold in the American imagination. Today's struggles over Elvis, in other words, are simultaneous with other struggles over public images, voices, and histories; over knowledge, identity, and ownership in America. Whatever their directions or resolutions (should they ever be resolved), these struggles are central to Elvis Culture's future, and by extension, the general future of image culture.

Elvis Inc.'s struggles to keep Elvis's image under lock and key testify to its subversive, rather than "official," multivalency. Greil Marcus says it best:

> Even as Graceland Enterprises, Inc., the corporation Priscilla Presley formed to market the legacy, gained increasing legal control over the image of Elvis Presley, its meanings spun further and further out of control. They cannot be controlled, any more than, in the beginning, Elvis Presley's body could stop moving; the shade of Elvis Presley is now an anarchy of possibilities, a strain of freedom less clear, but no less suggestive, than the man ever was.[41]

Elvis is everywhere not just because of EPE's fierce mass-merchandising schemes, but because his image provides intimate moments of joy, release, and pleasure for countless fans and innumerable others who have looked at Elvis and made whatever they see into whatever they want. Their multiple visions—their velvet paintings and home shrines, their museums and outdoor tableaus, their sculptures and pictures and quilts—have made Elvis into the "multifaceted icon" that EPE now aims to own and control. Seeing those visions—seeing velvet Elvises, for example—only as economic impediments, EPE fails to understand that an unharnessed culture of fandom has been absolutely essential to the sustenance of Elvis's popularity and celebrity for the past forty years.

elvis
Is America

At her roadside café and souvenir shop in Embudo, New Mexico, longtime fan Margaret Martinez used to sell velvet Elvises by the hundreds. In 1996, hers was just about the last store in the country to have any left, according to a fan from Boston who had called "every Elvis store in America" trying to find one and "was just in total paradise" when she scored the last velvet Elvis that Martinez had in stock. Martinez had been a fan of Elvis's since the mid-1950s, when she was in high school in Albuquerque, but she started "seriously" collecting Elvis stuff only after, as she put it, "we lost him." Her Elvisiana was a big part of La Iguana, an arts and crafts store she and her husband, Joe, ran out of their house on New Mexico Highway 68, midway between Taos and Santa Fe. Hundreds of Elvis album covers, prints, and posters plastered several of the gift shop's walls, alongside shelves of dolls, lamps, music boxes, pennants, busts, T-shirts, "Elvis at Embudo" gimme-caps, key rings, earrings, coffee mugs, Christmas ornaments, and *milagros*. La Iguana was a regular stopover for Elvis fans from all over America, who nicknamed Margaret the "Elvis Lady," and bought so much Elvis stuff that the Martinezes added Legend's Hideaway Cafe, a small restaurant overlooking the Rio Grande, where fans watched Elvis movies and munched on "Love Me Tender Burritos."

In one section of the gift shop, Martinez built her Elvis Shrine, an elaborate homemade altar featuring a large oil painting of Elvis flanked by a smaller picture of Jesus and rows and rows of votive candles, small statues of saints, dried flowers, personal photographs, and several velvet Elvises. Visitors to the store were invited to say a prayer and light a candle; after she was diagnosed with colon cancer in the mid-1990s, Martinez often lit candles and prayed that Elvis would intercede on her behalf. "His pictures and his music were a big comfort to her," recalls her husband. "She really believed in Elvis. She didn't think he was a god, or anything, but more like a real good friend." In April 1996, Margaret Martinez died at home, surrounded by her Elvis stuff. A few months later, her friends and family held a memorial service near her Elvis Shrine, paying tribute to the "Elvis Lady" and the popular culture icon she helped to construct.

At a fan gathering during Elvis Week 1993, Sam Phillips, the Sun Records owner with whom Elvis recorded his first rockabilly singles, spoke of the "sweet visual image of that little playboy, that powerful man, that love outstanding that was Elvis Presley." Phillips went on to remark:

(overleaf) *Elvis collection of Margaret Martinez on display in La Iguana gift shop, Embudo, New Mexico, photographed in 1996.*

Elvis shrine made by Margaret Martinez, Embudo, New Mexico,
photographed in 1996.

We carry on about Elvis Presley. Until you have the opportunity to be a part of this young man and his life, to be around him. . . . It is the most profound thing in the way of love, understanding, and fun since our great maker put his son Jesus Christ on this earth. I'm looking forward to seeing Elvis Presley reincarnated, and that would be in the memory of fans like you.

Admittedly, Phillips made his comments at a memorial service held on the sixteenth anniversary of Elvis's death, and the religious overtones of that ceremony were as inescapably present in his heartfelt eulogy as they were in those of the many others who paid homage to Elvis that day. Still, if Phillips cited Elvis's "sweet visual image" and the strength of his fandom, he also framed the persistent question of Elvis's contemporary presence and popularity, or the persistent presence and popularity of his image, within the realm of faith.

Mystery and wonder—the impossibility of ever knowing with fixed certainty what Elvis really means, the willingness to accept that, and the anticipation that this sort of pleasurable and also anxious uncertainty will continue—are strong currents within Elvis Culture. For more than forty years, Elvis fans have canonized his celebrity. If many of them worry about Elvis Inc.'s increasingly overbearing interpretive role in Elvis Culture, and resent the ways his estate aims to mediate their personal relationships with him, they continue to hold to an understanding of Elvis's ineffable complexity, his transcendent and mysterious significance. Indeed, I began this project in an epiphanic moment that left me wondering and leaves me believing that Elvis's meaning, and that of Elvis Culture, remains essentially enigmatic. Generally, this has not been an acceptable position to take: most of the radio, print, and television reporters I've talked with over the past few years, as well as various publishers, editors, and agents, have asked for a quick sound bite, an easy one-sentence answer to the seemingly straightforward question "Why Elvis?"

Hopefully, this book has enriched the query to point out the intellectual fallacy of the expectation that there *are* any simple sound bites about Elvis Culture, or easy assumptions to be made about his fans, his postmortem popularity, or popular culture in general. Hopefully, too, assertions of the abiding mystery of Elvis's meaning are not seen as anti-intellectual or ahistorical disclaimers or as glib ways to shrug off the complex understandings that his image and his fandom really demand. Rather than simply or completely reconciling the cultural significance of Elvis's multivalent image, this book has offered ways to think about how popular images are made meaningful in contemporary America.

Elvis Culture's continuity will have a lot to do with the emotive, pleasurable, personal, inexplicable, and transcendent meanings that Elvis's multifaceted image has inspired for the past forty years—the "love, understanding, and fun" that Sam Phillips described. Elvis Inc. may want to dismiss the faith and devotion of fans like Margaret Martinez, but fandom has been central to the popularity and sustenance that Elvis has enjoyed since the mid-1950s. Elvis, after all, is an American emblem, and debates and conflicts over who Elvis is and what he means are comparable to the debates and conflicts over what America is and what America means. If an "official" image of Elvis comes to dominate, one that translates exclusively in terms of dollars and profit, Elvis will just wind up joining all the other hollow American icons, from George Washington to JFK, who once satisfied our national craving for identity and definition. But if Elvis remains elastic, so that fans and others can continue to look at him and talk about him and remake him in terms of the history, complexity, mystery, pleasure, and pain that his image, and America's, demands, then Elvis may well survive into the twenty-first century as America's premiere icon.

NOTES

IMAGES OF ELVIS

1. Quoted in Julie Baumgold, "Midnight in the Garden of Good and Elvis," *Esquire*, March 1995, 99.
2. Eric Lott, *Love and Theft: Blackface Minstrelsy and the American Working Class* (New York: Oxford University Press, 1993), 92.
3. For information on Presley's television appearances, growing popularity, and critical reactions, see Patricia Jobe Pierce, *The Ultimate Elvis* (New York: Simon and Schuster, 1994), 104–33, and Peter Guralnick, *Last Train to Memphis: The Rise of Elvis Presley* (Boston: Little, Brown, 1994), passim.
4. "Presley Termed a Passing Fancy," *New York Times*, 17 December 1956, 28; Gould and Gross quoted in Guralnick, *Last Train to Memphis*, 285; Spellman quoted in "Spellman in Plea to Save U.S. Youth," *New York Times*, 1 October 1956, 10. On Elvis and television, see Karal Ann Marling, "When Elvis Cut His Hair: The Meaning of Mobility," in *As Seen on TV: The Visual Culture of Everyday Life in the 1950s* (Cambridge, Mass.: Harvard University Press, 1994), 164–201.
5. The best writing on Elvis's music is Greil Marcus, "Elvis: Presliad," in *Mystery Train: Images of America in Rock'n'Roll Music*, 3rd ed. (New York: Dutton, 1990), 120–75, 233–53.
6. Antonin Artaud, *The Theater and Its Double*, trans. Mary Caroline Richards (New York: Grove Press, 1958), 61.
7. "Face is Familiar," *Look*, 11 December 1956, 130; "Elvis—A Different Kind of Idol," *Life*, 27 August 1956, 101–9.
8. Hermann Nitsch, "The O.M. Theatre" (1962), in *Orgien Mysterien Theatre/ Orgies Mysteries Theater* (Darmstadt: Marz Verlag, 1969), 35–40, in *Theories and Documents of Contemporary Art*, ed. Kristine Stiles and Peter Selz (Berkeley: University of California Press, 1996), 747–50.
9. Michael Ventura, "Hear That Long Snake Moan," in *Shadow Dancing in the U.S.A.* (Los Angeles: Tarcher, 1985), 152; "Letters to the Editor," *Life*, 21 May 1956, 13.
10. Simon Frith, *Performing Rites: On the Value of Popular Music* (Cambridge, Mass.: Harvard University Press, 1996), 206; Greil Marcus, *The Dustbin of History* (Cambridge, Mass.: Harvard University Press, 1995), 140.
11. Unless otherwise noted, all quotes from fans, named or unnamed, stem from interviews with the author, conducted from 1993 through 1998, or from written surveys of Elvis fans collected during 1996.

12. Ventura, "Hear That Long Snake Moan," 153.

13. Julia Aparin, "He Never Got Above His Raising: An Ethnographic Study of a Working Class Response to Elvis Presley" (Ph.D. diss., University of Pennsylvania, 1988), 132; Guralnick, *Last Train to Memphis*, 443–45.

14. Lennon quoted in Sandra Choron and Bob Oskam, *Elvis! The Last Word* (New York: Citadel Press, 1991), 33; Gardner quoted in Guralnick, *Last Train to Memphis*, 464.

15. Cindy Hazen and Mike Freeman, *The Best of Elvis: Recollections of a Great Humanitarian* (Memphis: Memphis Explorations, 1992), xvii.

16. Quoted in Patricia Bunin, "Elvis Fans Still Love Him True," *Thomson News Group* (Pasadena), 7 January 1996, D5.

17. George Lipsitz, *Time Passages: Collective Memory and American Popular Culture* (Minneapolis: University of Minnesota Press, 1990), xiv; Kevin Quain, ed. *The Elvis Reader: Texts and Sources on the King of Rock'n'Roll* (New York: St. Martin's Press, 1992), 255.

18. Shirley Downing, "Notice to Offended Fans: Elvis Has Left the Gallery," *Commercial Appeal* (Memphis), 11 August 1997, A-1, 8; Fredric Koeppel, "Some Might Like to See What a Few Would Ban for 'Bad Taste,'" *Commercial Appeal*, 16 August 1997, C-3.

19. See David Morgan, ed., *Icons of American Protestantism: The Art of Warner Sallman, 1892–1968* (New Haven, Conn.: Yale University Press, 1996).

20. Neil Evernden, *The Natural Alien: Human Kind and the Environment*, 2nd ed. (Toronto: University of Toronto Press, 1993), 70–71.

21. Adam Sweeting, "Elvis Is Gone: But Will He Ever Really Die?" *Calgary Herald*, 16 August 1992, C5.

22. Janice Radway, "The Hegemony of 'Specificity' and the Impasse in Audience Research: Cultural Studies and the Problems of Ethnography," in *The Audience and Its Landscape*, ed. James Hay, Lawrence Grossberg, and Ellen Wartela (Boulder, Colo.: Westview Press, 1996), 235–45; Meaghan Morris, "Banality in Cultural Studies," *Block* 14 (1988): 15–26.

23. Joshua Gamson, *Claims to Fame: Celebrity in Contemporary America* (Berkeley: University of California Press, 1994), 6.

24. Theodor Adorno and Max Horkheimer, "The Culture Industry: Enlightenment as Mass Deception," in *Dialectic of Enlightenment* (1944; London: Verso, 1995), 120–67.

25. Jean Baudrillard, "The Precession of Simulacra," in *Simulations*, trans. Paul Foss, Paul Patton, and Philip Beitchman (New York: Columbia University Press, 1983), 4.

26. Michael Parenti, *Make-Believe Media: The Politics of Entertainment* (New York: St. Martin's Press, 1992), 12, 213.

27. Janice Radway, *Reading the Romance: Women, Patriarchy, and Popular Literature* (Chapel Hill: University of North Carolina Press, 1984), 16–17; Stuart Hall, "Culture, the Media, and the 'Ideological Effect,'" in *Mass Communication and Society*, ed. James Curran, Michael Gurevitch, and Janet Woolacott (Beverly Hills, Calif.: Sage, 1977), 315–49; John Fiske, *Television Culture*

(London: Routledge, 1987); Michael Schudson, "Delectable Materialism: Were the Critics of Consumer Culture Wrong All Along?" *American Prospect* 1 (1991): 26–35.

28. Wendy Steiner, *The Scandal of Pleasure: Art in an Age of Fundamentalism* (Chicago: University of Chicago Press, 1995), 156.

29. Guralnick, *Last Train to Memphis*, xiii; Greil Marcus, *Dead Elvis: A Chronicle of a Cultural Obsession* (New York: Doubleday, 1991), xx.

PAYING HOMAGE TO ELVIS

1. For the GracelandToo homepage, see http://oscar.teclink.net/~elvisgto/.

2. Elvis Aaron Presley MacLeod, "Walk a Mile in My Shoes" (Talk given at the University of Mississippi International Conference on Elvis Presley, 6–11 August 1995).

3. Scott Morris, "24 Hour Elvis," *Oxford American* 4 (1993–94): 34–41.

4. Paul M. Hirsch, "Processing Fads and Fashions: An Organization-Set Analysis of Cultural Industry Systems," in *On Record: Rock, Pop, and the Written Word*, ed. Simon Frith and Andrew Goodwin (New York: Pantheon, 1990), 129.

5. Mihaly Csikszentmihalyi, "Why We Need Things," in *History from Things: Essays on Material Culture*, ed. Steven Lubar and W. David Kingery (Washington, D.C.: Smithsonian Institution Press, 1993), 23; for an expanded discussion of the sociology of material culture, see Arjun Appadurai, ed., *The Social Life of Things: Commodities in Cultural Perspective* (Cambridge: Cambridge University Press, 1986); Mihaly Csikszentmihalyi and Eugene Rochberg-Halton, *The Meaning of Things: Domestic Symbols and the Self* (Cambridge: Cambridge University Press, 1981); Mary Douglas and Baron Isherwood, *The World of Goods* (New York: Basic Books, 1979); Grant McCracken, *Culture and Consumption: New Approaches to the Symbolic Character of Consumer Goods and Activities* (Bloomington: Indiana University Press, 1990); Daniel Miller, *Material Culture and Mass Consumption* (Oxford: Blackwell, 1987); and Susan Stewart, *On Longing: Narratives of the Miniature, the Gigantic, the Souvenir, the Collection* (Baltimore: Johns Hopkins University Press, 1984).

6. "Presley Spells Profit," *Newsweek*, 18 February 1957, 84, 86; statistics on postwar teens from Ed Ward, Geoffrey Stokes, and Ken Tucker, *Rock of Ages: The Rolling Stone History of Rock and Roll* (New York: Rolling Stone Press, 1986), 123.

7. Chester Morrison, "The Great Elvis Presley Industry," *Look*, 13 November 1956, 99–107; Louis M. Kohlmeier, "Heartbreak, Hound Dogs Put Sales Zip Into Presley Products," *Wall Street Journal*, 31 December 1956, 1, 8; "Presley Spells Profit," 86.

8. Howard A. DeWitt, *Elvis, the Sun Years: The Story of Elvis Presley in the Fifties* (Ann Arbor, Mich.: Popular Culture, Ink., 1993), 181, 188; Bob Masters, "Frenzied Elvis Fans Rock Youth Center," *Shreveport Times*, 16 December 1956, in *Elvis Album*, ed. Bill DeNight, Sharon Fox, and Ger Rijff (Lincoln-

wood, Ill.: Publications International, 1991), 74; William Steif, "Elvis Sings: 80 Cops Shield Him from Throng," *San Francisco News*, 16 October 1956, 1, 8. Quote about fan reactions from Morrison, "Great Elvis Presley Industry," 100.

9. Rosalind Cranor, *Elvis Collectibles* (Johnson City, Tenn.: Overmountain Press, 1987), 260; Steve Templeton and Rosalind Cranor, *The Best of Elvis Collectibles* (Johnson City, Tenn.: Overmountain Press, 1992), 104.

10. Quoted in "Presley Spells Profit," 86.

11. Loosely based on Williams's play *Battle of Angels* (1940), *Orpheus Descending* was substantially reworked to reflect contemporary concerns; see Tennessee Williams, "The Past, the Present, and the Perhaps," in *Orpheus Descending with Battle of Angels, Two Plays by Tennessee Williams* (New York: New Directions, 1958). *Orpheus Descending* was filmed as *The Fugitive Kind*, starring Marlon Brando, in 1959.

12. Schulberg's screenplay stemmed in part from his short story "Your Arkansas Traveler" (1953); see Budd Schulberg, *A Face in the Crowd, a Play for the Screen*, with an Introduction by Elia Kazan (New York: Random House, 1957), xvi–xvii, 127, 135, 144, and passim. On Griffith and Elvis, see Peter Guralnick, *Last Train to Memphis: The Rise of Elvis Presley* (Boston: Little, Brown, 1994), 206, 295.

13. Los Angeles critic quoted in Guralnick, *Last Train to Memphis*, 438; "idol worship" noted in "Elvis Worship," a UP article, date and publication unknown, in *Elvis Album*, ed. DeNight, Fox, and Rijff, 79.

14. "Elvis Worship," and "Elvis Fans Shape Up as 'Rebels' Who Can't Face Adult World," dates and publication unknown, in *Elvis Album*, ed. DeNight, Fox, and Rijff, 78–79.

15. Sinatra made these remarks in October 1957 and is quoted in Linda Martin and Kerry Segrave, *Anti-Rock: The Opposition to Rock 'n' Roll* (Hamden, Conn.: Shoe String Press, 1988), 46–47.

16. Rickie Solinger, *Wake Up Little Susie: Single Pregnancy and Race Before Roe v. Wade* (New York: Routledge, 1992), 13; Morrison, "Great Elvis Presley Industry," 102; "Elvis—A Different Kind of Idol," *Life*, 27 August 1956, 102–3.

17. Tom Corboy, director and producer, *Mondo Elvis: The Real-Life Rites and Rituals of The King's Most Devoted Fans*, 1984, distributed by Rhino Videos.

18. Howard Cosell, *Cosell* (Chicago: Playboy Press, 1973), 375. Despite their supremacy in America, sports fans remain relatively unanalyzed. For two very different approaches, see Rogan Taylor, *Football and Its Fans: Supporters and Their Relations with the Games, 1885–1985* (Leicester: Leicester University Press, 1992), which concentrates on English football fans, and Allen Guttmann, *Sports Spectators* (New York: Columbia University Press, 1986). See also George Vecsey, "Fans," in *Sport Inside Out*, ed. Daniel L. Vanderwerken and Stephen K. Wertz (Fort Worth: Texas Christian University Press, 1985), 122–31.

19. Joli Jenson, "Fandom as Pathology," in *The Adoring Audience: Fan Culture and Popular Media*, ed. Lisa A. Lewis (New York: Routledge, 1992), 9–29.

20. See, for example, Fred and Judy Vermorel, *Starlust: The Secret Fantasies of*

Fans (London: Allen, 1985), and *Fandemonium* (London: Omnibus Press, 1990); Sandy Troy, *One More Saturday Night: Reflections with the Grateful Dead, Dead Family, and Dead Heads* (New York: St. Martin's Press, 1991); and Rock Scully, *Living with the Dead: Twenty Years on the Bus with Garcia and the Grateful Dead* (Boston: Little, Brown, 1996). The best critical accounts on fandom are Lewis, ed., *Adoring Audience*, and Henry Jenkins, *Textual Poachers: Television Fans and Participatory Culture* (New York: Routledge, 1992). Interestingly, recent musicologists have produced some of the most compelling analyses of fans and fandom; see Susan D. Crafts, Daniel Cavicchi, Charles Keil, and the Music in Daily Life Project, *My Music* (Hanover, N.H.: Wesleyan University Press, 1993), and Robert Walser, *Running with the Devil: Power, Gender, and Madness in Heavy Metal Music* (Hanover, N.H.: Wesleyan University Press, 1993). For two studies of Elvis fans, see Julia Aparin, "He Never Got Above His Raising: An Ethnographic Study of a Working Class Response to Elvis Presley" (Ph.D. diss., University of Pennsylvania, 1988), and Adrienne Lynn Young, "Taking Care of Business: Elvis Fans and Moral Community" (Master's thesis, George Washington University, 1994).

21. Lawrence Grossberg, "Is There a Fan in the House? The Affective Sensibility of Fandom," in *Adoring Audience*, ed. Lewis, 50–65.

22. Quoted in Gordon Sinclair, "Sinclair Says Elvis 'Fine Lad,' Hopes to Last for 40 Years," *Toronto Star*, 29 October 1956, as noted in Ger Rijff, *Long Lonely Highway: A 1950s Elvis Scrapbook* (Ann Arbor, Mich.: Pierian Press, 1987), 110, and Guralnick, *Last Train to Memphis*, 488.

23. Greil Marcus, *Dead Elvis: A Chronicle of a Cultural Obsession* (New York: Doubleday, 1991), 179, 195.

24. Quoted in Laura Coleman, "Elvis Museum Honors Friend," *Commercial Appeal* (Memphis), 7 August 1992, A1–2.

25. Patrick Pacheco, "Fan Clubs—From Engelbert to Mr. Ed," *New York Times*, 4 November 1990, sec. 2, p. 1.

26. Statistics in "Where Elvis Lives," *American Demographics*, August 1993, 64. It should be noted that this survey is based less on data obtained from Elvis fans than that obtained from people who purchased items at Graceland's gift stores and filled out survey forms. For the 1993 survey at Graceland, see Young, "Taking Care of Business," 122–73.

27. Ed Will, "Long Live the Kings!" *Denver Post Magazine*, 1 August 1993, 10–13.

28. Quoted in Cindy Hazen and Mike Freeman, *The Best of Elvis: Recollections of a Great Humanitarian* (Memphis: Memphis Explorations, 1992), 176.

29. Albert Goldman, *Elvis* (New York: McGraw-Hill, 1981); for a blistering review, see Greil Marcus, "The Myth Behind the Truth Behind the Legend," *Voice Literary Supplement*, December 1981, reprinted in Marcus, *Dead Elvis*, 47–59; Whobrey quoted in Pacheco, "Fan Clubs," 1.

30. Anne Firor Scott, *Natural Allies: Women's Associations in American History* (Urbana: University of Illinois Press, 1992), 141–58 and passim.

31. Karal Ann Marling, "Elvis Presley's Graceland, or the Aesthetics of Rock 'n' Roll," *American Art* 7 (1993): 72–105, and *Graceland: Going Home with Elvis* (Cambridge, Mass.: Harvard University Press, 1996), 180–83 and passim.

32. Quoted in Christine Arpe Gang, "Elvisiana Excites the Trade Market," *Commercial Appeal*, 11 August 1997, C-1, 3.

33. Marling, *Graceland*, 69, 111–14; on Elvis and Nixon, see Egil "Bud" Krogh, *The Day Elvis Met Nixon* (Bellevue, Wash.: Pejama Press, 1994).

34. Quoted in Ted Harrison, *Elvis People: The Cult of the King* (New York: HarperCollins, 1992), 160.

35. Jean Norman, "Reg's Elvis Collection," *Australian Penthouse*, June 1996, 91.

36. For a gendered reading of record collecting, see Will Straw, "Sizing Up Record Collections: Gender and Connoisseurship in Rock Music Culture," in *Sexing the Groove: Popular Music and Gender*, ed. Sheila Whiteley (London: Routledge, 1997), 3–16; for two different accounts of art collecting and issues of class, see Stuart Plattner, *High Art Down Home: An Economic Ethnography of a Local Art Market* (Chicago: University of Chicago Press, 1996), esp. chap. 6, and A. Deirdre Robson, *Prestige, Profit, and Pleasure: The Market for Modern Art in New York in the 1940s and 1950s* (New York: Garland, 1995), 135–215.

37. Michel de Certeau, *The Practice of Everyday Life*, trans. Steven Randall (Berkeley: University of California Press, 1984), xiii–xiv, xvii.

38. Walter Benjamin, "The Work of Art in the Age of Mechanical Reproduction," in *Illuminations*, trans. Harry Zohn (New York: Schocken, 1968), 217–51.

39. Jean Baudrillard, "The System of Collecting," in *The Cultures of Collecting*, ed. John Elsner and Roger Cardinal (Melbourne: Melbourne University Press, 1994), 23.

40. For a similar account of how this works with "fans" of Vincent van Gogh, see Nathalie Heinich, *The Glory of Van Gogh: An Anthropology of Admiration*, trans. Paul Leduc Browne (Princeton, N.J.: Princeton University Press, 1996), 137–39. See also David Cheal, *The Gift Economy* (London: Routledge, 1988), Louis Hyde, *Imagination and the Erotic Life of Property* (New York: Random House, 1983), and Annette B. Weiner, *Indelible Possessions: The Paradox of Keeping-While-Giving* (Berkeley: University of California Press, 1993).

SAINT ELVIS

Portions of this chapter were originally published in "Elvis in the Public Sphere: Fans, Faith, and Cultural Production in Contemporary America," *Odense American Studies International Series*, Working Paper 24 (October 1996): 1–24.

1. Quoted in Ted Harrison, *Elvis People: The Cult of the King* (New York: HarperCollins, 1992), 53, 68.

2. A. J. Jacobs, *The Two Kings* (New York: Bantam, 1994); Louie Ludwig, *The Gospel of Elvis* (New Orleans: Summit, 1996).

3. Harrison, *Elvis People*, 9; Ron Rosenbaum, "Among the Believers," *New York Times Magazine*, 24 September 1995, 50–57, 62, 64; John Windsor, "Faith and the State of Graceland Enterprises," *Independent* (London), 15 August 1992, 33. See also Lucinda Ebersole, "The God and Goddess of the Written Word," and Gary Vikan, "Graceland as *Locus Santos*," in *Elvis + Marilyn 2 × Immor-*

tal, ed. Geri DePaoli (New York: Rizzoli, 1994), 136–45, 150–66; John H. Lardas, "Graceland: An Analysis of Sacred Space on the American Religious Landscape" (Paper presented at the annual meeting of the American Academy of Religion, 1995); Sue Bridwell Beckham, "Death, Resurrection and Transfiguration: The Religious Folklore in Elvis Presley Shrines and Souvenirs," *International Folklore Review* 5 (1987): 88–95; John Fiske, *Power Plays Power Works* (New York: Verso, 1993), 181–205; and Peter Stromberg, "Elvis Alive? The Ideology of American Consumerism," *Journal of Popular Culture* 24 (1990): 11–19.

4. James Wall raised these points at the conference "The Expression of American Religion in the Popular Media," held in Indianapolis in April 1993. See also Stewart M. Hoover, *Mass Media Religion: The Social Sources of the Electronic Church* (Newbury Park, Calif.: Sage, 1988), and Stewart M. Hoover and Knut Lundby, eds., *Rethinking Media, Religion, and Culture* (Thousand Oaks, Calif.: Sage, 1997).

5. Rosenbaum, "Among the Believers," 51; the fans pictured are Diane and Bert MacArthur of Little Rock, Arkansas. For a discussion of media assumptions of fan deviance, see Joli Jenson, "Fandom as Pathology: The Consequences of Characterization," in *The Adoring Audience: Fan Culture and Popular Media*, ed. Lisa A. Lewis (London: Routledge, 1992), 9–29.

6. Nathan O. Hatch, *The Democratization of American Christianity* (New Haven, Conn.: Yale University Press, 1989), 210.

7. Robert N. Bellah, Richard Madsen, William M. Sullivan, Ann Swidler, and Steven M. Tipton, *Habits of the Heart: Individualism and Commitment in American Life* (Berkeley: University of California Press, 1985), 220–21 and passim; Hatch, *Democratization of American Christianity*, 212, 218; Wade Clark Roof, *A Generation of Seekers: The Spiritual Journeys of the Baby Boom Generation* (New York: Harper & Row, 1993). Ideas of personal religious pluralism in complex industrial societies were first advanced in the works of Peter L. Berger and Thomas Luckman, see, for example, Berger, *The Sacred Canopy* (New York: Doubleday, 1967), and Luckman, *The Invisible Religion* (New York: Macmillan, 1967).

8. Edgar Morin, *The Stars*, trans. Richard Howard (New York: Grove Press, 1960), 71–108. The 1957 Elvis "church" is noted in Patricia Jobe Pierce, *The Ultimate Elvis: Elvis Presley Day by Day* (New York: Simon and Schuster, 1994), 136.

9. Colleen McDannell, *The Christian Home in Victorian America, 1840–1900* (Bloomington: Indiana University Press, 1986), and *Material Christianity: Religion and Popular Culture in America* (New Haven, Conn.: Yale University Press, 1995); David Morgan, ed., *Icons of American Protestantism: The Art of Warner Sallman, 1892–1968* (New Haven, Conn.: Yale University Press, 1996), and *Visual Piety: A History and Theory of Popular Religious Images* (Berkeley: University of California Press, 1998). See also David Halle's analysis of religious iconography in contemporary Catholic homes in *Inside Culture: Art and Class in the American Home* (Chicago: University of Chicago Press, 1993), 171–92.

10. McDannell, *Material Christianity*, 275; Celeste Olalquiaga, *Megalopolis: Contemporary Cultural Sensibilities* (Minneapolis: University of Minnesota Press, 1992), 38–39; Tomás Ybarra-Frausto, "Rasquachismo: A Chicano Sensibility," in *Rasquachismo: Chicano Aesthetics* (Phoenix: Movimiento Artístico del Río Salado, 1988), passim, and "The Chicano Movement/The Movement of Chicano Art," in *Exhibiting Cultures: The Poetics and Politics of Museum Display*, ed. Ivan Karp and Steven D. Lavine (Washington, D.C.: Smithsonian Institution Press, 1991), 132–34.

11. Laura Kalpakian, *Graced Land* (New York: Grove Weidenfeld, 1992), 16.

12. See, for example, Kay Turner, "Mexican-American Women's Home Altars: The Art of Relationship" (Ph.D. diss., University of Texas, 1990), and "Home Altars & the Art of Devotion," in *Chicano Expressions: A New View in American Art*, ed. Inverna Lockpez (New York: Intar Latin American Gallery, 1986), 40–48.

13. See, for example, John Fiske, "Cultural Studies and the Culture of Everyday Life," in *Cultural Studies*, ed. Lawrence Grossberg, Cary Nelson, Paula A. Treichler, Linda Baughman, and John MacGregor Wise (New York: Routledge, 1992), 154–73. While elaborating on the writings of Mikhail Bakhtin and Pierre Bourdieu to show "how the culture of the people denies categorial boundaries between art and life," Fiske nevertheless reinforces assumptions of class-based materialism and taste. He comments in particular on the ethnographic studies of Brett Williams, *Upscaling Downtown: Stalled Gentrification in Washington, D.C.* (Ithaca, N.Y.: Cornell University Press, 1988), and Odina Fachel Leal, "Popular Taste and Erudite Repertoire: The Place and Space of Television in Brazil," *Cultural Studies* 4 (1990): 19–29.

14. William A. Christian, Jr., *Person and God in a Spanish Valley*, new rev. ed. (Princeton, N.J.: Princeton University Press, 1989), 101.

15. Ralph Burns, caption to photographs, in *Elvis + Marilyn*, ed. DePaoli, 167.

16. Mary Lee Nolan and Sidney Nolan, *Christian Pilgrimage in Modern Western Europe* (Chapel Hill: University of North Carolina Press, 1989), 13, 36, 291–92.

17. Karal Ann Marling, "Elvis Presley's Graceland, or the Aesthetics of Rock 'n' Roll," *American Art* 7 (1993): 72–105. See also Marling, *Graceland: Going Home with Elvis* (Cambridge, Mass.: Harvard University Press, 1996).

18. On the lack of interest in Memorial Day celebrations, see Eugene Rochberg-Halton, "Communicating Democracy: Or Shrine, Perishing Republic," in *The Socialness of Things: Essays on the Socio-Semiotics of Objects*, ed. Stephen Harold Riggins (Berlin: Mouton de Gruyter, 1994), 315–16.

19. Christian, *Person and God*, 46, 85; Nathalie Heinich, *The Glory of Van Gogh: An Anthropology of Admiration*, trans. Paul Leduc Browne (Princeton, N.J.: Princeton University Press, 1996), 132. On *communitas*, see Victor Turner and Edith Turner, *Image and Pilgrimage in Christian Culture: Anthropological Perspectives* (New York: Columbia University Press, 1978), 20, and Vikan, "Graceland as *Locus Sanctus*," 159.

20. Stephen Wilson, "Introduction," in *Saints and Their Cults: Studies in Re-

ligious Sociology, Folklore and History, ed. Stephen Wilson (Cambridge: Cambridge University Press, 1983), 14.

21. Robert Orsi, "The Center out There, in Here, and Everywhere Else: The Nature of Pilgrimage to the Shrine of Saint Jude, 1929–1965," *Journal of Social History* 25 (1991): 222.

22. Quoted in Patsy Guy Hammontree, *Elvis Presley: A Bio-Bibliography* (Westport, Conn.: Greenwood Press, 1985), 126.

23. Poem noted in Van K. Brock, "Images of Elvis, the South, and America," in *Elvis: Images and Fancies*, ed. Jac L. Tharpe (Jackson: University Press of Mississippi, 1979), 118. See also Christine King, "His Truth Goes Marching On: Elvis Presley and the Pilgrimage to Graceland," in *Pilgrimage in Popular Culture*, ed. Ian Reader and Tony Walter (New York: Macmillan, 1992), 103. On votive offerings, see Wilson, "Introduction," 21.

24. Nolan and Nolan, *Christian Pilgrimage*, 67; Heinich, *Glory of Van Gogh*, 136.

25. The website for the First Presleyterian Church of Elvis the Divine is ⟨http://chelsea.ios.com/~hkarlin1.welcome.html⟩. On the revival at Lehigh University, which was organized by Norman J. Girardot for his course "Jesus, Buddha, Confucius, and Elvis," see Girardot, "But Seriously: Taking the Elvis Phenomenon Seriously," *Religious Studies News*, November 1996, 11–12. On Kapor, see Eugene Taylor, "Desperately Seeking Spirituality," *Psychology Today*, November–December 1994, 54–62, 64, 66, 68.

26. Girardot, "What Really Happened in Bethlehem? The Religious Power and Apocalyptic Pathos of the Religious Phenomenon" (Paper presented at the Third Annual Conference on Elvis Presley, Memphis, 15 August 1997). On similar forms of derision, see Heinich, *Glory of Van Gogh*, 129–30, and Olalquiaga, *Megalopolis*, 45–46. See also Greil Marcus, *Dead Elvis: A Chronicle of a Cultural Obsession* (New York: Doubleday, 1991), 74–85.

27. R. Laurence Moore, *Selling God: American Religion in the Marketplace of Culture* (New York: Oxford University Press, 1994), 256.

28. Elvis quoted in William Steif, "What Makes Elvis Presley Tick No. 3, the Pelvis Explains That 'Vulgar' Style," *San Francisco News*, 17 October 1956, 3.

29. Larry Geller and Joel Spector, with Patricia Romanowski, *"If I Can Dream": Elvis' Own Story* (New York: Simon and Schuster, 1989), 137–40, 187.

30. Maia C. M. Shamayyim, "Elvis and His Angelic Connection," *Angel Times* 1. (1995): 20–25, excerpted from *Magii from the Blue Star: The Spiritual Drama and Mystical Heritage of Elvis Aaron Presley* (Creston, Colo.: Johannine Grove, 1989). See also Raymond Moody, Jr., *Elvis After Life: Unusual Psychic Experiences Surrounding the Death of a Superstar* (Atlanta: Peachtree, 1987); Jack D. Mallay and Warren Vaughn, *Elvis: The Messiah?* (Mount Horeb, Wisc.: TCB, 1992); and Isabelle Tanner, *Elvis—A Guide to My Soul* (Dobbs Ferry, N.Y.: Elisabelle International, 1995). Fan quoted in Adrienne Young, "Taking Care of Business: Elvis Fans and Moral Community" (Master's thesis, George Washington University, 1994), 131. See also Catherine L. Albanese's analysis of Elvis's religiosity in *America: Religions and Religion* (Belmont, Calif.: Wadsworth, 1981), 318–20.

31. Fiske, *Power Plays*, 181.
32. Stromberg, "Elvis Alive?" 11–19; David Freedberg, *The Power of Images: Studies in the History and Theory of Response* (Chicago: University of Chicago Press, 1989), 432.
33. Michel de Certeau, *The Practice of Everyday Life*, trans. Steven Randall (Berkeley: University of California Press, 1984), 187; Morgan, *Visual Piety*, 4.
34. Fan quoted in Young, "Taking Care of Business," 123.
35. On similarities between Elvis's performance style and Pentecostalism, see Brock, "Images of Elvis," 101–7, and Albanese, *America*, 319.
36. On women and affectionate religion in the nineteenth century, see Ann Douglas, *The Feminization of American Culture* (New York: Knopf, 1977).
37. Fans quoted in Robert Hanks, "Radio: King Pawns," *Independent* (London), 7 July 1992, 16, and Young, "Taking Care of Business," 127.
38. Wilson, "Introduction," 6–7.
39. Mark Gottdiener, "Dead Elvis as Other Jesus," in *In Search of Elvis: Music, Race, Art, Religion*, ed. Vernon Chadwick (Boulder, Colo.: Westview Press, 1997), 189–200; Rosenbaum, "Among the Believers," 62, 64.
40. Rosenbaum, "Among the Believers," 52.

SEXING ELVIS

Portions of this chapter were originally published in "The Power of Elvis," *American Art* 11 (1997): 4–7.
1. Joni Mabe, "Introduction," in *Everything Elvis* (New York: Thunder's Mouth Press, 1996), 8. Unless otherwise noted, all quotes and comments from Mabe come from interviews with the author, November 1996. The title of this chapter is the same as Sue Wise, "Sexing Elvis," in *Women Studies International Forum* 7 (1984): 13–17, reprinted in *On Record: Rock, Pop, and the Written Word*, ed. Simon Frith and Andrew Goodwin (New York: Pantheon, 1990), 390–98.
2. Quoted in Lori Rozsa, "At Elvis U., the King Lives," *Miami Herald*, 13 August 1995, 10A.
3. W. P. Kinsella, "Elvis Bound," in *Elvis Rising: Stories on the King*, ed. Kay Sloan and Constance Pierce (New York: Avon, 1993), 82–95.
4. Janice Radway, *Reading the Romance: Women, Patriarchy, and Popular Literature* (Chapel Hill: University of North Carolina Press, 1984), 93; Tania Modleski, *Loving with a Vengeance: Mass Produced Fantasies for Women* (New York: Methuen, 1982), 113.
5. Adam Parfrey, "The Girlfriend Who Last Saw Elvis Alive Fan Club" and Debby Wimer, "Spanish Eyes," in *Cult Rapture*, ed. Adam Parfrey (Portland, Ore.: Feral House, 1995), 63–90; Lucy de Barbin and Dary Matera, *Are You Lonesome Tonight? The Untold Story of Elvis Presley's One True Love and the Child He Never Knew* (New York: Villard Books, 1987), xx, 39–41, and passim. On other types of female fan erotica, see Constance Penley, "Brownian Motion: Women, Tactics, and Technology," in *Technoculture*, ed. Penley Ross

and Andrew Ross (Minneapolis: University of Minnesota Press, 1991), 135–61, and Henry Jenkins, *Television Poachers: Television Fans and Participatory Culture* (New York: Routledge, 1992), 185–222.

6. On Janis Martin, see Ed Bayes, liner notes on the Bear Family, *The Female Elvis: Complete Recordings, 1956–60* (Rounder), and David Sanjek, "Can a Fujiyama Mama Be the Female Elvis? The Wild Wild Women of Rockabilly," in *Sexing the Groove: Popular Music and Gender*, ed. Sheila Whiteley (London: Routledge, 1997), 137–67. Madonna quoted in Leslie Bennetts, "k.d. lang Cuts It Close," *Vanity Fair*, August 1993, 94–98, 142–46. Susie Bright and Jill Posener, *Nothing But the Girl: The Blatant Lesbian Image, a Portfolio and Exploration of Lesbian Erotic Photography* (New York: Freedom Editions, 1996). On lang, see Victoria Starr, *k.d. lang: All You Get Is Me* (New York: St. Martin's Press, 1994).

7. Bangs quoted in Gregory Sandow, "Elvis Presley, Rhythm and Ooze," *Village Voice*, 18 August 1987, 71; Lester Bangs, "Where Were You When Elvis Died?" in *Psychotic Reactions and Carburetor Dung* (New York: Knopf, 1987), 212–16; George Melly, *Revolt into Style: The Pop Arts* (New York: Anchor, 1971), 34–35; Dave Marsh, *Elvis* (New York: Thunder's Mouth Press, 1982), 55. See also David R. Shumway, "Watching Elvis: The Male Rock Star as Object of the Gaze," in *The Other Fifties: Interrogating Midcentury American Icons*, ed. Joel Foreman (Champaign: University of Illinois Press, 1997): 124–43.

8. On "cock-rock," see Simon Frith and Angela McRobbie, "Rock and Sexuality," in *On Record*, ed. Frith and Goodwin, 371–89.

9. Linda Ray Pratt, "Elvis, or the Ironies of a Southern Identity," in *Elvis: Images and Fancies*, ed. Jac L. Tharpe (Jackson: University of Mississippi Press, 1979), 48–49.

10. On theories of gender transgression, see, for example, Teresa de Lauretis, *Technologies of Gender: Essays on Theory, Film, and Fiction* (Bloomington: Indiana University Press, 1987), 26; on "sexual mobility," see Miriam Hansen, "Pleasure, Ambivalence, Identification: Valentino and Female Spectatorship," *Cinema Journal* 25 (1986): 6–32.

11. Curtis W. Ellison, *Country Music Culture: From Hard Times to Heaven* (Jackson: University of Mississippi Press, 1995), 77. On Elvis's sexual affairs, see, for example, Patsy Guy Hammontree, *Elvis Presley: A Bio-Bibliography* (Westport, Conn.: Greenwood Press, 1985), 57, 78–79, and Peter Guralnick, *Last Train to Memphis: The Rise of Elvis Presley* (Boston: Little, Brown, 1994), 184, passim.

12. "Farewell to Priscilla, Hello USA," *Life*, 14 March 1960, 97–98.

13. Hanson, "Pleasure, Ambivalence, Identification," and *Babel and Babylon: Spectatorship in American Silent Film* (Cambridge, Mass.: Harvard University Press, 1991).

14. Moore and Atkins quoted in Howard A. Dewitt, *Elvis, the Sun Years: The Story of Elvis Presley in the Fifties* (Ann Arbor, Mich.: Popular Culture, Ink., 1993), 145, 160.

15. "Crazy Golden Slippers: Famous People Inspire Fanciful Footwear," *Life*, 21 January 1957, 12–13.

16. Lloyd Shearer, "I Remember Elvis," *Parade*, 29 January 1978, 4–9.
17. Elaine Tyler May, *Homeward Bound: American Families in the Cold War Era* (New York: Basic Books, 1988), 110–13; on *Playboy*, see Barbara Ehrenreich, *The Hearts of Men: American Dreams and the Flight from Commitment* (New York: Anchor, 1983), 43–47; on postwar attacks on homosexuality, see John D'Emilio, "The Homosexual Menace: The Politics of Sexuality in Cold War America," in *Making Trouble: Essays on Gay History, Politics, and the University* (New York: Routledge, 1992), 57–73.
18. "Teeners' Hero," *Time*, 14 May 1956, 53; Tony Zoppie, "Presley Thrills Crowd of 26,500," *Dallas Morning News*, 12 October 1956, as noted in Ger Rijff, *Long Lonely Highway: A 1950s Elvis Scrapbook* (Ann Arbor, Mich.: Pierian Press, 1987), 104; *Los Angeles Mirror News* quoted in Guralnick, *Last Train to Memphis*, 438. See also Linda Martin and Kerry Segrave, *Anti-Rock: The Opposition to Rock'n'Roll* (Hamden, Conn.: Archon, 1988), esp. 59–68.
19. Ferdinand Lundberg and Marynia F. Farnham, *Modern Woman: The Lost Sex* (New York: Grosset and Dunlap, 1947).
20. Amy Taubin, "My Elvis," *Village Voice*, 11 August 1987, 43.
21. Alfred C. Kinsey, *Sexual Behavior in the Human Male* (Philadelphia: Saunders, 1948); Kinsey, *Sexual Behavior in the Human Female* (Philadelphia: Saunders, 1953).
22. "Teeners' Hero," 53; "Letters to the Editors," *Life*, 21 May 1956, 14.
23. "Elvis—A Different Kind of Idol," *Life*, 27 August 1956, 101–9.
24. "Ain't Nothin' but a Hairdo," *Life*, 25 March 1957, 55–57; "Am I the Girl for Elvis?" *Movie Teen Illustrated*, March 1958, in *Elvis Album*, ed. Bill DeNight, Sharon Fox, and Ger Rijff (Lincolnwood, Ill.: Publications International, 1991), 111.
25. Wini Breines, *Young, White, and Miserable: Growing up Female in the Fifties* (Boston: Beacon Press, 1992), 158; Sanjek, "Can a Fujiyama Mama Be the Female Elvis?" 137–67. See also John Fiske, *Power Plays Power Works* (New York: Verso, 1993), 101–3.
26. Susan McClary, "Same as It Ever Was: Youth Culture and Music," in *Microphone Fiends: Youth Music and Youth Culture*, ed. Andrew Ross and Tricia Rose (New York: Routledge, 1994), 29–40; Robert Walser, *Running with the Devil: Power, Gender, and Madness in Heavy Metal Music* (Hanover, N.H.: Wesleyan University Press, 1993), 48–49.
27. Joanne Gottlieb and Gayle Wald, "Smells Like Teen Spirit: Riot Grrrls, Revolution and Women in Independent Rock," in *Microphone Fiends*, ed. Ross and Rose, 259; Trent Hill, "The Enemy Within: Censorship in Rock Music in the 1950s," *South Atlantic Quarterly* 90 (1991): 691. See also Jon Michael Spencer, "A Revolutionary Sexual Persona: Elvis Presley and the White Acquiescence of Black Rhythms," in *In Search of Elvis: Music, Race, Art, Religion*, ed. Vernon Chadwick (Boulder, Colo.: Westview Press, 1997), 109–20.
28. Quoted in Peter Whitmer, *The Inner Elvis: A Psychological Biography of Elvis Aaron Presley* (New York: Hyperion, 1996), 198.
29. See Laura Mulvey's discussion of the various discourses surrounding looking,

desire, and identification in *Visual and Other Pleasures* (Bloomington: University of Indiana Press, 1989), 18.

30. Quoted in Neal Gregory and Janice Gregory, *When Elvis Died* (New York: Pharos, 1980), 65.

31. Harry Medved and Randy Dreyfuss, *The Fifty Worst Films of All Time* (New York: Popular Library, 1978), 219–23.

32. James L. Neibaur, *Tough Guy: The American Movie Macho* (Jefferson, N.C.: McFarland, 1989), 190.

33. *Movie Mirror* noted in Patricia Jobe Pierce, *The Ultimate Elvis* (New York: Simon and Schuster, 1994), 173; for Elvis's mid-1960s mainstream media disappearance, see Stephen R. Tucker, "Visions of Elvis: Changing Perceptions in National Magazines, 1956–1965," in *Elvis,* ed. Tharpe, 27–39; for one analysis of tabloids, see S. Elizabeth Bird, *For Enquiring Minds: A Cultural Study of Supermarket Tabloids* (Knoxville: University of Tennessee Press, 1992).

34. Winner quoted in Greil Marcus, *Mystery Train: Images of America in Rock 'n' Roll Music,* 3rd ed. (New York: Dutton, 1990), 242; Melly, *Revolt into Style,* 34–35. For an analysis of male and female constructions of Elvis, see Wise, "Sexing Elvis," 390–98.

35. Frith and McRobbie, "Rock and Sexuality," 383; Melly, *Revolt into Style,* 37–38.

36. "The Girls of Rock," *Rolling Stone,* February 1969, passim. For an excellent rejoinder to the "girl rock fans are really just groupies" stereotype, see Cheryl Cline, "Essays from *Bitch:* The Women's Rock Newsletter with Bite," in *The Adoring Audience: Fan Culture and Popular Media,* ed. Lisa A. Lewis (New York: Routledge, 1992), 69–83.

37. Geldof quoted in *Melody Maker,* 27 August 1977, as noted in Theodore A. Gracyk, "Romanticizing Rock Music," *Journal of Aesthetic Education* 27 (1993): 45; Martin Scorcese's movie *The Last Waltz,* based on a 1976 concert by The Band, was released in 1978.

38. Sheryl Garratt, "All of Us Love All of You," in *Signed Sealed and Delivered: True Life Stories of Women in Pop,* ed. Sheryl Garratt and Sue Steward (Boston: South End Press, 1984), 144.

39. Barbara Ehrenreich, Elizabeth Hess, and Gloria Jacobs, "Beatlemania: Girls Just Want to Have Fun," in *Adoring Audience,* ed. Lewis, 84–106.

40. Frith and McRobbie, "Rock and Sexuality," 378.

41. Mabe, *Everything Elvis,* 25.

42. On fantasy, see, for example, Jean Laplanche and Jean-Bertrand Pontalis, *The Language of Psychoanalysis,* trans. David Nicholson-Smith (New York: Norton, 1973), and Victor Burgin, James Donald, and Cora Kaplan, eds., *Formations of Fantasy* (New York: Methuen, 1987). On Elvis fantasies, see Stephen Widener, "Fans, Fantasy, and the Figure of Elvis," in *Adoring Audience,* ed. Lewis, 107–34.

43. Wise, "Sexing Elvis," 393, 395.

44. Julie Hecht, "I Want You I Need You I Love You," *Harper's,* May 1978, 59–64.

45. Garratt, "All of Us Love All of You," 144.
46. Rena LaCaria, caption to painting, in *Elvis + Marilyn: 2 × Immortal*, ed. Geri DePaoli (New York: Rizzoli, 1995), 33. Her painting was seen only in the first few venues of the "Elvis + Marilyn" exhibition (which opened at the Institute of Contemporary Art, Boston, in 1994). Various images of a nude Marilyn Monroe, though, were not removed from the traveling exhibition.
47. Quoted in "Presley Show Impresses Even the Celebrities," in *Elvis Album*, ed. DeNight, Fox, and Rijff, 251.
48. Whitmer, *Inner Elvis*, 192; on Liberace, see Bob Thomas, *Liberace: The True Story* (New York: St. Martin's Press, 1987).
49. Camille Paglia, *Sexual Personae: Art and Decadence from Nefertiti to Emily Dickinson* (New York: Vintage, 1990), 115; Marjorie Garber, *Vested Interests: Cross-Dressing and Cultural Anxiety* (New York: Routledge, 1992), 363, 374.
50. Quoted in Kurt Loder, "Eurythmics: Sweet Dreams Come True," *Rolling Stone*, 29 September 1983, 22, 24, 29; Johnny Waller, *Sweet Dreams: The Definitive Biography of Eurythmics* (Wauwatosa, Wisc.: Robus, 1985), 87.
51. See *I Am Elvis: A Guide to Elvis Impersonators* (New York: Pocket Books, 1991); *The King and I: A Little Gallery of Elvis Impersonators* (San Francisco: Chronicle, 1992); and William McCranor Henderson, *I, Elvis: Confessions of a Counterfeit King* (New York: Boulevard, 1997).
52. Eric Lott, "All the King's Men: Elvis Impersonators and White Working-Class Masculinity," in *Race and the Subject of Masculinities*, ed. Harry Stecopoulos and Michael Uebel (Durham, N.C.: Duke University Press, 1997), 221.
53. Fans quoted in "Elvis Lives!" *The Gabrielle Show*, 26 November 1995, and Ed Will, "Long Live the Kings!" *Denver Post Magazine*, 1 August 1993, 10–13; Lynn Spigel, "Communicating with the Dead: Elvis as Medium," *Camera Obscura* 23 (1990): 194. See also Lynne Joyrich's analysis of the same Elvii convention, "Elvisophilia: Knowledge, Pleasure, and the Cult of Elvis," in *Differences: A Journal of Feminist Cultural Studies* 5 (1993): 73–91.

ALL-WHITE ELVIS

1. Quoted in Woody Baird, "Elvis Tribute Has a Different Mood," *Milwaukee Journal*, 15 August 1994, D-3.
2. See, for example, Ian F. Haney López, *White by Law: The Legal Construction of Race* (New York: New York University Press, 1996); Henry Louis Gates, Jr., ed., *"Race," Writing, and Difference* (Chicago: University of Chicago Press, 1985); Ruth Frankenberg, *White Women, Race Matters: The Social Construction of Whiteness* (Minneapolis: University of Minnesota Press, 1993); and Toni Morrison, *Playing in the Dark: Whiteness and the Literary Imagination* (Cambridge, Mass.: Harvard University Press, 1992).
3. Howard A. Dewitt, *Elvis, the Sun Years: The Story of Elvis Presley in the Fifties* (Ann Arbor, Mich.: Popular Culture, Ink., 1993), passim; Margaret

McKee and Fred Chisenhall, *Beale Black & Blue: Life and Music on Black America's Main Street* (Baton Rouge: Louisiana State University Press, 1981), 94–95; Nelson George, *The Death of Rhythm and Blues* (New York: Pantheon, 1988), 62.

4. Jon Michael Spencer, "A Revolutionary Sexual Persona: Elvis Presley and the White Acquiescence of Black Rhythms," in *In Search of Elvis: Music, Race, Art, Religion,* ed. Vernon Chadwick (Boulder, Colo.: Westview Press, 1997), 112–13.

5. Quoted in the *Charlotte Observer,* 26 June 1956, and *Portland* [Oregon] *Journal,* 3 September 1957, as noted in Ger Rijff, *Long Lonely Highway: A 1950s Elvis Scrapbook* (Ann Arbor, Mich.: Pierian Press, 1987), 75, 178, and Peter Guralnick, *Last Train to Memphis: The Rise of Elvis Presley* (Boston: Little, Brown, 1994), 369.

6. Norman Mailer, "The White Negro," in *Advertisements for Myself* (New York: Putnam, 1959, 311–31; Eric Lott, "All the King's Men: Elvis Impersonators and White Working-Class Masculinity," in *Race and the Subject of Masculinities,* ed. Harry Stecopoulos and Michael Uebel (Durham, N.C.: Duke University Press, 1997), 203. Keisker quoted in the *Memphis Press-Scimitar,* 28 July 1954, as noted in Rijff, *Long Lonely Highway,* 11.

7. On Sam Phillips's quote, see Greil Marcus, "Myth and Misquotation," in *The Dustbin of History* (Cambridge, Mass.: Harvard University Press, 1995), 36–46; on the music industry, see Russell Sanjek, updated by David Sanjek, *Pennies from Heaven: The American Popular Music Business in the Twentieth Century* (New York: Da Capo Press, 1996), 355, passim, and Barry Shank, "From Rice to Ice: The Face of Race in Rock and Pop," in *The Cambridge Companion to Rock and Pop,* ed. Will Straw and Simon Frith (forthcoming). For insights on contemporary biases in the mainstream recording industry, see Mark Crispin Miller, "The National Entertainment State III: Who Controls the Music?" *The Nation,* 25 August/1 September 1997, 11–16, and Armond White, "On the Charts, Off the Covers," *The Nation,* 25 August/1 September 1997, 16–17.

8. George Lipsitz, *Class and Culture in Cold War America* (South Hadley, Mass.: Praeger, 1981), 217; Little Richard, quoted in *The Rolling Stone Interviews,* ed. Sid Holt (New York: St. Martin's Press, 1989), 371.

9. Williams, in *Philadelphia Courier,* 22 December 1956, quoted in McKee and Chisenhall, *Beale Black & Blue,* 95–96; DeWitt, *Elvis, the Sun Years,* 178, 202. For more on Williams and Memphis media, see Miriam DeCosta Williams, "Between a Rock and a Hard Place: Black Life in Memphis During the Fifties," in *Memphis 1948–1958* (Memphis: Memphis Brooks Museum of Art, 1986), 66–83.

10. DeWitt, *Elvis, the Sun Years,* 178, 202; "Editor's Note," *Memphis Flyer,* 7–13 August 1997, 3.

11. Williams quoted in McKee and Chisenhall, *Beale Black & Blue,* 96; Greil Marcus, *Mystery Train: Images of America in Rock'n'Roll Music,* 3rd ed. (New York: Dutton, 1990), 166.

12. Trent Hill, "The Enemy Within: Censorship in Rock Music in the 1950s," *South Atlantic Quarterly* 90 (1991): 686.

13. Gilbert Rodman, *Elvis After Elvis: The Posthumous Career of a Living Legend* (New York: Routledge, 1996), 34–36. On rumors in general, see Patricia A. Turner, *I Heard It Through the Grapevine: Rumor in African-American Culture* (Berkeley: University of California Press, 1993).

14. Peter Whitmer, *The Inner Elvis: A Psychological Biography of Elvis Aaron Presley* (New York: Hyperion, 1996), 228, 288; Linda Martin and Kerry Segrave, *Anti-Rock: The Opposition to Rock'n'Roll* (Hamden, Conn.: Archon, 1988), 83; Carl J. Mora, *Mexican Cinema: Reflections of a Society*, rev. ed. (Berkeley: University of California Press, 1988), 98; Joanne Hershfield, *Mexican Cinema/Mexican Woman, 1940–1950* (Tucson: University of Arizona Press, 1996), 47–75.

15. José Agustín, *Contra la corriente* (Col. del Valle, Mexico: Editorial Diana, 1991); see, in particular, "Grandes bolas de fuego" ("Great Balls of Fire"), 78–80. On Elvis records, see Paul Dowling, *Elvis: The Ultimate Album Cover Book* (New York: Abrams, 1996).

16. On racist denial, see Haney López, *White by Law*, 144.

17. David C. Morton, with Charles K. Wolfe, *DeFord Bailey: A Black Star in Early Country Music* (Knoxville: University of Tennessee Press, 1991).

18. Milo M. Quaife, Melvin J. Weig, and Roy E. Appleman, *The History of the United States Flag* (New York: Harper, 1961), 143–45.

19. Jack Hitt, "Confederate Semiotics," *The Nation*, 28 April 1997, 11, 13, 15, 17; Doug J. Swanson, "Confederate Flag Symbolism Argued," *Denver Post*, 26 July 1997, 23A–24A.

20. Greil Marcus discusses "The All American Boy," released by Bill Parsons, in *Invisible Republic: Bob Dylan's Basement Tapes* (New York: Holt, 1997), 237; fan letter quoted in "Draft Board Has Headache, Named Elvis," undated newspaper article, in *Elvis Album*, ed. Bill DeNight, Sharon Fox, and Ger Rijff (Lincolnwood, Ill.: Publications International, 1991), 119.

21. Morrison, *Playing in the Dark*, 47.

22. Quoted in Julia Aparin, "He Never Got Above His Raising: An Ethnographic Study of a Working Class Response to Elvis Presley" (Ph.D. diss., University of Pennsylvania, 1988), 73, 75–76.

23. David Roediger, *The Wages of Whiteness: Race and the Making of the American Working Class* (New York: Verso, 1991), 19.

24. Haney López, *White by Law*, 167.

25. Quoted in Barry Shank, "Fears of the White Unconscious: Music, Race, and Identification in the Censorship of 'Cop Killer,'" *Radical History Review* 66 (1996): 124–45.

26. Rodman, *Elvis After Elvis*, 48; Alice Walker, "Nineteen Fifty-Five," in *You Can't Keep a Good Woman Down* (New York: Harcourt Brace Jovanovich, 1981), 3–20; Greil Marcus, *Dead Elvis: A Chronicle of a Cultural Obsession* (New York: Doubleday, 1991), 36.

27. Walker, "Nineteen Fifty-Five," 8; George, *Death of Rhythm and Blues*, 63.

28. DeWitt, *Elvis, the Sun Years*, 254.

29. Quoted in "Living Colour," *The Rough Guide to Rock* (http://www. roughguides.com); see also Shank, "From Rice to Ice."

30. Dave Marsh, "Introduction," in *Elvis* (New York: Thunder's Mouth Press, 1992), xi; Kevin Chappell, "How Blacks Invented Rock and Roll," *Ebony*, January 1997, 52–56; Public Enemy, *Fear of a Black Planet* (Def Jam Records).

31. Reid quoted in D. Fricke, "Living Colour's Time Is Now," *Rolling Stone*, 1 November 1990, 50–51; Rodman, *Elvis After Elvis*, 46; NdegéOcello quoted in George Plasketes, *Images of Elvis Presley in American Culture, 1977–1997* (Binghamton, N.Y.: Harrington Park Press, 1997), 59.

32. "Warm Winter Wonderlands," *Ebony*, January 1997, 58–60.

33. Adrienne Lynn Young, "Taking Care of Business: Elvis Fans and Moral Community" (Master's thesis, George Washington University, 1994), 13.

34. Nancy Rooks and Mae Gutter, *The Maid, the Man, and the Fans: Elvis Is the Man* (New York: Vantage Press, 1984).

35. Patricia Leigh Brown, "2 Kings: The Postal War over Elvis's Image," *New York Times*, 15 March 1992, 1, 31.

36. David Nicholson, "Please, Mr. Postman . . . ," *Washington Post*, 26 January 1992, C-5.

37. Alice Wondrak, "The King and His Progeny or 'Lisa Marie Presley Who?'" (Paper presented at the Rocky Mountain American Studies Association Annual Conference, 8 April 1995).

38. Quoted in Caroline Arthur, "Going to Graceland," *American Demographics*, May 1989, 48.

39. Bob Michals, "Oprah's Amazing Link to Elvis," *Globe*, 20 September 1994, 30–32.

40. The Michael Jackson Internet Fan Club can be found at http://fred.net/mjj/ michael.html.

41. Quoted in Vernon Ash, "Speak Out," *Memphis Times*, 9 August 1995, 4.

42. Quoted in *I Am Elvis: A Guide to Elvis Impersonators* (New York: Pocket Books, 1991), 49–51, and Roy Ames and Phil York, liner notes to *Sounds Like Elvis: Early Elvis Impersonators (1956–1977)* (Collectables Records).

43. Quoted in *I Am Elvis*, 58.

44. Lott, "All the King's Men," 203.

WHO OWNS ELVIS?

1. Jennifer Heath, *Black Velvet: The Art We Love to Hate* (Rohnert Park, Calif.: Pomegranate Artbooks, 1994), and conversation with author, 15 July 1997.

2. "Black Velvet" was written by David Tyson and Christopher Ward; © Bluebear Waltzes, CAPAC/SBK Blackwood Music Canada/David Tyson Music, P.R.O. For more velvet Elvis references, see George Plasketes, *Images of Elvis Presley in American Culture, 1977–1997* (Binghamton, N.Y.: Harrington Park Press, 1997), 47–48.

3. Quoted on *All Things Considered*, National Public Radio, 21 December 1995.

4. Kerri S. Smith, "Firm Keeps Eye on Elvis," *Denver Post*, 8 November 1996, 1-C, 4-C.

5. Siva Vaidhyanathan, "The New Imperialism: The Erosion of Fair Use, Free Expression and Public Discourse Through International Copyright" (Paper presented at the annual conference of the American Studies Association, Washington D.C., November 1997).

6. Peter Jaszi, comments at annual conference of the American Studies Association, Washington D.C., November 1997. See also James Boyle, *Shamans, Software, and Spleens: Law and the Construction of the Information Society* (Cambridge, Mass.: Harvard University Press, 1996).

7. Elvis at a press conference in New York in June 1972, as quoted in Patsy Guy Hammontree, *Elvis Presley: A Bio-Bibliography* (Westport, Conn.: Greenwood Press, 1985), 188.

8. James Elkins, *The Object Stares Back: On the Nature of Seeing* (New York: Harcourt, Brace, 1996), 31.

9. *I Am Elvis: A Guide to Elvis Impersonators* (New York: Pocket Books, 1991), 102.

10. David Sanjek makes similar remarks in " 'I'm Not a Musician, But I Play One on My Latest Recording': The Cultural Economy of Sound in Contemporary Popular Music," *Ethnomusicology* (forthcoming); see also Christopher Small, *Music of the Common Tongue: Survival and Celebration in Afro-American Music* (New York: Riverrun Press, 1987), 50.

11. Nicky Robertshaw, "The Wealth of the King," *Memphis Business Journal*, 16 June 1997, 1; Julie Baumgold, "Midnight in the Garden of Good and Evil," *Esquire*, March 1995, 99.

12. Sean O'Neal, *Elvis Inc.: The Fall and Rise of the Presley Empire* (Rocklin, Calif.: Prima, 1996), 63 and passim.

13. The Project on Disney, *Inside the Mouse: Work and Play at Disney World* (Durham, N.C.: Duke University Press, 1995), 39.

14. Quoted in Suzanna Andrews, "Making Elvis Pay," *Working Women*, September 1993, 52–55, 96–99.

15. Douglas Brinkley, "Dept. of Missed Opportunities," *New Yorker*, 18 August 1997, 25.

16. Whitney Smith, "Welcome to Tapeland," *Commercial Appeal* (Memphis), 16 August 1997, C-1, C-3.

17. Robert Frank and Eleena De Lisser, "Dueling Dreams: Dr. King's Heirs Fight Accusations of Greed over Theme-Park Plan," *Wall Street Journal*, 9 January 1995, A1, A7; Jesse Katz, "How Much Is that Velvet Elvis Really Worth?" *Los Angeles Times*, 4 December 1996, 45; Jody Callahan, "Board Split on Vision for Rights Museum," *Commercial Appeal*, 12 December 1996, 1B.

18. Linda Romine, "Elvis's Graceland Becomes Catalyst for City's Tourism Industry," *Memphis Business Journal*, 27 January 1997, 26; O'Neal, *Elvis Inc.*, 209.

19. Clifford Rothman, "Graceland, Preserving a Part of Elvis," *USA Today*, 8 August 1997, 6D; O'Neal, *Elvis Inc.*, 93.

20. See Donna Harraway's remarks on taxidermy in *Primate Visions: Gender,*

Race, and Nature in the World of Modern Science (New York: Routledge, 1989), 26–58.

21. Art Simon, *Dangerous Knowledge: The JFK Assassination in Art and Film* (Philadelphia: Temple University Press, 1996).

22. J. Thomas McCarthy, *The Rights of Publicity and Privacy* (Deerfield, Ill.: Clark Boarman Callaghan, 1997), 1:1-31-34, 1-40-44. The case was *Haelan Laboratories Inc.* v. *Topps Chewing Gum, Inc.*, 202 F.2d 866 (2d Cir. 1953), cert. denied 346 U.S. 816, 98 L.Ed. 343, 74 S. Ct. 26 (1953). The 1990s have seen similar cases involving the Three Stooges and Ernest Hemingway.

23. J. Thomas McCarthy, *The Rights of Publicity and Privacy* (Deerfield, Ill.: Clark Boarman Callaghan, 1997), 2:9-37; O'Neal, *Elvis Inc.*, 73.

24. McCarthy, *Rights of Publicity and Privacy*, 2:9-31-32, 9-38; Sinatra discussed on *Entertainment Tonight*, 28 May 1998.

25. Quoted in Marla Matzer, "Company Town," *Los Angeles Times*, 19 December 1996, D-1.

26. Quoted in Katz, "How Much Is that Velvet Elvis Really Worth?" 45.

27. Michael Davis, "Judge Won't Be Cruel: Velvet Elvis Nightclub Can Keep Name," *Houston Chronicle*, 31 December 1996, A-1.

28. Davis, "Judge Won't Be Cruel," A-1; Joseph Wharton, "All Shook Up: Elvis Estate Irked by Bar Name," *ABA Journal*, March 1997, 14; Debrett Lyons, "Elvis All Shook Up by the High Court," *European Intellectual Property Review*, October 1997, 613–17; Daniel Fisher, "Velvet Elvis Bar Wins Court Fight to Keep Name," *Commercial Appeal*, 31 December 1996, 4B. For the full decision, see *EPE Inc.* v. *Capece and Velvet Limited*, No. H-5-1197, 30 December 1996.

29. *EPE Inc.* v. *Capece*, No. 97-20096, 7 May 1998.

30. Quoted in Edward A. Mazza II, "Copyright Holders Wage War on Net," *Daily Yomiuri*, 21 January 1997, 9.

31. Gary Young, "Elvis Is Given Life After Death," *The Guardian*, 19 March 1997, 2–7; Dirk Beveridge, "Brit Shakes Up Presley Estate," *The Record Online* (19 March 1997): site at http://record.horacemann.org. For the full text of Justice Laddie's ruling, see the Elvisly Yours Web site at ⟨www.elvisly-yours.com⟩.

32. *Memphis Development Foundation* v. *Factors, Etc. Inc.*, 616 F.2d 956, 205 USPQ 784 (6th Cir. 1980), cert. denied 449 U.S. 953; discussed in McCarthy, *Rights of Publicity and Privacy*, 2:9-12-16.

33. "Role Dilemma Hinders Charity by Elvis Inc.," in *The Elvis Presley Burning Love Fan Club Newsletter*, March/April/May 1993, 5.

34. *The Elvis Presley Burning Love Newsletter*, December/January/February 1994–95, 2, 17.

35. Tom Walter, "TV Soaps Easily Slip into the Elvis Thing," *Commercial Appeal*, 16 August 1997, C-1, C-3. Thanks to *Days* fan Michele Bogart for sharing this scenario with me.

36. Clifford Rothman, "Music and Meatloaf Served à la Elvis," *New York Times*, 5 March 1997, C-8; Bill Ellis, "Sensible Elvis Inc. Aims to Grow Rock-Solid Empire," *Commercial Appeal*, 17 August 1997, A-1, A-19.

37. "Elvis Presley's Memphis to Open on Beale Street," *Business Wire*, 5 March 1997; letter to the editor, *Commercial Appeal*, 10 August 1997, B-7.
38. Ellis, "Sensible Elvis Inc.," A-19.
39. Robertshaw, "Wealth of the King," 1.
40. Quoted in Robertshaw, "Wealth of the King," 1.
41. Greil Marcus, "Introduction," in *Dead Elvis: A Chronicle of a Cultural Obsession* (New York: Doubleday, 1991).

INDEX